Heaven or Hell, the Future Depends on Our Choices

Miscellaneous Discussions on Needs, Technologies, Artificial Intelligence, and the Future of Human Society

I0131121

Zhen LUO

AMERICAN ACADEMIC PRESS

AMERICAN ACADEMIC PRESS

By AMERICAN ACADEMIC PRESS

201 Main Street

Salt Lake City

UT 84111 USA

Email manu@AcademicPress.us

Visit us at http://www.AcademicPress.us

ISBN: 979-8-3370-8924-9

Distributed to the trade by National Book Network Suite 200, 4501 Forbes Boulevard, Lanham, MD 20706

10 9 8 7 6 5 4 3 2 1

Author's Statement

———————————————⋙⋙⋙⋙⋙※⋘⋘⋘⋘⋘———————————————

Since the Industrial Revolution, scientific and technological progress has brought about a great improvement in people's living standards and cultivated people's reverence for science and technology. There are some people who even go to the point of blind worship and support technology as long as it seems "profound." Artificial intelligence (AI) is such a "profound" scientific and technological field. Moreover, AI is related to the problems that have been puzzling human beings for a long time, such as "What is the mind?" and "What is intelligence?" Thus, human society generally has an attitude of expectation and support for AI today. In addition, some investment stakeholders, for their own immediate interests, are eager to let the AI products they invest in occupy all applicable fields. They vigorously advocate for AI and build momentum for AI in society. All these factors have contributed to today's social atmosphere that caters to and expects artificial intelligence.

Now the social media atmosphere of advocating AI makes people ignore the huge threat of AI to human society. On the other hand, the level of AI technology has been rapidly improving, and AI applications are in rapid deployment in recent years. This makes the author worry sick about the future of human society. In the current state of society, without corresponding preparations and adjustments, artificial intelligence applications will occupy all aspects of society. This will lead to devastating turmoil in human society. In this paper, the author attempts to rationally analyze the relationship among human needs, scientific and technological progress, and artificial intelligence. A point of view is proposed that "it is urgent to limit the use of artificial intelligence in order to protect ordinary people, while our society is not ready for the advent of the era of using artificial intelligence in all aspects."

This kind of viewpoint naturally has a bit of an anti-AI sentiment, and it is easy to be labeled as "anti-intellectual" and ignored. For this reason, the author makes this statement. The author is by no means anti-intellectual. On the contrary, the author upholds "Tao"; in other words, advocates for science.

About twenty years ago, the author, Luo Zhen, studied at the School of Automation of Shanghai University and the Institute of Robotics of Shanghai Jiao Tong University successively. The author obtained a master's degree and a doctoral degree. Although he did not work in the field of artificial intelligence after graduation, he has always been interested in robotics and is not completely ignorant of the subsequent developments in the fields of robotics and artificial intelligence.

Due to the author's limited knowledge and wisdom, it cannot be said that every argument in the article is 100% sound. However, the views advocated in the article are all put forward by the author after trying to follow the fundamental principle of scientific exploration: "based on facts and evidence." The author made careful speculation based on what he knew about history and reality.

In addition, due to the lack of ways and means to obtain some of the original data from papers or reports, some of the data involved in this article are based on publicly available information on the Internet, for example, government websites. While the author tries to identify credible data based on a variety of online sources, he does not guarantee the 100% reliability of the data and information used. The author apologizes for any possible inappropriateness.

Please don't be offended if the arguments in the article offend your beliefs; the author does not intend to offend anyone, including you. After all, the author's insight is limited, and there may be biases in his mind of which he is not aware. Moreover, the sparks of human thought are bright and numerous. The author cannot take care of everyone's thoughts. The author is only expressing his concern for the future fate of mankind with his own superficial, piecemeal knowledge and wisdom.

Writing the article, the author hopes that everyone should also be "vigilant" besides "welcoming" AI, especially ordinary people, who account for the vast majority of the population. We strongly urge our society not to "blindly" welcome AI because of a lack of understanding of AI and before we are ready. After all, waiting until the time of social upheaval, or even collapse, is too costly to reflect on, and it may even be too late. There are some things in the world for which we have only one chance.

Preface

————————————————————

Science and technology are a double-edged sword, which can both benefit and harm people. "How to use science and technology" is a topic that needs to be seriously and prudently dealt with by human beings. As a category of science and technology, artificial intelligence (AI) cannot escape the fate of being a double-edged sword. AI simulates and tries to surpass the intelligence of human beings. The basis for human survival and development on the earth, or the most important difference between humans and animals, is that humans have superior intelligence. Therefore, the impact of artificial intelligence on human society might be much more far-reaching than that of many types of science and technology.

If human society is to use artificial intelligence thoroughly in all aspects of production, life, and security, then human beings need to make major adjustments in terms of cultural psychology and social systems such as economic operation mechanisms and wealth acquisition methods. Otherwise, it is likely to lead to turmoil and disasters in human society. If humanity does not treat artificial intelligence cautiously and only blindly encourages it, then, in the current situation where human society is not ready for the advent of the era of artificial intelligence, perhaps the next cruel social turmoil and social crisis will be caused by artificial intelligence.

Whether human beings are facing a gaping abyss or a broad road depends on how we choose to deal with AI. The purpose of this article is to make the following suggestions and appeals.

First, in the current situation that human society is not ready, we should use artificial intelligence technology prudently, especially in the field of wealth creation, such as factories, distribution and transportation, and the construction industry. We human beings must strictly restrict the use of artificial intelligence unless it is a very dangerous occasion, or an occasion that manual operation cannot meet the requirements for product accuracy, or an occasion that manual operation cannot meet social requirements for labor productivity, etc.

Second, all countries in the world should set up special committees to review the use of artificial intelligence and work together to establish corresponding international cooperation organizations. We, human society, should study which level of automation and intelligence can be put into use under the social conditions, such as employment rates, human working hours, and other demand factors. These committees should review the use of artificial intelligence in the production and circulation of material wealth and strictly assess the use of machines with artificial intelligence technology or powerful automated machinery in the fields of wealth creation. We, human beings, should strictly restrict the emergence of unmanned factories and impose heavy taxes on unauthorized or unnecessary unmanned factories.

Third, since our world is not ready to meet the advent of the era of comprehensive artificial intelligence, we call on ordinary people to boycott the products produced by unmanned factories unless they are licensed by special committees or it is proven that non-automation cannot produce such products that meet the requirements of users. We should reduce consumption in unmanned smart restaurants and smart stores now. For ordinary people, buying a product or service that can be produced efficiently with human participation but is now completely produced by artificial intelligence is to go against themselves.

Fourth, we should not be afraid of artificial intelligence either. We suggest that our society can allow or even encourage the development of certain artificial intelligence technologies and products applied in the field of consumer end users, such as nursing robots for the disabled and household service robots.

Fifth, our society can invest some resources to study the possible positive and negative effects of artificial intelligence and examine the social conditions for the thorough use of artificial intelligence in all aspects. We should work with the Artificial Intelligence Technology Review Committee and other institutions to provide suggestions on whether to welcome the era of comprehensive artificial intelligence and how to adjust the social operating mechanisms.

Today, human society as a whole has shown a certain fanatical expectation of artificial intelligence, including robots. The author hopes that society can treat artificial intelligence more rationally. Thus, the author pours cold water and voices a different view. It is hoped that decision-makers at all levels of society, including investors and other decision-makers, can have this view in mind and make more reasonable decisions. So, society can continue to prosper, and life can continue to be better.

Using AI to replace human workers in all kinds of fields is incompatible with the market economic system prevailing in the world today. It is also incompatible with the recognition of private property rights in today's human society. If our society chooses to implement the goal of using AI to replace human workers in all fields completely, it is necessary to adjust the social operating mechanisms. It will inevitably involve huge social upheaval. This kind of revolutionary and huge social change is the most terrifying. For the individual caught up in it, if he does not get it right, he will be crushed to pieces. Do not start such a revolutionary social change until you have sufficiently appropriate reasons. In particular, in the era of the global village today, the most appropriate response to replacing human workers with AI in all fields is for all countries to work in unison. In view of today's international situation, there are so many overt or covert quarrels, so much unrest happening, and so many wars going on. It's a headache just to imagine having all countries in lockstep. To depict it, the author uses three words: "difficult, difficult, and difficult."

The comprehensive use of artificial intelligence is likely to lead human society to an era of oligarchic rule in which there is a lack of effective checks and balances on public decision-making power. History tells us that we should not easily believe in those "saviors" actually consisting of power oligarchs, because in societies where so-called saviors existed, the lives of ordinary people were often bleak; not only were the basic material needs of survival often not met, but even daily complaints could not be spoken. Therefore, before human society has designed, argued over, and compromised on a reasonable social system that adapts to the era of comprehensive artificial intelligence, it is best not to engage in implementing comprehensive artificial intelligence, especially in the field of wealth creation and distribution.

As a conclusion, in the case that today's society is not ready, we should stop the current situation of disorderly, barbaric, and rapid development and application of artificial intelligence technology as soon as possible. The author believes that, at present, it is urgent to restrict and regulate the use of artificial intelligence to protect ordinary people!

In the past, humans realized the importance of protecting animals and plants; today, humanity has reached an age where it is necessary to protect ordinary people.

Abstract

AI is developing rapidly and has a tendency to surpass human beings in an all-round way. The author is concerned that the comprehensive use of AI may jeopardize the survival of ordinary people and may cause unrest and even the collapse of human society.

For human society, how should we judge something as good or bad, or what standard should be used to judge it? It is reasonable to judge something as good or bad by the standards of whether or not human needs are met. From a mechanical perspective, chapter 1 argues that human needs include food, heat preservation, rest, health, life continuity, housing, transportation, neuropsychological needs, knowledge and skills, etc. The application of artificial intelligence should be regulated, especially in wealth creation, until human society is properly prepared. The view in this paper can be easily interpreted as an opposition to science. Therefore, it analyzes the satisfaction of human needs in various historical periods and emphasizes the importance of the development of science and technology in meeting human needs. By analyzing the satisfaction of needs, this paper argues that in the absence of AI technology, or when AI is far from reaching the situation of fully surpassing human beings, human needs have been well met. Thus, human beings should not be in a hurry to use AI in all fields.

Considering that many people do not understand AI and the urgency of limiting the use of AI technologies, Chapter 2 gives an overview of the development and applications of AI, including robotics.

Chapter 3 deals with the issue of what a fully AI-powered society will look like. By discussing the structures of social organizations, it speculates on a potential social structure from a pessimistic perspective—an authoritarian social structure without checks and balances, which is very unfriendly to ordinary people. It aims to pour cold water on those who are overly optimistic, hoping that all will be more cautious in using AI.

Chapter 4 explores some potential issues that will arise from the adoption of comprehensive AI and discusses whether or not human society is ready for comprehensive AI, in which occasion it is appropriate to apply AI, and how to transition to comprehensive AI. This paper argues that comprehensive AI is incompatible with the prevailing market economy system and the private property rights system. Human society is not ready for comprehensive AI. Comprehensive AI will bring about a reshuffle of society, and it is difficult to avoid the occurrence of devastating social turmoil. Therefore, human society must be cautious about comprehensive AI and must not be blinded by immediate interests.

Chapter 5 is the conclusion.

The author does not guarantee that all the views in this article are reasonable, but only hopes that this article will arouse a cautious attitude toward the use of artificial intelligence.

Contents

1 Introduction to Scientific and Technological Progress and the Satisfaction of Human Needs

As we all know, almost since the first industrial revolution, the production efficiency of human beings has developed tremendously. The average wealth creation rate per person is dozens or hundreds of times faster than it was before the industrial revolution. In the past two to three hundred years, with the development of science and technology, there has been a great improvement in human living standards, medical and health standards, life expectancy, and so on. It can be seen that science and technology are important driving forces in promoting human society on the road to happiness.

Now that it seems that artificial intelligence (AI) technology is developing rapidly, human beings seem to have become more convenient in some aspects of life. Why does the author still say, as an alarmist, that if artificial intelligence technology is not dealt with well, it will lead to disasters for human society and even lead to social collapse? Isn't artificial intelligence technology also science and technology? Why is it that the previous technological developments have made human society prosperous and progressive, while artificial intelligence has the potential to lead to the collapse of society?

This chapter focuses on the question of why past scientific and technological progress and the previous industrial revolutions have not led to the collapse of human society but have created social prosperity. It analyzes and discusses human needs and the satisfaction of those needs in different eras and puts forward the following views.

The scientific and technological progress of the past has filled the "big hole" of people's various needs that were not met earlier.

With the progress of science and technology and the improvement of per capita productivity, many human needs have been met today.

We humans do need to push for continued advancement in science and technology to further better meet human needs.

1.1 Analysis of Human Needs

In our complicated, intricate, and ever-changing world, some people sing, some dance, some farm, some operate machines, some eat dog meat, some pet dogs, some learn, some preach... Through these complicated and intricate phenomena, we can find that all kinds of conscious behaviors are carried out to meet certain needs. These needs may be physical, material, spiritual, or psychological.

So, what is "need"? The word need can be used as both a verb and a noun. Literally, as a verb, need refers to demanding, indicating that there should be or must be. As a noun, it denotes something that is needed, a requirement that arises out of a need. The word need is used in many fields and has different meanings in different contexts, such as the field of market economy, which has its own meaning of "need," and the field of psychology, which also has its own meaning of "need." There are many discussions on needs, such as Maslow's division of human needs into five levels, which are physiological needs, safety needs, social (love and belonging) needs, esteem needs, and self-actualization needs. Since this paper mainly explores the relationship between artificial intelligence and human beings, it primarily analyzes "needs" from a mechanical perspective, and the "needs" in this paper mainly refer to the needs for material wealth and spiritual comfort.

Comment. Because people's behavior is closely related to brain thoughts, it seems to be difficult to distinguish between needs and desires sometimes. The point in this article is that needs and desires are related but different. For example, we humans need to eat every day, so the food we need to eat is the need. This food may or may not be required by human desires, but one thing is certain: eating is a need for the human body to maintain life functions. The point of this paper is that need is more inclined to an objective and reasonable requirement, while desire is more inclined to be a psychological appeal. So, if a person can only eat 3 kilograms of food in one day, but he gets 1 ton of food (assuming that it will be spoiled and inedible the next day), then a surplus of 997 kilograms of food is not a need, but only a person's desire (although from a marketing point of view, for the supplier, the goods sold are the needs of the customer). For example, limited by factors such as the size of the human body and other considerations, it is a relatively normal need for an ordinary family of five to have a few hundred square meters of housing today. It can enable the family to have several comfortable and breathable bedrooms, spacious and bright kitchens, clean and tidy bathrooms, comfortable and pleasant halls, quiet and suitable study rooms, appropriate storage rooms, utility rooms, and tool rooms, etc. It can make the living space spacious and comfortable. It will not cause excessive burden on daily cleaning and maintenance due to a too large area. But if someone desires to have millions of square meters of palace-style self-occupied housing, it can only be regarded as the venting of desire. In fact, just the burden of cleaning and maintenance of a house with millions of square meters is not something an ordinary family of five can afford. Millions of square meters of housing mean tens of thousands of rooms. Even if the family changes a room every day, how long would it take for a family of five to reach every room? From the perspective of quality of life, how much better is it to change rooms every day than to live in a fixed room for a long time? Of course, it is not better. Therefore, having a million-square-meter house can only be a catharsis of desire for a family of five, rather than the satisfaction of needs.

What are the material wealth needs and spiritual comfort needs of human beings? Here's a general mechanical analysis.

1.1.1 "Food" Needs

As the ancient Chinese saying that has been handed down for more than two thousand years, "food is the most basic need of human beings" (民以食为天). It can even be said that "food" is the basic need of all natural organisms, such as plants that absorb nutrients from the natural environment and animals that take in food. Let's do an analysis from a mechanical point of view.

As we all know, movement is an innate human ability. People can move and need to move. The human body needs to move from one spatial position to another, to speak and communicate in language, to get food, to eat, to breathe, to exercise, and so on.

There are many forms of movement of the human body, such as running, jumping, waving, writing and drawing, tapping on the keyboard, and other limb movements; facial expression muscle movements to express various emotions such as joy, anger, and sorrow; various eye movements to perceive and see our wonderful world; oral and vocal cord movements for language communication; and a series of digestive system movements such as chewing and gastrointestinal peristalsis for eating, digesting food, and excreting waste. There is respiratory movement to obtain oxygen and excrete carbon dioxide, and there are movements of the cardiovascular system to nourish all parts of the body.

Fig. 1.1.1 Walking and Pulling   **Fig. 1.1.2 Motion of the Stomach and Intestines**

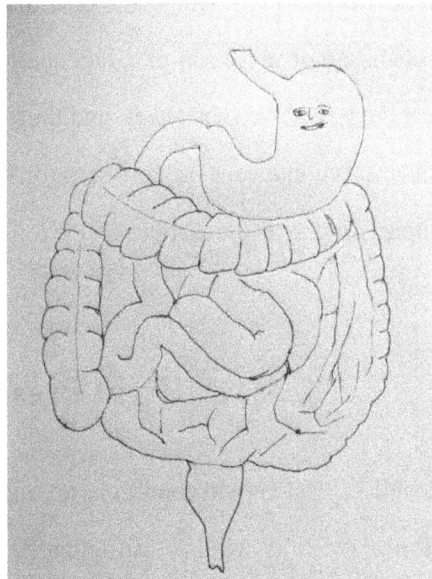

From the viewpoint of physics, when humans move, they need to overcome resistance to do work. On the other hand, the velocity or speed of the human tissues involved in the movement will also change over time, which means that the kinetic energy they have will change. According to the law of conservation of energy, if no work is done on it, the kinetic energy of an object neither comes out of thin air nor disappears into thin air. That is to say, when a person is moving, the constant change in the kinetic energy of the tissues involved in the movement usually means that the human body has done work. The human body needs energy to support its work. So, where does the energy needed for human movement come from? The energy required for human movement basically comes from chemical energy, that is, from the chemical energy released during the chemical reaction of nutrients such as sugars and proteins with oxygen to form substances such as water and carbon dioxide. And where do nutrients such as sugars and proteins come from? They come from the food we eat every day.

On the other hand, the human body is composed of many kinds of substances. Without these diverse substances needed for life, the human skeletal system, muscle tissue, digestive system, nervous system, and other tissue systems cannot be formed. Where did these substances that make up the human body come from? Just one word: "eat." Eating is the basic way for the human body to obtain the substances that make up the human body, including drinking.

Therefore, whether from the perspective of material composition or energy, "eating" is the basis for human existence. It can be seen that "food" should be the basic instinctive need of human beings. Of course, with the development of science and technology, the human body has more ways to "eat," such as injecting glucose and nutrient solutions.

In other words, the human body is actually a complex biochemical machine in the universe from a certain point of view. The human body is always carrying out complex biochemical reactions. These complex biochemical reactions maintain the vital functions of the human body and constitute the cornerstone of what makes a person human. In order to maintain the normal operation of these complex biochemical reactions, a variety of human needs have to be met. A chemical reaction must have reactive substances, and there is no chemical reaction without a reactive substance. The occurrence of a chemical reaction means the consumption of reactive substances. In order to provide those substances that participate in complex biochemical reactions and to replenish the reactive substances that are consumed, the human body has a "food" need.

1.1.2 "Heat Preservation" Needs

Chemistry knowledge tells us that certain conditions are required for chemical reactions to occur, such as temperature conditions. Many chemical reactions will have different reaction rates and generate different substances under different temperature conditions. As mentioned earlier, the human body is a complex biochemical machine, and many kinds of chemical reactions are carried out in the human body. It can be said that these many biochemical reactions in the human body reach reaction equilibrium at about 37°C; that is, the human body's vital functions work normally at 37°C. With too low or too high body temperature, it will lead to the imbalance of human biochemical reactions, which will then lead to disorders of vital functions and even be life-threatening in severe cases. Because the temperature range that maintains the equilibrium of various biochemical reactions and the normal vital functions of the human body is very narrow, only about one or two degrees Celsius, it can be said that human beings are temperature-sensitive and thermostatic biochemical machines.

No one is a closed, independent, and self-consistent world. Everyone will exchange substances or energy with the environment. Heat exchange will inevitably occur between the human body and the environment, such as heat convection, heat radiation, respiratory heat dissipation, and evaporative heat loss.

On the one hand, the biochemical reactions of the human body release heat. Thus, to maintain a normal body temperature, the human body needs to dissipate heat into the environment. When the human body feels hot, the nervous system regulates the body's physiological responses, such as sweating, to achieve evaporative heat dissipation.

On the other hand, the temperature of the natural environment changes every day. Usually, the temperature of the environment changes far more than the fluctuation of one to two degrees Celsius in normal body temperature. Substances or objects in nature are subject to heat exchange all the time. The ways of heat exchange include heat conduction, heat convection, and heat radiation. These heat exchange methods follow the objective laws of nature. For example, the law of heat conduction can be described and calculated by Fourier's law $dQ/dt = -kAdT/dx$, the law of heat convection can be described by Newton's cooling formula $q = h\Delta T$, and the law of heat radiation can be described by the formula of heat radiation $q = \varepsilon\sigma(T_1^4 - T_2^4)$. According to these formulas, the rate of heat exchange is positively correlated with the temperature gradient and temperature difference. The larger the temperature difference or the larger the temperature gradient, the faster the heat exchange rate is. Because the ambient temperature has a wide range of variations, the difference between the ambient temperature and the thermostatic human body temperature will vary within a large range. Different temperature differences further make the heat exchange rate different. For example, usually in winter, the ambient temperature is much lower than the body temperature. Therefore, compared to the warm environment in summer, the body dissipates heat faster in the cold environment in winter. As a result of this phenomenon, compared with summer, the surface temperature of the human skin is more likely to be lower than the normal temperature in winter. The thermoreceptors inside the skin will transmit stimulation signals to the nerve center when they feel the low temperature. Thus, it is more likely to feel cold for the human body in winter.

The law of heat exchange itself is not subject to human will, and the heat exchange between the human body and the environment must also follow the laws of nature. Although the human body will automatically produce some physiological reactions to "keep warm" according to the cold or heat felt, such as sweating and dissipating heat when at high temperatures, shivering and heat generation when cold, etc., the fluctuation of temperature in the environment of human survival is so big that it is far beyond the ability of the human body's own physiological regulation to keep thermostatic. The human body has neither dense fur to keep warm nor a very thick subcutaneous fat layer to keep warm. A person finds it difficult to survive in cold weather by relying on his or her own physiological reactions. The huge gap between the constant temperature requirements of the human body and the actual living environment, coupled with the physiological structural characteristics of the human body, makes people usually take certain non-physiological thermal insulation measures. Thus, the "heat preservation" needs of human beings are derived.

In the vast majority of cases, the ambient temperature is lower than the body's normal temperature. This means that the human body dissipates heat outwards in most cases. In order to maintain body temperature, there needs to be a heat source inside the human body. The heat source in the human body is the chemical reaction between the nutrients absorbed from food and the oxygen. Many times, the temperature is so low that the gap between the ambient temperature and the body temperature is too large. In the case of nakedness, the heat dissipation rate of all parts of the human body is greater than the speed at which the human body generates heat. In these times, if there are no heat preservation measures, the human body is likely to experience hypothermia, which can lead to dysfunction and physical problems. In these situations, heat preservation measures must be taken. The main measures include reducing the heat exchange rate and increasing the ambient temperature. Measures to reduce the rate of heat exchange include adding poor conductors of heat between the human body and the environment, reducing convection, and so on.

Sometimes the ambient temperature is too high, resulting in the phenomenon that the heat dissipating rate is slower than the heat generating rate for the human body. Sometimes the ambient temperature is even higher than the human body temperature. In this case, not only does the human body not dissipate heat to the environment, but the body may become a net heat absorber. In these situations, the main measure that can be taken is to try to reduce the ambient temperature of the human body. Of course, if the ambient temperature itself is lower than the body temperature, for example, lower than 37°C, one possible reason for the slow heat dissipation rate of the human body is that the human body is wearing too much insulating clothing. If so, trying to reduce the thermal insulation ability of clothing is a very natural and important measure that almost everyone will use. It is just as the saying goes, "wear less clothes if it is hot." If the ambient temperature itself is higher than body temperature, adding insulation is also a natural option. A typical application instance is that in the event of a fire, the human body can be wrapped in thick bedclothes moistened with water to help prevent burns and escape from the fire scene.

Human needs for "heat preservation" can be embodied in clothing needs, housing needs, air-conditioning needs, and so on.

First, we can create an individual micro-environment to preserve heat, such as using clothes and bedding to create a micro-heat preservation environment just covering one or two people. The materials used in clothes and bedding are poor conductors of heat, and they can also reduce heat transfer, such as heat convection. Thus, human beings have a demand for clothing, bedding, etc. It can be summarized by the need for "clothing," as in the Chinese saying "clothing, food, housing, and transportation."

Second, we can also create a small environment to preserve heat, such as using a house to slow down the impact of diurnal changes in the temperature of the external environment. A house can also protect the human body from scorching sun or rain, reducing the factors that interfere with the normal body temperature of the human body. We can also heat a small space through a fire or create a pleasant small living area through cold and hot air conditioning equipment, etc. In fact, according to the above-mentioned heat exchange formula, in the case of the human body being naked, as long as the temperature difference between the small environment in which the human body is located and the human body is such that the rate of heat dissipation of the human body is the same as the rate of heat generated by the human body itself, then the heat preservation needs of the human body do not need to be embodied in clothing needs.

For human beings on the earth today, in most cases, the ambient temperature is lower than the temperature required for "the rate at which the human body dissipates heat is equal to the rate at which the human body generates its heat." Since people often cannot stay in a house with a proper temperature, physical insulation measures such as clothing and bedding are very important basic needs of human beings. In other words, "clothing" is also a basic human need. Of course, the demand for this "clothing" can be eased and replaced by fires that appeared in primeval ages, houses that appeared in ancient times, air conditioners that appeared in modern times, and so on. In another way of understanding, houses, fires, air conditioners, etc. can also be regarded as "clothes" in a broad sense.

1.1.3 "Rest" Needs or "Body Recovery" Needs

The human body is a complex biochemical machine, and it is constantly undergoing biochemical reactions. Since the biochemical reactions are carried out, the reactants will inevitably be consumed, and the reaction products will also be produced. The blood circulation and other systems of the human body constantly transport nutrients and substances needed for biochemical reactions to the parts of the human body that need these substances and constantly remove waste products produced by biochemical reactions.

In the working process of the complex biochemical machine of the human body, when the human body tissues and organs are active, the rate of consuming reactants is often greater than the rate of transporting and replenishing, and the rate of producing waste is often greater than the rate of removal. Especially in the vigorous active state of large load, the rate of consuming reactants and producing waste products is much greater than the delivery rate of the circulating delivery system. It can easily lead to the lack of reactants required for biochemical reactions, such as muscle glycogen, liver glycogen, blood glucose, adenosine triphosphate (ATP), and creatine phosphate (CP). It also leads to the depletion of neurotransmitters, etc. It can also easily lead to the accumulation of certain metabolites, such as excessive lactate. Strenuous exercise is also easy to release a large amount of energy due to accelerated metabolism. It will increase the temperature, leading to physiological regulation of the nervous system and making the human skin sweat. Sweating can lead to the loss of water and electrolytes in the human body, which in turn causes the body's water and electrolyte imbalance. These can cause fatigue, discomfort, etc. Fatigue can be said to be one of the important cornerstones of human survival and reproduction. It can effectively restrain the behavior of the human body. It forces people to rest, to reduce the activity of tissues and organs, and reduce the level of metabolism. So, the delivery rate of the material delivery system in the body can be greater than the rate of consuming the reactants and generating the reaction products. Thus, it realizes the replenishment of the substances required by the tissues and organs and the cleaning of the reaction products. It ensures the material balance in the tissues and organs of the human body and ensures the normal biochemical reactions of the human body. Let's imagine that if the human body does not have a "sense of fatigue," it is easy for people to exercise excessively; that is to say, it is easy to lead to a serious shortage of reactants and excessive accumulation of reaction products, which in turn leads to a serious imbalance of human biochemical reactions and even triggers the collapse of human vital functions.

Therefore, people need to rest, and rest is a basic human need. When people are resting, the level of metabolism decreases. The body's circulatory system takes the opportunity to remove the waste products of the reaction, replenish nutrients to the body's tissues and organs, repair damaged parts, and so on. Almost everyone has experienced feeling tired after a long period of physical or mental work, or after strenuous exercise. They often feel vigorous, energetic, and refreshed after a good night's sleep.

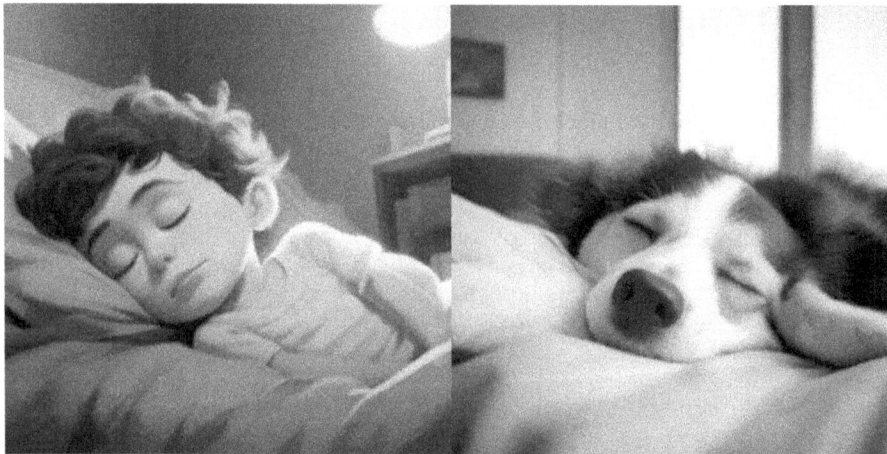

Fig. 1.1.3 Rest is a Basic Human Need

1.1.4 "Housing" Needs

As mentioned earlier, rest is a basic human need. Rest, including sleep, is actually a basic human behavior. When people are sleeping and resting, the perception of the human body is greatly decreased or even turned off. For example, when sleeping, visual perception is basically turned off, and auditory perception is also greatly decreased. Especially when the human body is in a deep sleep state, he or she may be deaf to the surrounding daily volume sounds. Obviously, in such a state, the human body seriously lacks the ability to prevent potential hazards. Especially in primeval ages with a large number of predators such as lions, tigers, and wolves, in such a state, people are easily hunted by predators and injured by snakes and insects. Therefore, it is very important to have a safe and comfortable place to rest that greatly reduces the existential crisis. So to speak, it is a basic human need to have a safe and comfortable resting place.

For the basic need of a safe and comfortable resting place, perhaps it can be expressed by the "housing" need in "clothing, food, housing, and transportation" that the Chinese often say. After human beings lived in caves and houses, they effectively isolated predators in nature through mountain walls, fences, and walls, etc. They could reduce the hunt from predators so that people could sleep and rest more at ease. By keeping the dwelling dry, tidy, and the ground hard, etc., the human dwelling is not suitable for the survival of insects, molds, etc. It will effectively reduce the potential harm of insects, ants, mold, and viruses, etc.

In addition to effectively reducing or even cutting off the danger of predators, from the perspective of physical space, caves and houses also create a small environment. Mountain walls, walls, and roofs make this small environment isolated from the natural environment to a certain extent. This isolation greatly weakens and mitigates the effects of drastic changes in the outside climate, thus providing a relatively friendly physical environment for people. Generally speaking, the temperature of the small environment will be relatively stable compared to the external environment. Moreover, the small space that is somewhat isolated from the outside world also allows people to more effectively use fires, air conditioners, etc., to adjust the temperature of the living environment. It is conducive to meeting the basic needs of human beings in terms of "heat preservation." In addition, it can also protect people from uncomfortable weather conditions such as summer exposure and cold rain. It also makes the dwelling a suitable place to entertain friends and family and to meet the social, belonging, and emotional needs of human beings.

With the development of human production technology, especially after entering the era of civilization, people gradually have more and more diverse material wealth, including food, labor tools, daily necessities, handicrafts, decorations, and so on. Obviously, there needs to be a place to store these material possessions. The physical isolation of housing brings certain "privacy," which is particularly suitable for storing people's material wealth. Moreover, the physical isolation of housing allows people to keep the house dry and the ground hardened, making it difficult for insects, ants, and molds to survive, which is more conducive to the long-term safe preservation of material wealth.

Human activity requires energy and time, and activity can make people tired. People will have the idea of lying flat and being lazy sometimes. So it is natural that human beings spend most of their time in and near their homes outside of work. Therefore, a safe and comfortable living environment is very important for human beings. What makes up a comfortable living environment? Comfortable tables, chairs, mattresses, and other resting utensils, convenient access to water and food, fresh air, and a beautiful environment are all important components of the basic housing needs of human beings.

Housing Needs
$\left\{\begin{array}{l}\end{array}\right.$
Safety Residence

Spatial Isolation: Create a Small Living Environment
and Facilitate Interpersonal Communication

Privacy: Storage of Private Material Wealth

Comfortable Living Environment

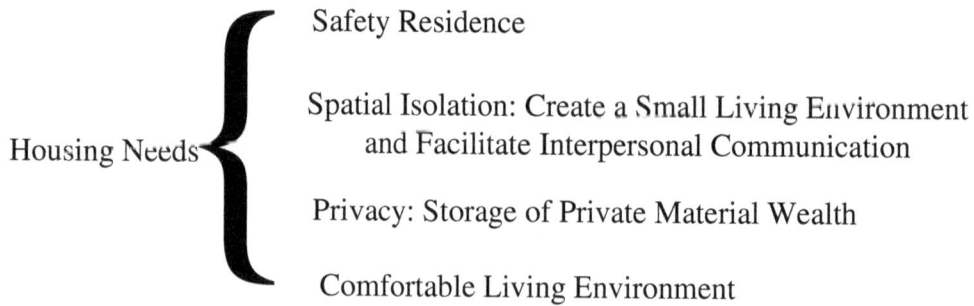

Fig. 1.1.4 Housing Needs

1.1.5 "Health" Needs

Health needs are basic human needs.

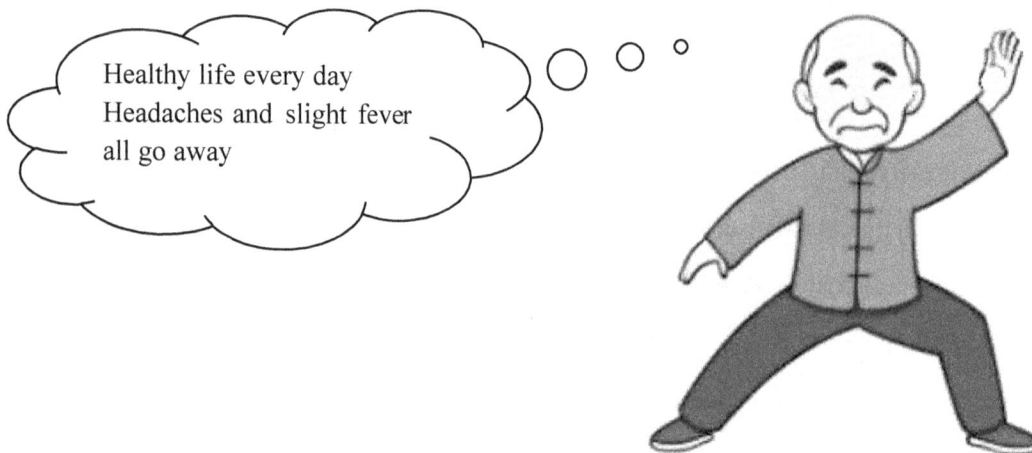

Healthy life every day
Headaches and slight fever
all go away

Fig. 1.1.5 Health Needs Are Basic Human Needs

From the perspective of material existence, the "living" person is a person in the strict sense. The "dead" person is a corpse, not a person who can move and think in the strict sense. If people want to live and live well, they must have a healthy physical state. Health is the basic need of people.

When a person has a healthy body, he is more likely to be happy. Maybe it is because "when there is a problem with some tissues and organs in the human body, if uncomfortable nerve stimulation is produced in the corresponding position of the human body, it will help the person take corresponding measures and improve the possibility of survival," or because "in the sick tissues and organs of the human body, there may be certain substances that will lead to uncomfortable stimulation of the nervous system." When a person is sick, he or she feels uncomfortable and painful. I think every adult has a deep understanding of the pain when sick. Thus, once a person loses his health, the feeling of pain follows, and happiness naturally goes away.

It can be said that the human body is quite tenacious because it has its own immune system and can complete a certain degree of self-repair. The human body can also be said to be fragile. In this world, there are too many existences that can harm human health. Almost everyone suffers or will suffer from headaches, brain fever, or other diseases. For example, according to online data, a person suffers from a cold and fever two to four times a year on average.

We live in an environment where there are millions of species of organisms. There are mutually beneficial and parasitic relationships between these diverse biological populations. Human beings do not remain aloof from the world. Not all creatures in nature are beneficial to human beings. There are many kinds of organisms that can even endanger the survival of human beings. In particular, the immune system of the human body is powerless against the invasion of many viruses and bacteria; for example, the vast majority of people are not immune to HIV.

The human body itself is a complex biochemical machine. Appropriate substance intake is required to maintain the balance of the body's complex biochemical reactions. In the real world, there are many kinds of substances that can interfere with the normal biochemical processes of the human body. Just because of this, when we take chemistry classes, we will see the knowledge of "so-and-so substance is toxic," and we can often hear about incidents such as death from being bitten by poisonous snakes and death from eating poisonous mushrooms by mistake.

In the process of human life, human cells are also constantly dividing, regenerating, and dying. This life activity of division, regeneration, and apoptosis of human cells is controlled by genetic material. Speaking of genetic material, on the one hand, the process by which genetic material controls cell metabolism is affected by the material conditions around the genetic material. It may be for this reason that at certain stages of fetal development, the ingestion of certain drugs by pregnant women can lead to malformations of fetal development. On the other hand, in the process of controlling cell metabolism by genetic material, the genetic material of some cells may also undergo mutations due to some interference, and the mutation of this genetic material may also lead to certain lesions in the human body.

The human body is composed of many substances. The bones, muscles, and skin of the human body have a certain physical strength to resist external forces, but this strength is very limited. When the human body is subjected to an external impact that exceeds the strength limit of its tissues and organs, it will suffer physical injuries, such as skin bleeding, sprains, fractures, etc. Some of this physical damage is recoverable, while some is non-recoverable. When it comes to the severity of the injuries suffered, they can range from short-term pain to lifelong disability or even death.

The main substance that makes up the human body is organic matter. Many of these organic substances are very easy to change; for example, after a certain part of the human body is raised to more than 70 or 80 degrees Celsius, the vital substances that make it up are easy to change, resulting in the loss of vitality of the corresponding part. Therefore, it is common to see cases of burns. Most of the substances that make up the human body are water. Water freezes below zero degrees Celsius. The freezing of water in the human body will damage the corresponding human cells and tissues,

11

so frostbite often occurs in cold weather.

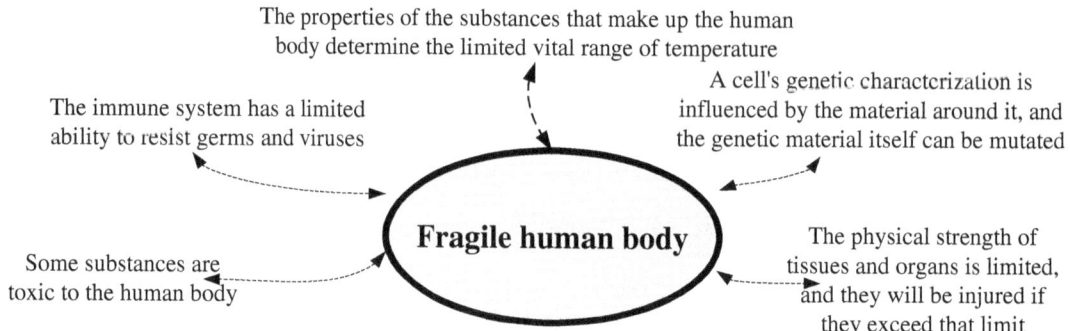

The properties of the substances that make up the human body determine the limited vital range of temperature

The immune system has a limited ability to resist germs and viruses

A cell's genetic characterization is influenced by the material around it, and the genetic material itself can be mutated

Fragile human body

Some substances are toxic to the human body

The physical strength of tissues and organs is limited, and they will be injured if they exceed that limit

Fig. 1.1.6 Vulnerable Human Body

In view of the various factors that affect human health in reality, we need to take corresponding measures to deal with them. In other words, the basic need for health gives rise to a wide variety of derived needs. These derivative needs include the need for pre-prevention, the need for treatment during the event, the need for post-event recovery or daily life assistance, as well as the need to master relevant medical and health knowledge and apply that knowledge.

The needs of pre-prevention can be divided into many kinds, such as the need for a pleasant living environment, the need for exercising and strengthening the body, the need for preventive isolation measures during the epidemic of serious infectious diseases, the need for safe food to prevent diseases from entering by the mouth, the need to control diet to prevent diseases of the digestive system and cardiovascular system, the need to control the dietary ratio to prevent malnutrition and nutritional imbalance, and the need for human body heat preservation. These needs can also be further subdivided and derived, such as the demand for exercise, from which the demand for fitness methods, fitness equipment, and fitness venues can be derived.

The needs of treatment include the needs of doctors to examine, diagnose, and formulate treatment plans; the needs of drugs used to treat diseases; the needs of treatment equipment; the needs of treatment operations; the needs of treatment sites; the needs of energy used in treatment; and so on.

There are also many needs in the post-event stage, such as the need for convalescent care and the need for daily assistive devices. The needs for daily assistive devices include glasses, wheelchairs, prostheses, hearing aids, etc.

In addition, in a sense, being strong is also a component of physical health. In order for people to live better and happier, they need to have relatively easy access to the material things they need for survival. A strong body is obviously conducive to the acquisition of living materials. Imagine if a person is so weak that he can't breathe even when he climbs a few steps up the stairs, and his strength is so small that he can't hold a bowl of soup, and he feels that he can't stand up when he wears a thick coat in winter. How can life be convenient in such a physical state? Can such a body be considered healthy? Therefore, a strong body is also a health requirement, which directly affects people's ability to survive. The need for physical strength further produces the demand for exercise, the demand for fitness food, the demand for exercise venues, the demand for exercise equipment, the demand for exercise measurement tools, the demand for exercise clothing and protective gear, the demand for exercise skills and exercise courses, the demand for body movement function research, sports rehabilitation, and so on.

Longevity is also a health need. First of all, people have to live long enough to reach adulthood and have children. Second, it takes a long enough time for people to master modern scientific knowledge and life skills so that they can participate in wealth production and maintain the survival of individuals, families, and societies. Moreover, people must live long enough to have the opportunity to fully see and enjoy the wonders of the world and to come into the world without complaints or regrets. Therefore, longevity, or maintaining youthful vitality, is also a basic need for human health. To achieve longevity, one needs to have the means to survive the illnesses and disasters that people often face, to have the means to maintain their youthful vitality, and so on.

1.1.6 "Life Continuity" Needs

The reason why a multicellular race of advanced beings can exist for a long period of time is that the race of advanced beings can reproduce. Similarly, the development and prosperity of human society are also inseparable from life reproduction. Thus, the demand for "life continuity" is not only the basic need of human individuals but also the basic need of human society as a whole.

Subject to the extremely complex and large body compared to a single cell, subject to the complex metabolic processes, etc., a large number of cells that constitute a complex multicellular life form will gradually age and languish over time. Many components that affect vital functions cannot be cleaned up completely. The tissues and organs that make up the body cannot be fully renewed over time, and the tissues and organs will eventually gradually move away from the most energetic state, resulting in the overall vital function of a body gradually declining after developing to a certain extent. Finally, the body will be completely incapacitated and die. As a result, the natural lifespan of both humans and advanced animal individuals is very limited. In fact, the lifespan of a short-lived multicellular individual is measured in days or even hours, while the long-lived advanced animal can live for hundreds of years at most. The lifespan of an individual is insignificant compared to the history of the existence of a race that is tens of thousands, hundreds of thousands of years, or even hundreds of millions of years. Therefore, the constant reproduction of new life individuals and embarking on new life processes continuously is the only way for advanced beings to exist for a long time. Lives that do not have the ability to reproduce will soon disappear in the long river of history. The ability to reproduce offspring is fundamentally determined by genetics, so it can be said that reproduction is a need engraved in genes.

The world we live in is constantly changing. The sun's radiation is constantly changing. The inclination of the Earth's axis of rotation relative to the ecliptic plane fluctuates periodically. The Earth's crust is constantly moving, and it is just as the Chinese saying goes, "Seas change into mulberry fields and mulberry fields into seas." The climate and environment of various regions are also constantly evolving. Some places may have been abundant in precipitation, water, and grass thousands of years ago, but now they have become arid and semi-arid desert areas. As the climate changes, so does the type of possible food. The ability of higher life forms, such as digestion, must also adapt to the change. Otherwise, they will die out in the long course of history. The pathogenic microorganisms in the environment of higher life forms are also constantly evolving, which requires the immune system of higher life forms to have the corresponding adaptability. The so-called "innate" abilities of higher life forms are mainly determined by genetic material such as genes. For a specific higher life individual, the genes and other genetic material it possesses are basically constant after birth. As mentioned above, different living environments require higher organisms to adapt with different "innate" abilities. That is to say, individuals need to have slightly changed genetic material from their ancestors to adapt to the changed environment.

Asexual reproduction is basically a copy of the previous generation of life forms, with few changes. It is relatively difficult for such life forms to adapt to an environment that has undergone great changes, and it is naturally easier to disappear in the long river of history. For higher life forms, because there are often a large number of cells together to start a new life process in the process of asexual reproduction, even if a few cells have mutated, they are often covered up by a large number of original replicating cells, and it is difficult to show mutations, such as trees planted with branches, sweet potatoes planted with vines, and potatoes planted with tubers. In fact, in some agricultural production, the stable and unchanged characteristics of asexual reproduction are often used to ensure the widespread planting of improved varieties; for example, asexual reproduction is often used to ensure the quality of durians produced by improved durian planting.

Sexual reproduction means that the genetic material of the offspring has changed compared to that of the parent. The sexually reproducing individual is developed from a single fertilized egg cell. The fertilization process is accompanied by genetic recombination. Therefore, the next generation reproduced sexually is more likely to develop certain mutations in genetic traits. Sexual reproduction causes many changes in the offspring relative to the parents. Among these many changes, it is more likely to have a new trait that will help the new organism adapt to the changed environment. Such new life forms are naturally more likely to survive. Of course, it may allow the population to perpetuate, or it may be classified as a new race because the change is too great. In fact, for today's higher life forms, sexual reproduction is absolutely dominant.

Since humans reproduce their offspring sexually as the result of evolution, sex has become a basic need for healthy young adults. Imagine that if sexual activity is painful and sad, it will make people instinctively avoid sexual activity, which in turn will lead to the extinction of the population. Therefore, realistic sexual activities are basically exciting and

14

pleasurable. That's exactly why healthy young adults will instinctively engage in sexual activities and produce offspring. Thus, human life can continue.

Human beings have a strong ability to create wealth and resist other predators. People do not need to be born with the ability to walk and run quickly, like animals such as horses. Human children are weak, but they can survive and grow under the protection of parents and elders. On the other hand, the size of the adult body limits the size of the newborn baby. Moreover, one of the most important advantages that humans possess over various higher animals is a well-developed brain. The developmental characteristics of the human brain make the head of the human fetus large at birth. Under the constraints of body size, human beings cannot wait for the fetus's locomotor organs to develop relatively strong before being born. Otherwise, the probability of dystocia may be greatly increased, and the survival of the race may be endangered. Perhaps these are the reasons why newborn babies are so weak. The delicate nature of human newborns has created the need for human beings to raise young children. To raise the next generation, love and hard work are needed from parents, elders, and society.

In the process of creating an offspring and raising young children, many needs have been identified, such as the need to organize and maintain the family, the need for birth assistance, the need for care for pregnant women and infants, the need for medical health care for minors, the need for minors to enhance their physical and athletic abilities, and the need for minors' scientific and cultural education and skills training.

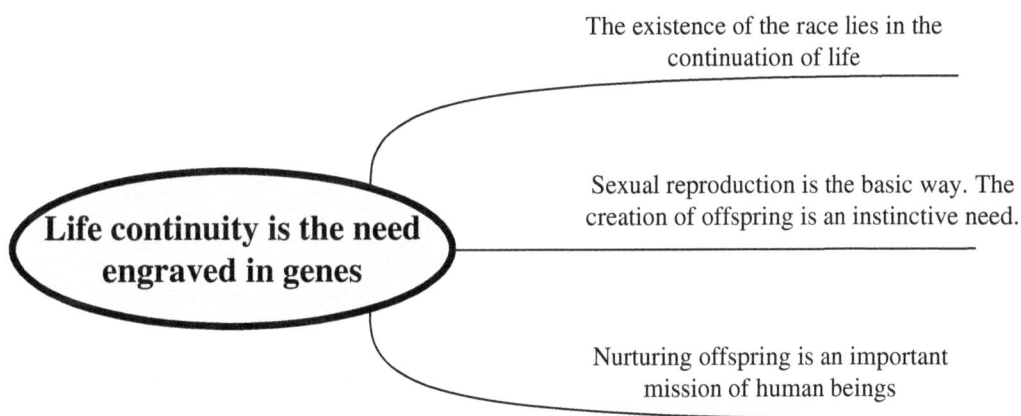

The existence of the race lies in the continuation of life

Sexual reproduction is the basic way. The creation of offspring is an instinctive need.

Life continuity is the need engraved in genes

Nurturing offspring is an important mission of human beings

Fig. 1.1.7 Life Continuity Is the Need Engraved in Genes

1.1.7 "Transportation" Needs

A person's dwelling is often just a small space. In this small space, it is difficult for people to obtain all kinds of wealth to meet the needs of life. People usually need to go to the vast world outside their homes to obtain food, create wealth, learn knowledge, develop various abilities, satisfy spiritual needs, and so on. The ancient sages of China paid attention to "reading ten thousand books and traveling ten thousand miles." Traveling to see the world and experience nature can expand people's horizons, broaden people's knowledge, and cultivate people's sentiments. In modern times, people often need to work a few kilometers or even tens of kilometers away from their homes every day and need to buy daily necessities from shops several kilometers away. All of this gives rise to a need for "transportation," which can be classified as the need for the "transportation" of human beings.

Since entering civilized society, the social division of labor has become increasingly detailed. The materials that people need for work and life are likely to be produced by other people hundreds or thousands of kilometers away. Mobilizing and transporting the materials that people need from thousands of kilometers away, or sending goods to distant places, is another important aspect of the "transportation" need, which can be classified as the "transportation" need of objects.

People's transportation needs are mainly reflected in several aspects: safety, comfort, speed, low cost, etc., while the transportation needs of objects are mainly reflected in low cost, light load, speed, and reliability. People have created a variety of means of transportation, such as boats, cars, and airplanes. This leads to the need to manufacture various vehicles for transportation, the need to build and maintain transportation facilities, the need to design and organize the transportation system, and the need for traffic management, etc.

In addition, we can define the concept of "transportation" more broadly. As we all know, the business behaviors of human society are accompanied by the exchange of data and information; the exchange of data and information is required for the dissemination of knowledge in human society, and the exchange of data and information is required for social activities between two people who are far away. The "transportation" demand for data and information has prompted people to create a variety of remote data information exchange technologies and methods, such as beacons, postal letters, telegrams, telephones, network communications, etc. It then derives the corresponding needs of data and information exchange technology, such as the development and production needs of network communication equipment, the operation and maintenance needs of communication systems, and so on.

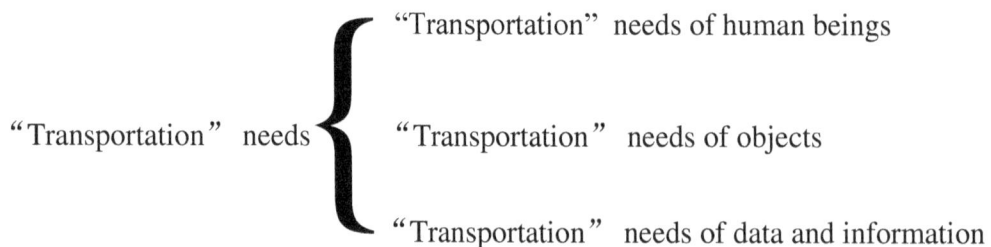

$$\text{"Transportation" needs} \begin{cases} \text{"Transportation" needs of human beings} \\ \text{"Transportation" needs of objects} \\ \text{"Transportation" needs of data and information} \end{cases}$$

Fig. 1.1.8 "Transportation" Needs

1.1.8 "Neuropsychological" Needs

As the saying goes, people have seven emotions and six sensory pleasures. People's actions are often controlled by these seven emotions and six sensory pleasures. The psycho-emotional needs of people, i.e., the "neuropsychological" needs of people, are also basic needs. Human "neuropsychological" needs include not only those directly related to human neurostimulation but also those that are social, loving, recognized, respected, and secure.

In the struggle for survival in the natural world, in most cases, it is easier for living individuals who can draw on advantages and avoid disadvantages to continue their lives. The behavior of seeking advantages and avoiding disadvantages is determined by the human nervous system. Thus, it is very important to meet people's neuropsychological needs. Some people even regard the satisfaction of certain needs in the "neuropsychological" aspect as more important than life itself. There is a widely known poem, "Life is precious, love is more expensive"; this "love" is a neuropsychological demand.

The following is a brief discussion on the pursuit of advantages and avoiding disadvantages. Most higher animals will instinctively seek advantages and avoid disadvantages, and humans are the same as those higher animals. However, sometimes, due to the complexity of the situation that needs to be dealt with, people are not always able to accurately pursue the advantages and avoid the disadvantages. It may be difficult to determine which choice is advantageous and which choice is harmful. After all, there are often many uncertain factors that will affect the future outcome. In a certain situation, there is a contradiction between the interests of the individual and the interests of the group; for example, in the following case (*Note: the following assumptions are only used to discuss the choice of advantages and disadvantages and do not represent the real combat power of humans and wolves*).

Suppose that in a primitive age, when people were extremely sparsely populated, five men in the prime of life who had no modern weapons in their hands encountered a pack of wolves. If these men work together desperately against the wolves, the foreseeable result is that they may resist the wolves' attack, but at the cost of almost all of them being injured, and some even have a certain chance of losing their lives. If they give up resisting and escape, as long as one runs fast enough and is lucky enough, he won't even be injured except for tiredness, but there is a high probability that someone will die, and the probability that everyone can escape safely is very small. Everyone thinks he is fast enough, even though that's not necessarily the case. Under such circumstances, for these five people, no matter what kind of choice they make, there is great uncertainty in the future, whether it is better to run away or resist together. It is really difficult to say which behavior is the most advantageous for everyone and what is really "drawing on advantages and avoiding disadvantages."

Now suppose that it is a family that encounters the wolf pack. The family consists of an old man, an old woman, two young men, two young women, and five children. Suppose that if the escape strategy is adopted, old men and young men will basically not be injured and can survive, while women and children will most likely be hunted by wolves, and families will be broken and will not continue. If the resistance strategy of all is adopted, there is a high probability that the wolves will finally retreat, and most of the women and children will be protected; the adult men may be injured, and someone may lose his or her life. If the old man and woman stay to fight against the wolves and cover the others to escape, the result is that the old man and woman are most likely to die, but the young and children can be safely evacuated, which is almost the best outcome for the continuation of the family. For the old man, there is a contradiction between the choice that is conducive to his personal survival and the choice that is conducive to the survival of the family. The benevolent see benevolence, and the wise see wisdom.

Now let's go back to the issue of the human body's pursuit of advantages and avoidance of disadvantages.

The human body is a complex biochemical machine. If the central nervous system, i.e., the decision-making system of the human body, can perceive the situation when the human body is in a suitable and comfortable state, it is obviously conducive for people to pursue advantages. If the central nervous system of the human body can perceive such conditions when the biochemical machine of the human body is out of balance or reaches certain warning conditions, it is obviously conducive for people to avoid disadvantages. Let's list some of the categories of neurostimulation related to biochemical activities, life, health, and so on.

When the stomach is emptied, the human body will normally produce an uncomfortable hunger stimulus, reminding the body that it is time to eat. Thus, the human body is not prone to nutrient deficiency. On the contrary, people who cannot have an appetite are prone to serious "emptiness" of the body, which can easily lead to physical problems. Obviously, it is difficult for people who cannot have an appetite to survive and have descendants.

An uncomfortable bloating sensation is also very important for a person when eating too much food. It is a reminder to stop eating. After all, the stomach and intestines have their own capacity limits. It is not good to eat too much. If the food eaten exceeds the limit, it will also cause physical problems.

When a sharp object squeezes the body, or when a large amount of pressure is applied to a part of the body, the nerves of the human body produce uncomfortable, painful stimuli. This painful stimulus is an effective reminder that it is time to take measures, including taking action to prevent injury and applying nursing care to the injured part to help the body recover.

When the temperature of the environment is low, according to conditions such as temperature, humidity, and airflow, the human body will produce sensations of coolness, cold, shivering from the cold, or painful and biting cold. It does help to remind the human body to take measures to preserve heat quickly.

When the human body is full of urine, the human nervous system produces a sense of urgency to urinate. This reminds the body that it is time to urinate and prevents damage to human health due to large amounts of urine staying in the body for a long time.

When the stool stored in the large intestine reaches a certain level, the human body will perceive various types of discomfort, such as abdominal pain and urgency. This also reminds the body that it is time to excrete. After all, if stool stays in the human body for too long, it will be detrimental to health.

When a part of the body is dysfunctional, the central nervous system of the human body can often feel uncomfortable nerve stimulation. Depending on the situation, these uncomfortable nerve stimuli include sensations such as warmth, bloating, itching, and pain. Through these nerve stimuli, the human body can often feel the discomfort more accurately. It is obviously beneficial for the human body to take reasonable treatment measures. Of course, it also brings desperate pain to some patients.

When people consume appropriate foods such as sugar, it produces a sweet and comfortable feeling. This feeling of comfort helps people develop an appetite for suitable food, which naturally contributes to human survival. Think about it: if people feel unbearable as soon as they eat suitable foods such as sugar, then how can they eat and supplement the nutrients needed to maintain the balance of the body's biochemical reactions, and how can they activate the body's vital functions?

When it comes into contact with rotten food and gases, the human body will feel uncomfortable sensations such as "smelly," "bitter," and "nauseating." These uncomfortable sensations can help humans avoid problematic foods and prevent food poisoning from occurring.

…

There are many kinds of sensations or stimuli that are directly related to the body's biochemical reactions. It is precisely because of these stimuli that people can effectively make decisions and behaviors that seek advantages and avoid disadvantages. Of course, these stimuli are not all 100% reasonable. After all, the ability of the human body, a biochemical machine, is also limited, and the internal discrimination ability of the human body is limited. For example, some foods that the human body feels "smelly," especially some fermented things, are actually foods that the human body can accept, such as pickled stinky birds of the Inuit, stinky fish from Northern Europe, and the fruit "durian" loved by many Southeast Asians and Chinese. Another example is that the human body will develop pathological pleasure and addictive dependence on many drugs that are harmful to health. However, in ancient nature, it was difficult for humans to come into contact with substances with serious toxicity. In fact, it is the improvement of modern chemical purification technology and synthesis capacity that is the key to the spread of drugs among certain populations in some countries. In other words, in a purely natural environment, the stimulation sensations related to the body's vital functions and the balance of biochemical reactions are actually quite effective.

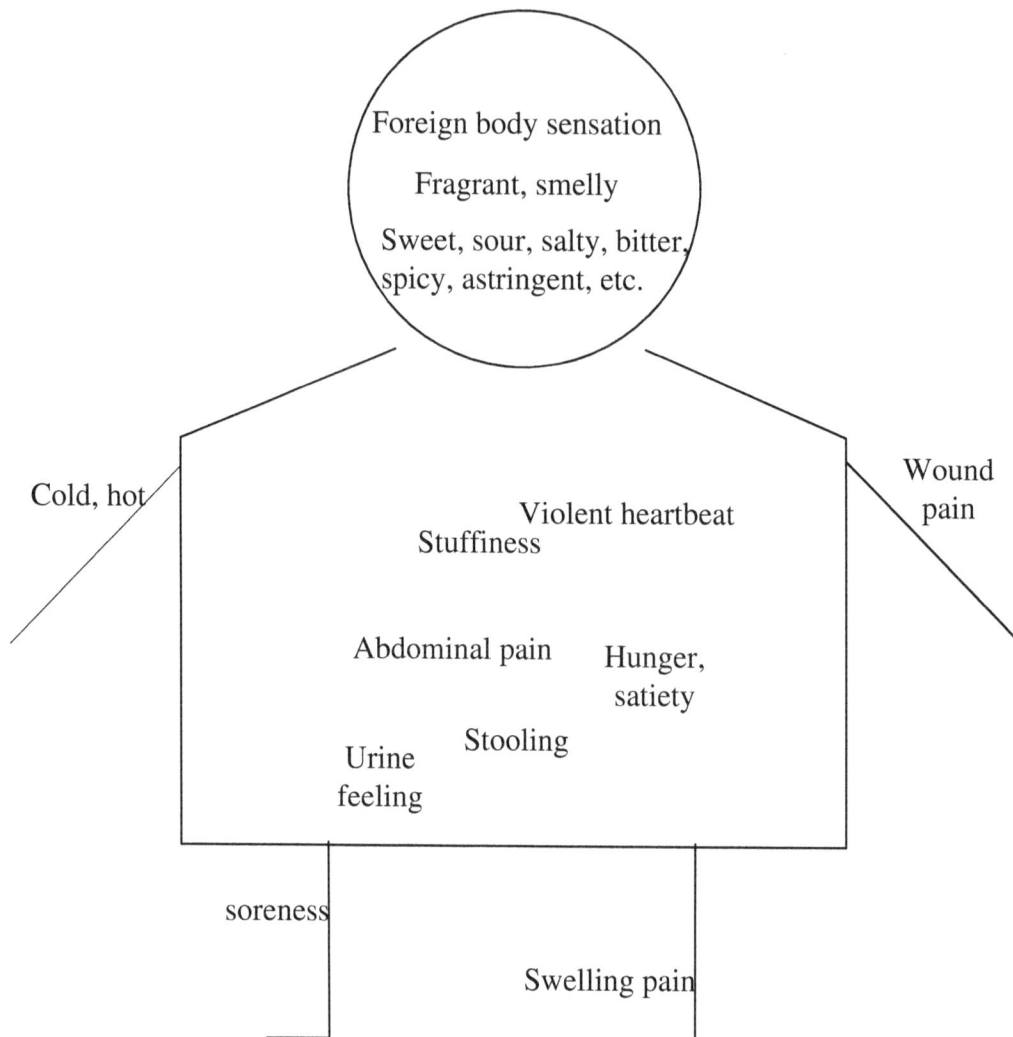

Fig. 1.1.9 Nerve Stimuli Contribute to Seeking Advantages and Avoiding Disadvantages

The various stimuli related to biochemical reactions and the memory of the central nervous system for these actual stimuli make higher animals instinctively seek advantages and avoid disadvantages, which naturally helps them survive and reproduce better. For example, suppose that a bison A has developed a fearless lifestyle habit with no sense of crisis due to the lack of pain and other neurostimulation responses that should make it uncomfortable. The other bison, B, has a sensitive sense of pain and has been trained to have a sense of crisis since he was a child, and he is careful about his surroundings. Bison A has no discomfort with the bite of the predator lion due to the lack of pain and other sensations. Thus, even if a lion arrives, bison A will not run away and will even let the lion bite it. Bison B has a keen sense of nerve, has an obvious sense of fear of danger, and will frantically flee when it finds a lion approaching. Bison B will even resist frantically due to nervous reactions such as nervousness and fear when it fails to escape. Obviously, Bison B has a higher chance of survival in nature than Bison A. It is clear that Bison B is more likely to survive to adulthood. Therefore, under the same fertility conditions, Bison B obviously has a higher chance of successful reproduction.

Perhaps the many stimuli related to human vital functions and the balance of biochemical reactions are the underlying basis for human beings to produce seven emotions and six sensory pleasures. For example, after the tempering of the environment, with the frustrations and lessons learned in the process of growing up, people and some higher animals will have a sense of fear of certain types of phenomena. The so-called "newborn calves are not afraid of tigers" is an exact depiction of this phenomenon. Newborns have no fear of many things that are dangerous due to a lack of experience. In fact, as long as we pay attention to the news, we often see incidents such as young children fearlessly climbing onto the windowsill of tall buildings to play. The human brain has a strong memory, logical thinking ability, and plasticity. It can classify events and phenomena according to empirical knowledge and distinguish which things are dangerous and which are safe. Therefore, with the accumulation of life experience, people's fear or alertness of dangerous things will slowly form. For example, car drivers sometimes encounter this situation: when a driver's nerve center suddenly perceives a driving danger that may lead to a traffic accident, they tend to experience an adrenaline rush, produce nervous emotions, and quickly take measures to avoid the danger.

Moderate tension, vigilance, and fear of dangerous things contribute to the survival and reproduction of living organisms. In the same way, animals and humans who can produce pleasant emotions for a comfortable environment and suitable food will be more likely to successfully choose to live in an environment conducive to survival, which naturally helps to improve the chances of survival and the chances of retaining offspring.

From the primitive clan and tribal society to today's society with many types of occupations, the cooperation between individuals and social groups is the cornerstone of the survival and development of human society. In a sense, people can even be seen as social animals. In fact, when people are born, they are weak and blank slates. Through the nurturing and teaching provided by parents and elders, the knowledge and skills acquired by a person can grow. Being able to transmit and accumulate knowledge is the basis for the development of human society, and the transmission and accumulation of knowledge is based on the social nature of human beings. In fact, primates are basically social. It can be seen that human sociality may have been engraved in the genes for a long time. The sociality of a person means that a person has a social need.

What are the social needs of people? Loneliness is an emotion that people don't like very much, so people have social needs. Even if one is the so-called "social phobia," he or she still has social needs. People love to be recognized and respected by others. People have a need for respect, including being respected and respecting others. People have a need for love, including a desire to be loved, a desire to have a lover, a desire to have someone to rely on, and a desire to be relied on. People also need to have a sense of belonging, spiritual comfort, security, and respect that comes from participating in group activities.

The human body's need for survival has derived the need for safety, including the need for safe access to food, the need for safe rest, and the need for safe leisure and entertainment. Due to the development of social civilization and the

21

increasingly complex and refined social division of labor, people's demand for security has also developed. Stable, reliable, and promising jobs are people's security needs. Survival security is people's security need after old age. Survival security after unemployment is a security need. Medical security is also a security need, and so on.

1.1.9 "Knowledge and Skills" Needs

An important point that distinguishes human beings from animals is that human beings have developed civilization and created a variety of production technologies, production tools, and living utensils, which can meet people's material needs in many aspects. Human beings have developed a variety of ethical and moral norms and have developed a variety of leisure and social entertainment, which, in a sense, have promoted the satisfaction of spiritual needs. Human beings are no longer just like animals, eating, surviving, and reproducing. Human beings acquire material wealth not only for survival but also for recreation. Human beings use wealth to understand the world and to explore the world. There are many kinds of wealth created by human beings, and the vast majority of material wealth can hardly be created by relying on the innate instinctive ability of human beings. In the current field of wealth creation and distribution, which requires quite complex skills, only through a long period of study and training can people master enough knowledge and skills. With knowledge and skills, people can find their own jobs and earn the material wealth needed for themselves and their families. Therefore, the acquisition and possession of "knowledge and skills" are basic survival needs of modern humans.

In fact, it is not only human beings who need to acquire "knowledge and skills" in order to survive. Even if it is a higher animal, it needs to be trained from an early age to acquire survival skills. For example, African lion cubs have mastered excellent hunting skills under the guidance and training of adult lions, while lions raised by people are not good at hunting, which indicates that lions also need to learn survival skills.

With the accumulation and development of human scientific, technological, and cultural knowledge, human beings have more and more knowledge content. Today, the total amount of knowledge possessed by human beings is as vast as a misty ocean compared to individuals. Basically, everyone can only master a small part of it in their entire life. Moreover, scientific and cultural knowledge is constantly evolving. So, it is difficult for human beings to acquire sufficient scientific and cultural knowledge just through the words and deeds of their parents. As a result, human society has generated needs for special masters and teachers, who teach the knowledge and skills of later generations and train and exercise the self-learning ability of later generations. Therefore, the demand for "knowledge and skills" has derived many needs for education and training resources, such as the needs for teachers, schools, and teaching equipment.

In addition, due to the wide variety of derivation and subdivision of human needs, and the many things that can be improved in the satisfaction of needs, the needs of human "knowledge and skills" also cover the needs for research and development of new knowledge and new products.

1.2 Introduction to Scientific and Technological Progress and the Satisfaction of Human Needs

1.2.1 The Historic Eras of Mankind Based on Science and Technology

There are many theories about the history of modern human beings' emergence on Earth. Some say that it is about 200,000 to 300,000 years. Some say that it is more than 100,000 years. Some say that it is about 70,000 to 80,000 years, and so on. However, various theories basically agree that modern humans have been on Earth for tens of thousands of years.

In the tens of thousands of years since the emergence of human beings, the development of human society, especially the ability to obtain living materials, is closely related to the science and technology mastered by human beings. The level of scientific and technological development is concentrated in what kind of tools human beings use. From the perspective of the tools used, the history of modern human beings is often divided into the Paleolithic Age, the Neolithic Age, the Bronze Age, the Iron Age, and the era of industrial machine mass production. Of course, it is very likely that another era of artificial intelligence will be added now. The author's expectation is that human society must not rush into the era of comprehensive artificial intelligence before we are ready. It is in line with archaeological findings to divide human history into stone tool ages, bronze tool ages, and iron tool ages, according to the tools used by humans at that time. In fact, the ancient Chinese book "Yue Jue Shu" (越绝书), which was written about 2,000 years ago based on oral tradition and historical documents, also describes the development history of the tools used by human beings from stone tools to jade, to bronze tools, and finally to iron tools. In the book "Yue Jue Shu," philosopher Feng Hu told the king of State Chu, "At the time of Xuanyuan, Shennong, and Hux, stones were used to make tools … By the time of the Yellow Emperor, jade was used to make tools, and trees were cut down to build palaces … At the time of Emperor Yu, people used copper to make tools, chisel Yique … At this time, iron tools (weapons) were used …" (《越绝书》记载了风胡子对楚王说的话：“时各有使然。轩辕、神农、赫胥之时，以石为兵，断树木为宫室，死而龙臧。夫神圣主使然。至黄帝之时，以玉为兵，以伐树木为宫室，凿地。夫玉，亦神物也，又遇圣主使然，死而龙臧。禹穴之时，以铜为兵，以凿伊阙，通龙门，决江导河，东注于东海。天下通平，治为宫室，岂非圣主之力哉？当此之时，作铁兵，威服三军。天下闻之，莫敢不服。此亦铁兵之神，大王有圣德。”)

1.2.2 The Importance of Written Characters

Looking back at history, we must mention the invention and influence of written characters. In recent thousands of years, sages from all over the world have invented and created their own written characters. Thus, things, including knowledge, observations, ideas, and so on, can be recorded in writing. It has greatly promoted the accumulation and dissemination of human knowledge. It has provided wings for the rapid development of human science, technology, and civilization.

Since the invention and popularization of written characters, to train skills and transfer knowledge for newcomers, human beings can no longer rely solely on the extremely limited ways of word of mouth and hand-to-hand teaching. After all, teaching by word and deed also has its own shortcomings. For example, a master may forget to pass on some knowledge and skills that he has mastered or even his own exclusive creations and discoveries due to negligence. A master may not be able to pass on the relevant knowledge because he has not encountered a suitable teaching situation. The apprentice or student may also fail to effectively master some knowledge and skills because of his or her own learning ability and the practical environment. This may result in the transmission of knowledge and skills being interrupted and knowledge being lost.

The invention and use of written characters have enabled people to learn not only from the teachers around them but also from unknown people and the ancients. For example, people in the European Renaissance period are said to have learned knowledge from ancient Greek scholars. Nobel laureate Tu Youyou was inspired by the Taoist Ge Hong about 1,700 years ago. She referred to Ge Hong's medical book "Handbook of Prescriptions for Emergencies (Reserve Emergency Prescription Behind the Elbow)" (《肘后备急方》), which mentioned that the juice extracted from Artemisia can treat malaria and discovered and refined the effective ingredient artemisinin for the treatment of malaria.

The invention of written characters has also facilitated communication between people around the world. In modern times, the combination of written characters with transportation and communication technology has enabled people to quickly understand the situation in distant places, the development of distant societies, and the scientific and technological progress of distant peoples.

The invention of written characters has promoted the satisfaction of needs for "knowledge and skills," as well as the satisfaction of spiritual needs, and so forth.

1.2.3 Overview of Scientific and Technological Progress and Demand Fulfillment

In the first section, we make a simple mechanical analysis of human needs, such as food, heat preservation, rest, housing, transportation, health, life continuity, neuropsychology, knowledge and skills. Among these needs, food, heat preservation, housing, transportation, and health are directly related to materials. For human beings, the ability to obtain and use materials is determined by the science and technology mastered by them. Among these, the advancement of medical and health technology can make it easier and safer for people to achieve "life continuity" and meet the "life continuity" needs of human beings. The advancement of science and technology and the increase in labor productivity have also allowed human beings to have more leisure time and create many leisure and entertainment methods to meet neuropsychological needs. The improvement of science and technology and labor productivity also enables people to have more time and ways to learn and master knowledge, using more and better practical materials to train skills. Thus, people can better understand the world and meet the needs of human beings in terms of "knowledge and skills."

In the various eras before the modern industrial revolution, due to the limitations of science and technology, human beings were deeply affected by the external environment in terms of material acquisition. In particular, there was often a large-scale famine in the event of a flood, drought, war, or other man-made disaster. In general, in those times, the satisfaction of human needs was unstable. Due to the limited variety of goods, many needs were in a state of serious dissatisfaction. Food and heat preservation were the regular and universal pursuits of ordinary people around the world during those times.

The era of modern scientific and technological civilization, embarked on by scientists such as Galileo and Newton about three to four hundred years ago, has brought the development and progress of science and technology into the fast lane. In the last few hundred years, especially in the last two hundred years, mankind has made a large number of scientific discoveries, such as electromagnetic phenomena, electrons, atoms, antibiotics, the double helix structure of cellular DNA, and so on. As a result, mankind has established a relatively comprehensive scientific research and education system.

The development of science and technology has greatly promoted the development of productivity and helped mankind to develop a variety of products to meet people's needs. Since the beginning of the industrial revolution more than 200 years ago, mankind has carried out several industrial revolutions. In the past 200 years, mankind has developed and applied various technologies such as steam technology, chemical technology, electromagnetic technology, internal combustion engine technology, electronic technology, biochemical technology, and information technology. As a result, the productivity of human labor has increased rapidly, not only in terms of the tremendous increase in labor productivity but also in the creation of many kinds of new products to meet the various needs of human beings. Thus, the situation of human beings in terms of "clothing, food, housing, and transportation" has been greatly improved, and many needs have actually been relatively well met.

In a considerable number of developed countries in Europe and the United States, there has been no large-scale famine for more than one to two hundred consecutive years. The nutrition of ordinary people has also kept up, and malnutrition has become relatively rare. Even if malnutrition occurs, it is likely that they listen to some one-sided body shaping and aesthetic views and engage in dieting on their own. Now the general situation is that a large number of ordinary people are worried about overnutrition, and they have to try their best to resist the temptation of food to lose weight and shape.

People's heat preservation needs have also been met to a large extent; for example, many ordinary families in the United States are even using high-energy-consuming heat preservation methods. They often adjust the air temperature of their large houses to be very comfortable. Whether it is summer or winter, they only need to wear thin clothes indoors.

Modern, convenient, and high-speed transportation helps to meet transportation needs to a large extent. Ordinary people usually no longer rely mainly on two legs to travel but take motorcycles, cars, subways, trains, airplanes, and other means of transportation. The speed at which people move in space has been dramatically enhanced. For example, by taking the high-speed train, people can travel from Shanghai to Beijing in just four to five hours. By plane, you can fly from Beijing to London in one day. As for the transportation of goods, the reality is that people in the United States can quickly receive customized clothes, shoes, and hats made in China, and Chinese people can eat fresh fruits from Chile, half a world apart. In terms of "travel," it can be said that human beings have realized the ancients' dream of "visiting the North Sea in the morning and traveling to Cangwu at dusk."

The advancement of science and technology has also enhanced people's ability to resist diseases. The health needs of humanity have been met to a considerable extent. The average life expectancy of the people of many countries today has reached the age of about 80, instead of only 30 to 40 years of average life expectancy or even less, as in ancient times. Ordinary people can basically live to the time point when they are close to the aging point of the body before they die. Most people no longer die in the prime of life or before. According to the optimistic estimates of some experts, it is likely that humans will soon be able to master the ability to maintain their youthful vitality and further prolong their lives. If it is realized, it will inevitably turn the human desire for "immortality" into a realistic need for "immortality."

The progress of science and technology has also brought many new ways of entertainment and leisure to human beings, such as movies, television, and computer games. They enhance the satisfaction of neuropsychological needs.

1.2.4 Science and Technology Are Not Only About Artificial Intelligence

In the past, relying on the power of science and technology at their disposal, human beings have become the kings of the earth. The continuous progress of science and technology is also constantly affecting the systems and operational modes of human society. The tremendous progress of science and technology has greatly promoted the satisfaction of various human needs. Of course, so far, there are still many unmet needs of human beings, such as some diseases that are difficult to cure. Thus, human beings still need to move forward in the field of science and technology.

Science and technology have brought great convenience and improvement to human life. Thus, human beings generally have a warm welcome attitude towards science and technology. In particular, artificial intelligence technology, which seems to be magical, has recently become the hottest technology field. It is highly sought after by capital, government, and public authorities.

However, in this article, it is firmly suggested that the development of AI, and especially its application, should be slowed down. In the current situation, as human society is not yet prepared, we should stop blindly pursuing artificial intelligence technology. There are many types of science and technology; we don't have to focus on the use of various artificial intelligence technologies.

Yes, the so-called artificial intelligence technology can improve labor production efficiency. However, is it meaningful for human society to improve labor productivity by introducing artificial intelligence technology to transform a factory that originally needs to hire a lot of human workers into an unmanned factory with only one capitalist remaining? The answer is no. Opening our eyes to the whole world, under today's social operating systems, this so-called improvement in labor productivity is simply a nightmare for the vast majority of people.

In fact, from the perspective of human development history, from the process of satisfying human needs, and from the current living conditions of human beings, human beings do not need to use artificial intelligence for comprehensive automation and unmanned operations in most production fields and can basically meet human needs. Indeed, in the early stage of the development of human society, before entering the era of industrialization, and even before the limited computer automation in certain fields of wealth creation, it was indeed necessary to develop production technology and improve labor productivity to meet human needs. Even today, there is a need to continue to improve labor productivity and reduce the labor intensity of human workers in many areas. However, it should not be forgotten that even with the development of science and technology today, improving labor productivity and reducing the labor load of the human body still do not mean the development and application of artificial intelligence technology. According to the reality of today's society, in many fields, artificial intelligence is not actually needed to meet the needs of human beings.

With the current state of human society, in the field of wealth creation, human beings must not continue to pursue the improvement of labor productivity under the mode of developing comprehensive unmanned factories without restraint. In some fields, the introduction of high-level artificial intelligence beyond the human brain will only put a shackle on humanity and bring disaster to humanity. In the current state of development of human society, blindly pursuing and developing artificial intelligence technology to realize the so-called artificial intelligence unmanned production system with "ultra-high labor productivity" that only the capitalists are left with will have a very high probability of causing serious social problems and even leading to social collapse. This is the reason why this article has reservations about the use of AI technology.

1.3 Overview of the Satisfaction of Human Needs in Primitive Times

1.3.1 Overview of the Paleolithic Age

In the first tens of thousands of years when modern humans appeared on the earth, due to the lack of scientific and technological knowledge accumulation, the tools at the disposal of human beings were still very rudimentary, and humans were in the Paleolithic Age.

In the Paleolithic Age, the tools used by humans were very crude. Especially in the early Paleolithic period, human beings only used direct hitting to make tools. In the Paleolithic Age, in general, if a blade was made by hitting stones or aggregates, then it was considered that the tool manufacturing process was finished successfully.

In the Paleolithic Age, there were very few types of stone tools in human possession. Tools can be mainly divided into three categories: chopping tools, scrapers, and pointed tools. Among them, chopping tools are used to chop trees to make wooden sticks, cut animals, dig plant roots, smash nuts, etc. Scrapers are used to cut meat, scrape bark to make bamboo or wooden tools, and scrape animal skin, etc. Pointed tools are used to peel animal skins, dig up bones for meat, etc. Choppers and sticks were the main tools used by humans in hunting at that time.

For most of the Paleolithic period, the only tools used for hunting, except for throwing stones and sticks, were melee assault weapons. The beasts were generally very alert. Therefore, it was usually not easy for humans to get close to them and carry out attacks. Consequently, it was not easy for the human ancestors of the era to obtain food through hunting.

In that time, clothing used to protect against the cold was mainly made of animal skins and leaves. Since the cutting edges of stone and bone tools were not very sharp, it was naturally quite time-consuming and laborious to make clothes. For reference, you can refer to the process of making animal skins (http://www.genhe.gov.cn/News/show/599115.html) by the Evenks. The Evenks need to spend a few days drying the animal skins in the first step. In the second step, they need to scrape the dry skin to remove the grease. The third step is to soak the oil-removed dried skin for several days until it is soft. Then the fourth step is to repeatedly scrape the skin to remove the moisture. The fifth step is to roast it dozens of times with smoke. Each time, it is smoked for about five hours. Finally, the sixth step is to scrape the hide with a special tool and rub it with hands until it is very soft. It takes about 12 to 13 days for the last step. Thus, the whole process of making a skin takes dozens of days. Even in terms of the above time-consuming process, it is just the cost of so-called "primitive" manual craftsmanship in modern times. The tools they use are much better than those of our Paleolithic human ancestors. As mentioned in the article "Animal Skin Culture" (http://www.genhe.gov.cn/News/show/599115.html) on the website of the Root River City Government, the woman in the illustration uses a metal knife that is much more advanced than stone tools.

In the late Paleolithic period, the technology mastered by human beings improved, and human beings mastered indirect striking methods and secondary repair techniques. By striking indirectly, one can create long, thin stone chips, and the blade is easier to sharpen. By using the indirect striking method, it is easier to control the shape and more efficient than using the method of direct strikes. In addition to the smashing tools, scrapers, and pointed tools, tools such as carvings, stone balls, stone cones, stone saws, bone spears, bone needles, and bone swim bladders had also been invented. People also invented the long-range weapon of the bow and arrow. Bone swim bladders made it easier for people to catch fish. Bows and arrows are ranged weapons that allow humans to attack from a distance, making it easier to launch effective lethal attacks on beasts before they are alert. Compared to wooden sticks, the piercing ability of bone spears is more likely to inflict more damage on beasts. Compared to previous eras, these tools have greatly improved the efficiency of human hunting and fishing. Of course, this improvement is only compared to earlier times. People still relied on physical fitness and luck to obtain food, and they still had to rely on the heavens to reward food. Bone needles allowed people to sew clothes. In this era, the tools used by humans were still very rudimentary. Labor was all based on manual physical ability, which was time-consuming and labor-intensive. Travel still relied on two legs. It relied on physical strength to carry prey, plants, roots, fruits, and other items. In order to get enough food and clothing, human beings had not had an easy time.

In general, human beings' ability to obtain and use materials was still very weak throughout the Paleolithic Age. So people were often exhausted and tired of solving the problem of food and clothing. In that era, humans mainly obtained food through gathering and hunting. At that time, people's food preservation technology was still very low. There were no refrigerators, and there were no large quantities of table salt that could be used to marinate food for long-term preservation. In warm and hot weather, whether the food was animal meat, plant stems, leaves, or fresh fruits, it would often rot and deteriorate in a few days. So in those days, especially in warm and humid weather, people literally had to go hunting and gather food every day. Wild animals, on the other hand, tended to be alert and agile, so hunting was not an easy task, and humans often needed to fight wits and patience with animals. Outside the tropics, plant growth had a distinct seasonality due to changing weather. After autumn, it was often difficult to collect enough delicious stems, leaves, fruits, and seeds during the cold winter because the fruits and seeds fell and rotted. Moreover, the use of rudimentary wooden, stone, or bone tools, or even the excavation of wild plant roots by hand, was very inefficient. Therefore, although in the early days of modern human existence there were many wild animals and plants and a sparse population, and most of the time human food was relatively abundant, because they relied on nature for food, the food supply was not very stable, and people had to be busy looking for food almost every day.

Due to the rudimentary tools of clothing making in the era, making clothes was time-consuming and laborious. Therefore, in the cold season, heat preservation was often a big issue for human ancestors.

As for the health needs of human beings, because the accumulation of human knowledge in that era was extremely limited, the level of science and technology was very low, and there was little health knowledge and medical methods, people were easily frustrated by injuries and diseases. At that time, the satisfaction of human health needs was a big hole. In terms of life expectancy indicators, which can better reflect the health status of a society, in general, the data of the era were not very good. Due to the lack of actual records, modern people can only speculate and estimate the lifespan of humans in primitive times by observing fossilized teeth, so there are various estimates and theories about human lifespan. The author has not studied archaeology, and here is only a loose account based on information on the World Wide Web. According to the statements about the average life expectancy of human beings in the era that can be searched on the Internet, some say fifteen or sixteen years old, and some say between twenty and thirty years old. Among them, the low value of the average life expectancy estimate is even only about ten years old, and the highest estimate is about thirty-five years old. Due to the influence of injury, disease, heat and cold, and other factors, it is possible that 40 to 50 percent of people in the era did not live to be 15 years old. Referring to the lifespan of ancient human beings recorded after the technological progress of later generations, it is basically certain that "the average life expectancy of human beings in the Paleolithic Age was very low." Moreover, whether it is "overestimated" or "underestimated," it can be seen that for the vast majority of people in the Paleolithic Age, the satisfaction of needs for health and longevity is extremely lacking.

1.3.2 Overview of the Neolithic Age

About 10,000 years ago, humans entered the Neolithic Age. The main characteristics of the Neolithic Age are the emergence and widespread use of polished stone tools, the emergence of agriculture and animal husbandry, which gradually became the mainstream of food production in human society, the beginning of human settlement, the storage of food, and the development of pottery and textile technology. Of course, as for the phenomenon of settlement, this article does not deny that it also existed in earlier times, and even among birds, there are many that live in the same place all year round; let alone people, as long as the local area can always meet the needs of survival, why should they migrate? Moreover, the speed and ability of people to cross mountains and rivers are not as strong as those of many birds.

According to some studies, in the first tens of thousands of years after the emergence of modern humans, the population grew relatively slowly. The total population remained very small for a long period. But over time, by about 10,000 years ago, it was estimated that the global population had grown to about four million. Such a population size means that the total demand for food by human beings was already very large at the time, especially in some densely populated areas or on the edge of habitable areas, and the pressure and difficulty for human beings to obtain enough food through fishing, hunting, or gathering were great.

Why is it speculated that about 10,000 years ago, there was great pressure and difficulty for humans to obtain enough food through fishing, hunting, or gathering?

It is because humans do not have the same strong ability to digest the dry and withered stems and leaves of many types of plants as cattle and sheep, and the types of plant-based food sources for humans are quite limited, and the yields of these naturally growing plant-based foods are usually low. In the primitive era, the quantity of human-edible parts of each plant was often very limited. This is because wild plant varieties with edible parts for humans were not artificially bred and improved, and because there were often many other species competing for sunlight and fertility in the natural environment. In addition, in the case of natural growth, the density of these foodborne plants was often not very high. They were often scattered in clusters in the east and west. Thus, the food yield per unit area of land was usually very low. In the article "Population, Resource Consumption and Energy Conversion" (http://old.lifeweek.com.cn//2005/0113/10836.shtml), it is mentioned that "in the stage of collecting food, only 0.4–20 kg of dry matter can be produced per hectare of land per year." Of course, it cannot be denied that in some regions, food production per unit land may be much higher than the estimates in this paper, such as breadfruit trees in some Pacific islands that can produce up to 2,400 kilograms of breadfruit per acre. However, for most areas where human beings live, the dry matter yield estimate per unit land in the article should be reasonable. For example, the original wild corn should be a good example. Fig. 1.3.1 compares the shape of the cob of wild maize teosinte with the shape of the modern corn cob. Wild corn teosinte has only a handful of seeds, and it's completely incomparable to modern corn. As for the size of the cob, the teosinte seed grains are not larger than the modern corn seed grains, and one can imagine that the ratio between the teosinte cob and the modern corn cob is simply more exaggerated than the size ratio between humans and elephants. Thus, we can imagine how low the yield of corn must have been when humans first domesticated corn thousands of years ago (there is much information and many pictures about wild corn on the Internet, such as the article "Chinese scientists successfully retrieved the genetically lost high-protein gene from the ancestor of corn" (https://www.cas.cn/cm/202211/t20221117_4855089.shtml). According to the article "Population, Resource Consumption and Energy Conversion," one square kilometer of land only produced 40–2,000 kg of dry matter in the primitive era, which could only feed several people.

Cob of Wild Corn Teosinte   Cob of Modern Corn

Fig. 1.3.1 Comparison of the Cob of Wild Corn Teosinte and the Cob of Modern Corn

In places where plants are naturally randomly distributed, people often need to do ergodic searches to gather food.

Let's estimate the time required for searching 1 square kilometer of land thoroughly. If a person can traverse 1 square meter of land per second (equivalent to walking at a speed of about 1 meter per second), and the time spent purely traversing the land to collect food is 6 hours per day, then it takes 46 days to traverse a square kilometer of land without repeating the route. The actual potential scenarios may differ from the assumptions. If the field of vision is broad and the distribution of foodborne plants is concentrated, the traversal time may be much less than assumed. If there are shrubs and vines all over the place, and the visibility is poor, then the traversal speed may be much slower than assumed. If there is only grass on the land and the grass is very tall, as in the scene "wind blows, grass low, cattle and sheep visible," it is estimated that it will take about the same amount of time to collect food as assumed. Thus, from the perspective of traversal time, collecting food in primitive times was very time-consuming and labor-intensive. Moreover, the human-edible stems, leaves, and seeds of plants are generally very popular with birds, beasts, insects, and ants; that is, human beings also face a huge team of competitors such as birds, beasts, insects, and ants. Plant stems, leaves, and seeds also have the problem of a collection window, which will fall and rot if they are not picked in time.

Therefore, this paper argues that the pressure on humans to obtain food through collection was quite great. Especially for the collection of cereal seed foods that could be stored for a long time after drying and were suitable for preparing grain for winter and spring, it was very likely that, because people had to spend a lot of time on the way, the seeds had fallen to the ground or been eaten by birds and insects before they could collect a large amount.

On the other hand, the population was not evenly distributed. In relatively densely populated areas, there might be less prey. In the end stage of the Paleolithic and the beginning stage of the Neolithic Age, humans invented the bow and arrow, a long-range shooting weapon. After entering the Neolithic Age, the stone tools polished by humans were sharper than in the past. The hunting efficiency of humans was greatly enhanced. As a result, at the beginning, many tribes had easier access to food. The factor "lack of food" that limited population growth was alleviated, and the population naturally increased. In some densely populated areas, over time, human settlements were no longer far apart. As the population increased, the number of people involved in hunting naturally increased. This was likely to result in the prey being hunted rapidly and in large quantities. Over time, the number of prey available in some densely populated areas had been greatly reduced by the rapid rate of hunting. In addition, it is likely that there were constraints between different human settlement groups, such as the existence of mountains and rivers. It was likely that a human settlement group could only hunt in a very restricted area for a certain period of time. In some areas, humans encountered a new problem after the advancement of hunting technology: it was difficult to find prey.

Of course, it might also be because of the change in climate 10,000 years ago, which made it difficult for some animals and plants in some regions to survive, and the corresponding prey naturally became less. Naturally, people living in such areas had fewer sources of food, and they were under more pressure to obtain food.

Under the pressure of seeking food, reducing working time, and improving efficiency, about 10,000 years ago, human society in many regions of the world began to carry out agricultural revolutions. Some archaeological studies indicate that the agricultural revolution likely began on the edge of the regions suitable for human existence. In these fringe areas, the pressure on human survival was often greater than in the central area. Of course, there was also a possibility that there happened to be some whimsical human ancestors at that time who observed and practiced that crops could be cultivated and some animals could be domesticated, and that the cultivation of crops and livestock was more secure in terms of food supply stability than gathering and hunting, so the agricultural revolution began. Humans began to clear the land, plant and cultivate plants, and grow delicious and long-lasting food crops and sweet fruits and vegetables. Humans also began to domesticate animals such as pigs, cows, sheep, chickens, and ducks. In this way, people could not only get meat and egg food when they needed it, but also pigs, cows, sheep, chickens, ducks, geese, and other animals could convert plants, insects, and ants that are difficult for humans to eat and digest into meat and egg food that humans need, which is equivalent to broadening the diet of human beings in a sense. By the way, dogs were probably domesticated tens of thousands of years before the agricultural revolution to serve as watchmen and hunting assistants.

The agricultural revolution dramatically increased the amount of food produced per unit of land, providing humanity with a new, relatively stable, and generally predictable supply of food. The Agricultural Revolution allowed humans to harvest enough food on a small plot of land near their habitat as planned and no longer had to wander the mountains and fields in search of food by luck, nor did they have to spend their energy on the way to find food every day. The popular science article "Population, Resource Consumption and Energy Conversion" (http://old.lifeweek.com.cn//2005/0113/10836.shtml) mentions that "in the era of farming, without the help of fossil fuels and chemical fertilizers, the dry matter yield per hectare has increased to 50–2,000 kg, which has increased by hundreds of times." In fact, with the cultivation and optimization of crops and the improvement of farming technology, the dry matter yield in some regions in later generations may be higher than that mentioned in the above article; for example, some studies say that after the Song Dynasty, some areas in southern China have produced more than 200 kilograms of grain per mu, which is equivalent to more than 3,000 kilograms of grain per hectare. The scientific and technological progress represented by the agricultural revolution has provided a food basis for human beings to continue to grow after reaching a certain population.

About the end of the Paleolithic or early Neolithic Age, humans invented and created pottery. The emergence of pottery has provided better conditions for human beings to store food and other items. For example, by storing dried rice in a pottery jar and covering the lid, people need not worry about the rice being stolen by mice, which was safer and more hygienic. People could also use clay pots to carry water and hold water, eliminating the trouble of having to run to the river or pond every time they needed to drink. Pottery also allowed people to have more ways to cook. People could use clay pots to cook rice, boil meat, boil vegetables, boil milk, etc. In this way, human cooking techniques became more varied. People could have more diverse taste enjoyment, and it increased human happiness. Moreover, cooking in clay pots may be healthier than simply using fire to roast food. The invention of pottery caters to the multifaceted needs of human beings. Even one important reason why the ancient Chinese sage "Shun" was able to ascend to the throne of emperor was that he made excellent pottery. In addition, the changes in the form and nature of the material brought about by the firing of pottery might have inspired the imagination of people's creations.

The construction of pottery often took a lot of time and manpower, so the potter was objectively required to settle down within a certain period of time. For planting crops, there was a lot of work to be done, including clearing the land, sowing, weeding, insect removal, driving away birds and beasts, caring for crops, harvesting, and so on. A harvest cycle is often half a year or one year. Furthermore, the cultivated land was more convenient to plough and sow. Thus, the planting industry practitioners also needed to settle down. Some of the animals raised by humans are not suitable for mobile grazing. For example, pigs and chickens are not suitable for nomadic herding but are suitable for animal husbandry. To raise these animals, people also needed to settle down. With the progress of science and technology and the improvement of productivity, people had more material wealth, which was quite troublesome to move, and it was a pity to abandon it. It objectively reduced people's desire to migrate and flow to a certain extent. Moreover, the people who had settled down were able to spend more energy to improve their living conditions and could make their living environment relatively safer and more comfortable.

Over time, the territory of human beings gradually expanded from warm places to places with four seasons. Compared with many higher animals, the human body is characterized by the lack of dense body hair to keep out the cold. It raises the question of how people can meet the needs of the body to "keep warm" in the cold winter. In order to keep warm, people lived in caves, lit fires, and put on clothing made of fur and leaves, as well as shoes, hats, and other garments. Fire and clothing, respectively, represent the milestones of scientific and technological progress in the early days of mankind. Of course, "fire" had been mastered by earlier humans much earlier than the advent of modern Homo sapiens, and clothing was invented in the Paleolithic period.

In the Neolithic Age, humans developed textile technology. In addition to meeting people's needs for "food," the agricultural revolution in the Neolithic Age also included the cultivation of cotton, hemp, mulberry, and other plants, as well as the domestication of silkworms. All these promoted the development of the textile industry, enriched the source of human clothing, and provided a new way for people to make clothes and bedding to meet the needs of "heat preservation." The textile processing of the Neolithic period can be found in many articles, for example, "Ancient Textiles of Ancient Achievements" (https://www.ciae.com.cn/detail/zh/4497.html) on the website of the China Agricultural Museum, which shows the simple textile processing of kudzu vine.

In the Neolithic Age, people also invented and created many other types of tools, such as rattan baskets that could be used to carry and store items and fishing nets. These inventions objectively facilitated the lives of human beings in the Neolithic Age and greatly helped meet human needs.

1.3.3 A Brief Analysis of the Satisfaction of Human Needs in Primitive Times

In the primitive times of Homo sapiens, that is, in the Paleolithic and Neolithic periods, it could be said that human beings lived in an environment full of crises, such as food crises caused by unstable food sources, meteorological crises caused by weather changes, health crises caused by germs and viruses, casualties caused by predators, and crises caused by conflicts between different human tribes. For most people in that era, it was difficult to meet almost all kinds of needs in a good and stable manner, and scientific and technological progress was urgently needed to meet the various needs of human beings.

In the Neolithic Age, although there were ships like canoes in some areas, people were terrestrial after all. So, as far as human beings as a whole, human "travel" almost completely relied on their legs and carried goods on their shoulders, which belonged to a typical "transportation mainly relying on walking." Animals such as donkeys, horses, camels, and other animals that could be used for carrying are said to have been domesticated by humans for only about several thousand years, almost from the time when humans opened the light of civilization.

The athletic abilities and physical capabilities of individual humans limit the results of hunting activities. Humans hike at a speed of four or five kilometers per hour. Since one has to rest in frequent breaks, this speed will slow down when people carry heavy objects. As a result, the distance that hunters in ancient times could leave their home every day was extremely limited. Usually, ten to twenty kilometers was already a very long distance. In fact, for reference, even during the Spring and Autumn Period and the Warring States Period, which was over 2,000 years after the advent of civilization, the regular marching distance of infantry units with heavy weapons was defined as one "she" in China, and the length of one "she" was equivalent to 30 li at that time, which is only about 12.5 kilometers today. Although the factor of encampment had to be considered for the march of an army, the march of an army was one-way in a day, and the hunting journey was often a round trip. Thus, the historical fact can confirm that people should have had very limited space for daily hunting in ancient times. Moreover, people have physiological limits. An adult man is quite strong enough to walk a long distance of more than 10 kilometers with a prey weighing about 50 kilograms on his back. If the weight is increased a little more, such as to 100 kilograms, and a person can walk such a long way, then the person can be considered to be super strong against nature. This physiological limit of man restricts the range of hunting activities. Moreover, except for the cold season, especially in summer, if fresh meat cannot be properly treated, it will often spoil and rot after a day or two. Therefore, for the women and children who remain in their places of residence, it is of little use for the hunters to travel far to hunt. Therefore, this paper argues that the scope of people's daily hunting activities is very limited. The existence of these constraints affects the potential outcomes of human hunting. After all, it is not always possible to find prey in a small area, let alone hunt successfully.

Before the agricultural era, people relied on gathering and hunting. People often faced the situation of sparsely distributed edible fruits, seeds, stems, and leaves for gathering. For hunting, sometimes it was easy to find prey, and sometimes it was hard to find prey. Both gathering and hunting had a lot of unreliability and instability. As a result, human beings might face a lack of adequate food from time to time. With the absence of effective means of preserving food, human beings may often be in a state of hunger and fullness. Therefore, food needs should not always be well and stably met.

Later, in order to obtain a stable and reliable food supply, people began to clear trees and weeds, plant and cultivate cereals, and domesticate animals. This is the agricultural revolution that began about 10,000 years ago. In contrast, it is clear that hunting was usually more time-consuming and laborious, far less convenient than the use of livestock and poultry kept around. The collection of scattered wild fruits and seeds was basically far less reliable than the cultivation of grains, fruits, and vegetables that had been domesticated and cultivated. Agriculture, including cropping and animal husbandry, had greatly increased food production per unit area of land, i.e., increased population carrying capacity per unit area of land. The agricultural revolution is an epoch-making progress in science, technology, and industry in the history of human development.

However, due to the limited accumulation of science and technology in the early stage of the agricultural era, although people invented and created a lot of tools, they could only make and use some relatively simple labor tools for a long period of time, mainly stone, wood, and bone tools. The labor efficiency was not very high. In the early days, agricultural work was very dependent on human physical ability. Before entering the era of civilization, the degree of domestication of crops was still relatively low, and the technology of scientific cultivation and breeding was also low. Although the annual yield of food per unit land after the agricultural revolution was often one or two orders of magnitude higher than that in the gathering era, compared with modern agriculture, the yield was generally still very low. Moreover, at that time, the means and ability of human beings to resist disasters were quite weak. Droughts, floods, and insect and locust plagues that occurred from time to time affected the food harvest. So, in the early days of agricultural society, human food needs were not always satisfied.

Since many preys lost their living space in the agricultural planting area, humans in agricultural planting areas had become vegetarian, and the proportion of meat in people's food intake was much lower than before the agricultural era. Some studies have also suggested that for a long time after entering the agricultural era, the average nutritional status of human beings was worse than before the agricultural era. However, the conclusion cannot deny that the agricultural revolution brought about real social progress. The reality was that due to climate change and population growth, it was no longer possible for our ancestors in many regions to obtain enough food to maintain basic satiety if they continued to hunt and gather only for food. As mentioned above, "Population, Resource Consumption and Energy Conversion" stated that "during the food gathering stage, only 0.4–20 kg of dry matter can be produced per hectare of land per year." According to the estimate, one square kilometer of land could only feed several people. In some areas, population densities were likely to be high enough to reach the limits of the carrying capacity of the land under natural conditions. The food available through gathering and hunting was likely to be unsustainable, and people often went hungry. Therefore, although agriculture has made a large number of people vegetarian, in the case of population growth, agriculture has maintained the state of basic human satisfaction and survival and has made great contributions. Without agriculture, it was very likely that the situation of meeting human food needs would be worse, at least not sufficient to support the subsequent population growth.

It may be questioned why this article argues that human needs for food were not always met in the early days of the agrarian era. Although the population increased in the early agricultural era, the population density was still very low compared to modern times. There were a lot of wastelands. Why not cultivate more land and raise more livestock to improve the supply of food and prepare for disaster prevention?

There may be questions. Although the population had increased in Neolithic times, the population density was still very low compared to modern times. There were many wastelands. Although the yield per unit area of land was a little lower, why not cultivated more land and raised more livestock to improve the supply of "food"?

Indeed, it is natural to think of producing and stocking up on enough food. In the face of some disasters, human beings are very weak, especially in ancient times when productivity was relatively low. For example, if a somewhat big flood came, which often happened, it was likely that even the shelter would be washed away, and no matter how much food storage was prepared, the food storage might be washed away completely as well. Furthermore, there was no need to plant too much. After all, food has a shelf life. Even if dry rice and other grains can be stored for a relatively long time, they will become aged grain after two or three years, and they are no longer suitable for consumption. In Neolithic times, since there was not much trade, there was really no need to plant too many crops. After all, planting crops was quite hard, and it was all blood and sweat. It would be a waste to put too many crops in the warehouse and wait for them to naturally spoil. The more important reason of all was that in the early days of the agrarian era, the tools used were very simple, the labor efficiency was very low, and it was very hard to grow crops. There was a shortage of manpower. The land one farmer could cultivate was very limited. For a farmer, too much land is useless; what he can do is see the wastelands, and he is unable to cultivate them.

Let's take ancient China as an example for discussion. In the Neolithic times of China, i.e., in the first few thousand years of the agrarian era, it was said that there was no invention of the plow that could utilize animal power, and the main agricultural tool used by people was "Lei Si." Lei Si could be used to turn the soil. Fig. 1.3.2 below shows the agricultural tools Lei Si excavated from the archaeological excavation of the Hemudu site. Compared with modern machine farming, the productivity of the early rudimentary labor tool Lei Si is extremely low. Using Lei Si, the dependence on human physical strength was very heavy. The rudimentary tools of labor greatly limit the size of the land that a man can cultivate, and thus the amount of food he can produce.

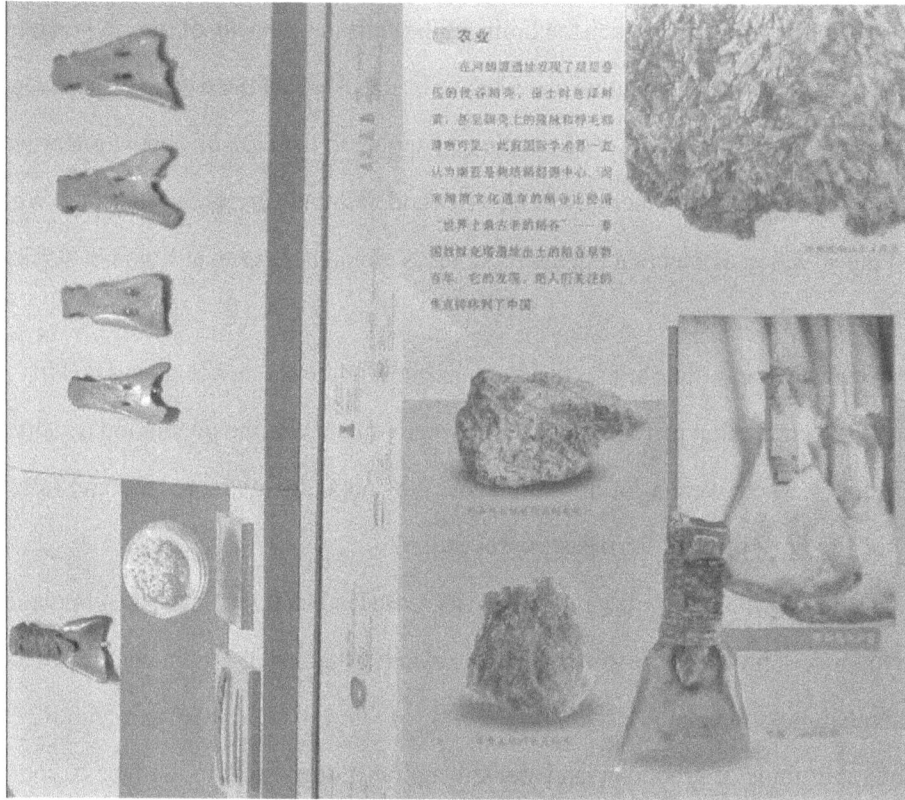

Fig. 1.3.2 Ancient Agricultural Tools 5,000 to 7,000 Years Ago (Picture from the Zhejiang Provincial Museum)

Since Lei Si, made of stone or bone, had long been eliminated from the historical stage, the following discussion is based on a kind of similar tool: the hoe, an iron tool with higher efficiency. Why is it thought that iron hoes are more efficient than Lei Si? It is because the strength of steel materials is much higher than that of stone and bone. The cutting edge of the hoe can be made sharper, and it is easier to chisel the soil. The soil is turned without worrying about the hoe being broken or damaged. The dry, large soil blocks can also be easily broken with the hoe, so that the loosening step of planting crops can also be completed easily.

According to the author's experience of living in rural Zhejiang thirty to forty years ago, if a hoe is used to turn over the soil in the paddy field, an adult man might turn over half a mu of land a day, and he would be exhausted after finishing the work. About thirty years ago, in the countryside of Jinhua, Zhejiang Province, the cultivation of sporadic vegetable fields of tens of square meters was basically completed with hoes. Considering that the feelings may be different for different people, the following estimate of the labor efficiency of the hoe is from the perspective of time and energy.

Let's start with an estimate from a temporal perspective. Turning over the paddy field land with a hoe includes the following actions: raising the hoe to increase the potential energy, swinging the hoe hard to crack the ground, prying the soil after the hoe to the end, and pulling the soil. Even if one completes the set of movements quickly and periodically, it takes about two seconds for a period. If the required depth of turning is deep, the width of the hoe used is generally not more than 10 cm, and the length is generally about 30 cm. Now assume that each hoe can turn over an area of about 200 square centimeters of land, which is almost equivalent to the area of 14 centimeters by 14 centimeters. The actual operation may not be able to achieve such an area; different soil conditions and different hoe swing strength will affect the area of land that can be turned under a hoe. The above assumption means that it uses the hoe 50 times and takes about 100 seconds to turn over a square meter of land. A half-mu of land, i.e., 333 square meters of land, has to be turned over for more than nine hours with a tool hoe, and the physical consumption of the human body is very huge. In fact, for this kind of laborious physical work, even if one works effectively for six hours a day, plus the time for eating, drinking, and resting, people almost have to be busy from morning to night all day.

Let's discuss it from the perspective of energy. The thickness of the paddy soil cultivation layer is about 15 to 20 cm. Assume that the depth of soil turned over with a hoe is 15 cm and that turning the soil with a 15 cm depth is equivalent to raising the soil by 15 cm. Since the density of paddy soil is about 1.2 to 1.5 grams per cubic centimeter, 1.35 grams per cubic centimeter is taken. Following the work formula, the work w_1 to turn over a half-mu land is as follows.

$$
\begin{aligned}
w_1 &= mgh_w \\
&= \rho v g h_w \\
&= \rho S h_h g h_w \\
&= 1350 kg/m^3 \times 1000000 m^2 / 1500 / 2 \times 0.15m \times 9.8m/s^2 \times 0.15m \\
&= 99225J
\end{aligned}
$$

Assume that each turning over is equivalent to turning over a square soil block with an area of 200 square centimeters and a height of 15 centimeters; that is, each square meter of land needs to lift the hoe 50 times. Assume that the mass of the hoe is 1.1 kg, and the lifting height of the hoe is 1 meter (in fact, many people use the hoe to carry out deep soil ploughing, and the hoe is raised higher than the human head). Then the work of lifting the hoe w_2 is as follows, where t represents the number of times.

$$
\begin{aligned}
w_2 &= nsmgh \\
&= 50t/m^2 \times 1000000m^2 / 1500 / 2 \times 1.1kg \times 9.8m/s^2 \times 1m/t \\
&\approx 179667J
\end{aligned}
$$

Suppose that the work done by swinging the hoe is the same as that of lifting the hoe; then the total work done w_{all} is as follows.

$$
\begin{aligned}
w_{all} &= w_1 + 2w_2 \\
&= 99225J + 2 \times 179667J \\
&= 458559J
\end{aligned}
$$

It is estimated that the efficiency of converting energy into mechanical energy in the human body is about 10% to 30%. Thus, 20% is taken here. The internal energy consumed by the human body during action is as follows:

$$
w_{in} = w_{all} / \eta = 458559J / 0.2 = 2292795J
$$

The inner energy 2,292,795 J is about 548 kcal. Generally speaking, light manual workers consume 2,400–2,600 kcal a day, and heavy manual workers consume 3,000–3,400 kcal. According to the relevant classification criteria, work such as typing on a keyboard meets the criterion for light physical work. When hoeing, people are standing and moving, and they also need to bend down frequently. Obviously, the human body itself has reached or even exceeded the standard of light physical labor by removing the series of actions of swinging the hoe and digging the ground. Coupled with the energy consumption of hoeing and digging the ground analyzed above, in addition to the consumption factors such as the need for the human body to overcome the suction and resistance between the soils in the process of hoeing, it is very heavy physical labor for adults to turn over half a mu of paddy land a day with a hoe.

Moreover, for rice from sowing to being eaten, it not only needs to turn the soil, but also to loosen the soil, raise seedlings, transplant seedlings, weed, apply farm fertilizer, manage water, harvest, thresh, dry, mill rice, and perform other tedious work. Furthermore, much work is constrained by the solar terms and agricultural time. Therefore, as far as the adult labor force in Neolithic times is concerned, converted into the area of rice fields that are intensively cultivated with hoes in later generations, it was already very remarkable that one person cultivated rice with a field of ten to twenty mu. Of course, land area with extensive cultivation may be much larger than the above, but extensive cultivation will also lead to much lower yields. Referring to the data of about 200 kilograms per mu of intensively cultivated rice fields in ancient China after the Song Dynasty, it was possible, but with difficulty, for an adult man in Neolithic times to produce 2,000 or 3,000 kilograms of rice per year. Of course, 2,000 kilograms of rice was enough to feed a family of six with four children. But for a family, it was not only necessary to obtain staple food, but also to have vegetables to eat, to plant cotton and linen and other crops for weaving, to carry out cotton and linen textile work, and to build labor tools, etc. At intervals such as two years or three years, it was also necessary to renovate the thatched shed. Of course, the specific time interval of the renovation depended on the climatic conditions and the materials used. In addition, although there was little trade at that time, because of the division of labor in society, people also needed to prepare some goods in exchange for certain items that they could not produce, such as those engaged in cultivation might need to exchange some pottery from potters.

According to the previous discussion and analysis, it was obvious that in Neolithic times, human beings must have still been busy supporting their families; that is, busy meeting their food needs.

In primitive times, humans' houses were rudimentary, and the housing conditions were very poor. People lived in caves, thatched sheds, etc. Fig. 1.3.3 below shows the appearance of the thatched-roof huts lived in by the ancestors of the Hemudu period in China about 5,000 to 7,000 years ago. The advantage of a thatched hut without mud walls is that it provides shelter from the wind and rain, and it is particularly breathable. The disadvantage is that it is very cold when the cold snap comes in winter. In addition, thatched huts need maintenance from time to time, which is very labor-intensive. In fact, it is not that there isn't a human tribe that is still in the stage of primitive society in modern times; for example, the primitive Indian tribes in the Amazon jungle and some Khoisan tribes on the African continent. The living conditions are still very simple in these tribes today. Compared with the living conditions of people in modern developed areas, they are simply extremely poor. So, on the whole, the housing needs of people in that era were not met very well.

Fig. 1.3.3 Schematic Diagram of the Restoration of the Stilt-Style Housing in Hemudu (Picture from Zhejiang Provincial Museum)

In primitive times, human beings had extremely limited scientific knowledge and means in terms of health and hygiene. People did not have microscopic observation equipment, and the human eye could not see viruses and germs at all. At that time, there were no antiseptic and anti-inflammatory substances such as disinfectant alcohol. Humans did not know the scientific principles of chemical reactions. As a result, people at that time were often unable to accurately diagnose the cause of disease. Because there was not enough scientific explanation, it was natural that many people would explain the causes of diseases from the perspective of gods, witches, and other metaphysical beliefs. At that time, what most human beings could do was to try to treat injuries and diseases with existing substances in the surrounding environment, such as roots, stems, leaves, and sap of plants, based on macroscopic experience. The legendary Shennong classified and characterized plants by tasting hundreds of herbs, and his work was already the pinnacle of science that human beings could achieve at that time. The existing substances in nature are often complex in composition, and the active ingredients contained in them for specific diseases are often very few, and the effect of drug treatment is often non-ideal. Because the cause was not clear, symptomatic treatment was often not possible, so the treatment effect on the disease was often very poor. Due to the lack of disinfectants and anti-inflammatory drugs, people were easily infected and inflamed after serious injuries. At that time, people lacked daily scientific and health knowledge, and daily sanitation methods could basically be said to be nonexistent, such as no toothpaste and no toothbrushes. People usually drank unclean raw water every day. All of these factors would erode people's health. In primitive times, for the health needs of human beings, people were helpless and passive most of the time. They almost did not know how to meet the needs of health. For human beings at that time, health and longevity could basically only be regarded as a matter of fate.

1.4 Analysis of the Satisfaction of Human Needs in the Pre-Industrial Civilization Era

With the development of agriculture and the advancement of tools and instruments, people's ability to conquer nature is getting stronger and stronger, and the population is increasing. The increasing number of inter-clan exchanges and tribal mergers among human clans has led to more and more information to be transmitted and things to be recorded, and word of mouth can no longer meet the requirements of human society. It is generally said that about four or five thousand years ago, the ancestors of human beings in the two river basins, ancient Egypt, the Yellow River Basin, ancient India, and other places successively invented and created writing, and the social system completed the evolution from the form of clans and tribes to the form of states, and mankind entered the so-called era of civilization.

Due to the increase in labor productivity, there are people in society who can specialize in research or have more time to conduct research. The growth of the human population—compared with the population of antiquity—has led to a dramatic increase in the size of the population involved in the development of production technology and scientific research. Thanks to the great role of written characters in promoting the accumulation and dissemination of human knowledge, the general trend is that after entering the era of civilization, mankind's science and technology are developing and progressing at an accelerated pace, and mankind's material life is becoming richer and richer.

1.4.1 Material Improvements Propelled Human Society forward

The birth of the civilization era can be said to be closely related to the development of science and technology, and the development of science and technology is closely related to the breakthrough progress of tools and materials. The invention and development of metallurgical technology, such as copper smelting technology, which was first developed at the end of prehistory, brought about breakthroughs in tools and machinery. With the accumulation of practical experience, human beings have gradually developed fairly mature bronze crafts. The maturity of bronze technology greatly improved the performance of the tools and weapons used by human beings at that time and enhanced their ability to adapt to nature and conquer it. With bronze tools, it was much easier and more convenient for humans to hunt and prepare food. Copper cookware and tableware have been developed, which have facilitated people's lives to a certain extent. The ancients also used copper to make some bronze agricultural tools, and the use of bronze tools in agricultural production helped to improve labor production efficiency.

However, due to the limitations of production conditions, including mining and smelting, and the relatively small reserves of copper ore, the cost of copper in early civilization should be said to be quite high, and the application of various copper tools is still relatively limited. Even with modern prospecting technology, the current global proved copper reserves are only about 800 million tons. As a large country, China only has about 30 million tons of copper reserves, and the copper reserves in relatively populated places outside the Qinghai-Tibet Plateau are only about 8 million tons. Therefore, the copper production of the Bronze Age in history was actually not too much. For example, according to the slag stock of Tonglu Mountain in Daye, Hubei Province, an important copper-producing area in ancient China, the cumulative copper production is estimated to be only about 120,000 tons, and the production age of the mine was from the Western Zhou Dynasty to the Han Dynasty, spanning about 1,000 years. Thus, it can be estimated that the mine only produced an average of 100 tons of copper per year. The Song Dynasty had the highest annual copper production in ancient China, and only about 13,000 tons of copper were produced in the highest production year. Generally speaking, copper is somewhat expensive. Copper is more likely to be used in weapon manufacturing and some important vessel manufacturing in the early days. For example, one main material used in weapon manufacturing by the Qin Kingdom during the Warring States Period was bronze. Coupled with the performance constraints such as hardness and wear resistance of copperware, there were few copper tools used in agricultural production. In fact, because copper has relatively noble characteristics, from the Spring and Autumn Period to the Qing Dynasty, copper had been the main material of China's circulating currency for more than 2,000 years.

For more than 3,000 years, people have mastered the technology of smelting iron. Compared with copper, iron has a higher hardness in terms of physical properties, so the cutting edge of iron tools can be sharper, and iron agricultural tools are less susceptible to deformation and damage due to the influence of hard objects such as stones in production. Moreover, in nature, iron ore reserves are hundreds of times higher than copper ore reserves. Iron ore is much more abundant and easier to obtain than copper ore. As a result, iron quickly developed into the mainstream material for making tools after humans mastered the technology of smelting iron.

China's historical book "Guo Yu · Qi Yu" (《国语·齐语》) more than 2,000 years ago recorded that Guan Zhong said to King Qi Huan Gong about 2,700 years ago, "inferior metal is used to cast hoes, yi, and jin, and try loam," in which "inferior metal" refers to iron, "yi" refers to a tool used to weed and level the land in ancient times, and "jin" refers to a tool that was used to cut down trees in ancient times. In the following Warring States Period, iron agricultural tools had already been widely used in China. Iron tools provide strong cutting, load-bearing, wear resistance, and other capabilities.

Iron tools greatly expanded the production capacity of human beings and significantly improved human labor productivity.

Whether it is copper or iron, it has the ability to shape that stone, bone, and other materials do not possess. It was convenient for people to manufacture tools of various shapes and greatly facilitated the invention, creation, and production of different kinds of tools. The discovery and improvement of these materials gave wings to the development of ancient science and technology and contributed to the satisfaction of human needs.

1.4.2 The Satisfaction of "Food" Needs

Agricultural planting can be basically divided into four stages: soil preparation, planting, maintenance, and harvesting. Among them, in ancient times, soil preparation was basically the most physically demanding step, including the elimination of weeds to reduce the competitors of crops, loosening the soil to facilitate the growth of crops, regulating proper soil moisture, etc. The tasks of weeding and loosening soil can be accomplished by ploughing and sowing. In the early stage of the agrarian era, the work of plowing the land was done by pure human power with the help of agricultural tools such as Lei Si. Obviously, human laborers were particularly tired naturally, and labor productivity was low. Later, about four to five thousand years ago, the plough was invented. The plough was pulled by cattle, horses, mules, and other animals that are much stronger than human beings, and labor productivity was naturally greatly improved. In addition, the diet of animals such as cattle and horses is different from that of humans, and they can eat the stems and leaves of grass that cannot be digested by humans. So there is no need to worry about cattle and horses eating up all the food produced. For example, in China, from the Spring and Autumn Period, ox-drawn iron plows had been used to plough land. They increased the labor productivity of cultivated land by more than five to ten times compared with manual reclaiming. It objectively reduced people's labor intensity and allowed people to have more rest time. From the perspective of society as a whole, society can organize more manpower to produce more of other daily necessities, which facilitates people's lives.

In the early years of civilization, human needs for food were not always met steadily and adequately. Due to the constraints of relative scarcity and other limitations in the production of bronze, it was difficult for bronze to be widely used in agricultural production in various places. In the early years of civilization, the smelting and making of iron tools were not well mastered by humans, and the agricultural tools used by humans were often made of wood, stone, or bone. In the early age of civilization, the tools used by human beings were also relatively rudimentary and inefficient. Human beings were relatively weak in their ability to resist disasters, and floods, droughts, and locust plagues might have brought devastating blows to agricultural production in a certain region in the year they occurred. In addition, wars between tribes and countries that occurred frequently would mobilize and consume a large number of young and middle-aged laborers, and it seriously affected agricultural production. Furthermore, the planting and harvesting of crops in areas where wars occurred were often affected by confrontation and destruction between the two armies, which could easily lead to a shortage of food supply. Population growth and the decline of wild huntable animals would also affect the availability of meat for everyone, and it was not uncommon for the nutritional ratio to be poor. In the historical book "Historical Records" written by Sima Qian more than 2,000 years ago, the allusion used to describe the reason for the downfall of King Zhou of the Shang Dynasty is "Wine Pool Meat Forest." Though the allusion was to preach people against wasting and living extravagantly, it reflected that the ordinary people of ancient China more than 3,000 years ago were not always able to meet the needs of "food." Think about it: if people were always well-fed, the food composition was ideal, and the proportion of delicious meat in the food was high, people would not regard the king's luxury as an unforgivable sin. People might think, "The king loves to drink wine and eat meat so much." "Will he be overnourished?" "Will he suffer from cardiovascular diseases?" "Will he be unhealthy?"

With the improvement of transportation technology, especially shipbuilding and navigation technology, and the improvement of understanding of the world, human beings can carry out more distant voyages and explorations. With the contact and economic and trade exchanges of various human groups scattered around the world, people in various regions have obtained many species that are suitable for local cultivation and originally grown in other parts of the world, which greatly enriches human diets and expands the range of human food. For example, it is generally believed that the Han Empire, whose capital was Chang'an, introduced many new species from the west to the Central Plains during the reign of the Western Regions, such as grapes, cucumbers, walnuts, and carrots. Thus, people in the Central Plains could enjoy a wider variety of cuisines. Spices from all over the world were exchanged and spread to each other, making it possible for people all over the world to enjoy more delicious food. At the end of ancient civilization and the beginning of modern society, after the relatively closed Americas were discovered and established a connection with the people in Europe, Africa, and Asia, crops such as corn, potatoes, and sweet potatoes native to the Americas were spread to all parts of the world. Due to their adaptability to the land and climate, their spread has greatly contributed to the increase of total world food production, contributing to the satisfaction of human food needs.

In the era of ancient civilizations, for thousands of years, people had mastered the technology of large-scale production of table salt. Salt intake can help the body's electrolyte balance, and moderate intake is beneficial to human health. Salt can not only make food more delicious but also help the long-term preservation of many foods. For example, by salting vegetables, the shelf life of some vegetables can be extended from a few days to several months or even longer. By treating meat with salt, the edible shelf life of meat can be extended from a few days to several years; for instance, the shelf life of Chinese and Spanish ham can be up to two or three years. The use of salt can also make certain things into food for human consumption, such as using table salt to treat fresh jellyfish, which has a certain amount of toxicity, to remove the toxicity of fresh jellyfish and make jellyfish edible and delicious. The technology of large-scale acquisition of table salt, coupled with the development of skills to use it, has also greatly improved the satisfaction of human food needs.

Over thousands of years, humans have developed a variety of food processing techniques that have greatly enriched people's recipes. For example, it is said that more than 2,000 years ago, the King of Huainan in the Han Dynasty and his disciples invented the method of making tofu in the process of seeking alchemy (in modern terms, it means conducting scientific exploration experiments). The invention of tofu promoted the consumption of soybeans and turned soybeans into a more delicious delicacy. For another example, four to five thousand years ago, the pastoral area developed the technology of making yogurt, which met the flavor needs of many people for milk products and enriched the variety of milk for human consumption. Human beings have mastered the technology of making sugar and developed the production process of many kinds of sugars, such as sucrose and maltose. Sugar is a delicacy that brings people a sense of sweetness and happiness. All in all, in the history of ancient civilization for thousands of years, human beings have developed a wide variety of food processing technologies, and through different treatments of various ingredients, people have developed a variety of cuisines, including staple foods, fruits and vegetables, pastries, and snacks, expanding the scope of human food enjoyment.

The development of metal smelting technology has provided people with cookware that has better thermal conductivity. For example, with the help of the prosperity of the iron and steel metallurgical industry, China achieved the popularization of iron pots in the Song Dynasty about 1,000 years ago. Ordinary people used iron pots for cooking. The iron pot has excellent thermal conductivity, which facilitates people using various cooking methods such as frying, deep-frying, stir-frying, and boiling, while clay pots are only more suitable for boiling, and stoves are only suitable for baking. The popularization of iron pots has facilitated the processing of people's meals and promoted the production of various delicacies. It can be said that the popularization of the iron pot has provided a material tool foundation for the development of diversified cuisines in China. It allows people to better enjoy food and promotes the satisfaction of human food needs.

In general, the satisfaction of human food needs was inadequate in the ancient civilization era. Except for the aristocracy and wealthy, who accounted for a small number of people, the majority of ordinary people were not always able to meet their food needs, which was mainly reflected in the hardships of food acquisition, the instability of food supply, the shortage of food supply, and the unreasonable ratio of nutrients. In the entire ancient civilization era, the agricultural tools used by human beings were not machines, and the power required to operate the tools came from people or livestock. So, the physical requirements were relatively high. The process of human beings obtaining food was very difficult. A poet of the Tang Dynasty wrote, "Who knows the dished food, each grain is from hard work." People in agricultural areas often faced malnutrition caused by an insufficient proportion of meat. For example, even due to too little meat protein intake and nutritional imbalance in ancient Japan, the height of Japanese people was generally severely short. Due to the fragile ability to resist disasters at that time, floods, droughts, locusts, wars, etc., could bring catastrophes and great instability to the supply of human food. Moreover, in the ancient civilization era, the transportation technology and conditions were poor, and it was often difficult to transfer enough food from other areas in time when one area encountered a famine. Compared with the present, the technical level of food production in ancient times, including variety improvement, fertilizer supply, heat preservation, pest control, etc., was relatively low. The grain yield per mu was even less than one-third of the current yield. The carrying capacity per unit of land was much lower than that of now. For example, in the middle of the Qing Dynasty, the average cultivated land per person in China was only two to three mu, and the population had basically reached the land carrying limit at that time. Coupled with the annual payment of government taxes, even if a slight natural disaster or something else happened, ordinary people would starve. Even in Europe, where the population density was relatively low, there were many famines in history, such as famines in the United Kingdom, France, Spain, and other regions in the Middle Ages. Even in the middle of the nineteenth century, when the world industrial revolution had begun in some countries and regions, there was a great famine (failure of the potato crop) in Ireland.

1.4.3 The Satisfaction of "Transportation" Needs

In early civilization, about four to five thousand years ago, vehicles such as chariots had already been invented. Early chariots might have often been used for warfare and hunting. For example, Qi, the King of Xia, about four thousand years ago, what he said in a war had been recorded in the pre-war proclamation of "Shang Book · Xia Book · Gan Oath," and he mentioned something related to chariots: "If the soldiers driving cannot make the chariots and horses move properly, you have violated orders." Vehicles can carry people and goods, which greatly facilitate the satisfaction of human transportation needs and make people's travel easier, especially for cargo transportation. In order to facilitate land passage and transportation, some ancient human civilizations built many roads, such as ancient Rome, which built a huge road network, and the Qin Empire, which built gallop roads to all parts of the country with the capital Xianyang as the center on the basis of the old Six Kingdoms roads. The ancients developed ox carts, horse-drawn carts, donkey carts, and man-powered wheelbarrows. They greatly facilitated people's travel and cargo transportation and contributed to the satisfaction of transportation needs.

After entering the era of civilization, mankind also continued to develop shipbuilding and navigation technology. Relying on water power and wind power, the use of ships improved the transportation capacity of people and goods. For the convenience of transportation, human beings have even opened up a lot of canals, such as the Qin Dynasty opening up a canal named Lingqu connecting Central China and Lingnan, and Emperor Yang of Sui presiding over the construction of the Grand Canal connecting the Yangtze River and the Yellow River. Shipping provides a low-cost way of long-distance transportation that greatly facilitates exchanges around the world. In ancient Greece and Rome, their ships traveled through the Eastern Mediterranean. After Columbus, explorers, colonists, and traders from Western Europe used ships to travel the world. In ancient times, there were also merchant ships between China and Southeast Asia, the Arab region, and other places. People also often used small boats for short-distance transportation. For example, in order to facilitate the passage of people and goods, they often used boats to ferry across the rivers and lakes where it was difficult to build bridges or where the cost of building bridges was too high. Just like in ancient China, the rivers and lakes located in densely populated areas often had ferries and employed full-time ferrymen. Ancient Chinese literati left a lot of poems involving ferries, such as Li Qingzhao in the Song Dynasty, who wrote a popular poem involving crossing the water, "Like a Dream Order": "Have had all the fun, went back home by a boat, strayed into the depths of the lotus flowers. Scrambled and rowed the boat. Scrambled and rowed the boat. Startled a shoal of gulls and herons." In addition, people had been using boats to shuttle back and forth on the surface of the water to catch fish for a long time. The development of ancient shipbuilding and shipping technology had greatly contributed to the satisfaction of human transportation needs.

However, limited by the physical limitations of livestock and the technical ability of means of transportation, ancient transportation using animals directly, vehicle transportation, shipping, and other means was still far from perfectly meeting the needs of human beings.

First of all, the transportation speed was relatively slow. For example, horseback riding is almost the fastest mode of transportation. It can run 20 to 70 kilometers per hour, and a horse can run 60 to 100 kilometers at once. The distance of 150 to 200 kilometers a day is almost the upper limit. For medium and long-distance transportation, generally speaking, the speed of horse-drawn carriages is about 10 kilometers per hour, and they can travel about 80 kilometers a day. In ancient times, the average speed of a sailing ship was about 15 kilometers per hour. These speeds of transportation made long-distance transportation somewhat costly, and they could not meet the demand for time-sensitive transportation.

Second, the transport capacity is limited. Livestock such as mules, horses, camels, and cattle have a limited load-bearing capacity and can carry a few hundred catties at most. Vehicles are changed to rely on the ground's load-bearing capacity, and people or livestock mainly work to overcome friction. The load capacity of vehicles is higher, and the load capacity of vehicles can generally reach one to two tons. The carrying capacity of ships is larger, and the carrying capacity of a single big ship in ancient times was generally dozens of tons. For example, the carrying capacity of a big ship on the Yangtze River in the Western Han Dynasty was about twenty to thirty tons, and the carrying capacity of the ships for transporting tribute grain on the Yangtze River in the Tang Dynasty was about one hundred tons. Although the Song Dynasty built a large ship with a carrying capacity of about 550 tons, the carrying capacity of the ships for transporting tribute grain on the Yangtze River was generally less than fifty-five tons. Moreover, the larger the ancient ship was, the more crew members were required. In the early Qing Dynasty, a boat with a load of about thirty-five tons was allocated ten to twelve crew members on the Grand Canal. That is to say, the per capita carrying capacity of a single ship was only a few tons. In addition, ship transportation is limited by river and sea waterways, and vast land areas cannot be reached.

After all, there are many places where there are no suitable waterways.

Third, the comfort level is relatively low. The bumps in horseback riding, camel riding, etc., are very strong, and long-distance travel is not easy. Moreover, the stirrup was not invented until about 2,000 years ago during the Han Dynasty. In the era before the use of stirrups, the safety and comfort of riding horses were naturally less than ideal. Ancient vehicles and ships, limited by transportation capacity and economy, usually were not equipped with many luxurious enjoyment facilities because they all needed to occupy the load capacity. Thus, the comfort was generally not very good. It can be seen that the comfort of travel in ancient times was generally not good, and the journey was often linked to fatigue.

1.4.4 The Satisfaction of "Housing" Needs

In the era of ancient civilization, especially in the middle and late stages of the past two to three thousand years, the housing of the nobles and the powerful was relatively good, and they often lived in palaces and castles. For the houses of the nobles, in the Yellow River Basin and the Yangtze River Basin, it was more common to see houses similar to the palace style of the Forbidden City in Beijing, built with wood, bricks, tiles, stones, etc. In Europe, palaces were more often built with materials that do not decay, such as stone. Of course, in the Middle Ages, most castles in Europe were actually built of wood and rammed earth.

In the era of ancient civilization, subject to the level of productivity, for most ordinary people, a palace-style house like the Forbidden City could not be afforded at all because the materials were too expensive and the construction cost was too high. For example, in ancient China, the materials used in the construction of palaces were "gold bricks," and they were very expensive. Zhang Wenzhi of the Ming Dynasty mentioned in "Please Increase the Burning Labor Price" that for the gold brick of two chi and two cun square (about 0.7 meters in length and width, and about 0.1 meters in thickness), the official price of 0.32 tael of silver was too low, and for each brick, the merchant would lose as much as 0.7 tael of silver. This means that the cost of each brick was about one tael of silver. By the way, in the early years of Emperor Qianlong, the price of this kind of gold brick agreed upon by the Ministry of Internal Affairs was 0.91 tael of silver. According to the annual income of ordinary people in the lower classes, even if they didn't eat or drink, they could only buy about 30 gold bricks a year. How could it still be used to build houses? Of course, the answer is no.

As for ordinary people, in the ancient civilization era, the housing in various places was very different due to special factors such as climate, water, and soil. For example, from two to three thousand years ago, the people in the Loess Plateau took advantage of the loess characteristics of strong uprightness and easy excavation, mainly by digging caves to meet their living needs. The advantages of caves are that they are warm in winter and cool in summer. People in arid desert areas often lived in flat-roofed adobe houses. Due to the lack of cement, waterproof paint, and other waterproof materials, the buildings in places that receive a lot of rain are often made of brick or rammed earth, and they usually have sloping roofs and eaves.

Due to the different acquisition costs of various materials, the housing of people with different economic conditions would be quite different. For example, regular strips of stone, brick, tile, and thick hard log pillars were relatively expensive to obtain. In ancient civilizations, only wealthy families with strong economic strength or religious institutions and public organizations with financial resources were able to use them to build houses. Poor families often used materials whose costs were very low or even almost non-existent to build their dwellings, such as mud and sand, pebbles from nearby riverbanks, ordinary timber, thatch, and straw.

For the wealthy people of ancient China, they often used bricks to build walls for their houses, and the bricks used were generally cyan bricks. There were many specifications of blue bricks; taking the small cyan bricks in Suzhou as an example, the average size was about 220 mm x 110 mm x 54 mm. Chen Congzhou et al. mentioned in the article "The Price of Bricks in the Song and Ming Dynasties" that when rebuilding the North Temple Tower in Suzhou, some bricks of the Song and Ming dynasties were obtained, and the bricks of the Song Dynasty were printed with words such as "donate 1,000 bricks, 30 coins per piece," and the bricks of the Ming Dynasty were printed with words "Donate 12 taels of silver to make 4,000 bricks." According to the proportion of about 1,000 copper coins equal to one tael of silver in the Ming Dynasty, the price of bricks in the Ming Dynasty was about 3 copper coins a brick. Taking the construction of a square house with almost three open faces as an example, the outer profile is calculated as 10 meters by 5 meters. Assuming that the outer profile wall is made of bricks, the wall thickness is about 220 mm, and the average height of the wall is about 3 meters, then it can be calculated that the total volume of the wall is about 20 cubic meters, which is about the volume of 15,000 small cyan bricks in Suzhou. Excluding the space occupied by the mud and sand plaster joints required for bonding, it is estimated that about 13,000 bricks will be used. To buy 13,000 pieces of small cyan bricks, it needed 390,000 copper coins in the Song Dynasty and 39 taels of silver in the Ming Dynasty. The daily salary of the people in the Shaoxing period of the Southern Song Dynasty was estimated at two to three hundred copper coins. If the daily salary of 250 coins was taken, it was necessary to work for 1,560 days without eating or drinking to buy these cyan bricks, which is about four years. In the Ming Dynasty, street vendors earned about 20 taels of silver a year, and street vendors needed to work for two years to buy these bricks. Of course, building a Chinese-style brick house also requires a large amount of wood, tiles, and other materials. Furthermore, people needed to pay money to hire plastering craftsmen and carpentry masters, etc. Moreover, a person cannot live without eating or drinking, and he has to bear the daily living expenses of the family. So, for ordinary people, building a brick house was also a big burden. Thus, people living in a brick house must be relatively wealthy or have rich ancestors. Most of the people with ordinary and lower incomes lived in tiled or thatched houses with rammed earth walls. Of course, there were also people in some areas who lived in slab houses supported by wooden pillars. Poor families were likely to live in thatched huts supported by a few timbers with only simple processing.

The situation in medieval Europe was not much different from that in China. The aristocracy, who made up a tiny minority of the population, lived in large palaces, while the vast majority of the ordinary and lower classes lived in cramped thatched huts. In the Middle Ages, European peasants mostly lived in low-slung longhouses, which were about 10 to 20 meters long and about 5 meters wide. These longhouses were largely built from local materials. Frames were built with stones or trees that could be found everywhere, and roofs were laid with thatch. These longhouses tended to be mixed-use houses where livestock and people lived at opposite ends of the house. The middle of the houses was often directly connected, and a house usually only equipped with one or two doors. As for the disadvantages of living together with humans and animals, everyone can imagine them. One of the advantages of living together was that it could effectively prevent thieves from stealing livestock because the owner lived on the side, and the owner could find out easily if there was a slight movement. It was naturally more difficult for thieves to steal. Second, it helped to survive the cold winter. The heat emitted by the combustion of fuel in the furnace could be shared by people and animals in the house, and the heat emitted by people and livestock bodies was dispersed in the same room to help people and animals huddle for warmth.

In ancient civilizations, electricity had not yet been scientifically recognized and used by humans, and there were no electric lights, so most of the houses were relatively dim. At that time, there were naturally no modern household appliances such as microwave ovens, ovens, dishwashers, refrigerators, and washing machines. People's housework was relatively heavy. Without temperature control technology such as modern air conditioners, it was difficult to adjust the temperature in the room to reach a pleasant level, and it was normal for the house to be very cold or very hot. The comfort of mattresses and bedding was generally not very high. Generally speaking, subject to the level of science and technology or productivity in the ancient civilization era, the living conditions of most people were relatively poor, cramped, and simple. It was still far from satisfying people's housing needs.

1.4.5 The Satisfaction of "Heat Preservation" Needs

Since the primitive era, human living areas have covered various climatic zones, such as tropical, subtropical, temperate, and cold zones. Except for the tropics, other climatic regions have relatively cold weather, especially in winter. Even in the two river basins and the Eastern Mediterranean coastal areas where it is relatively warm, people still need to take some measures to maintain body temperature, not to mention the people in the Yellow River basin, Eastern Europe, Northern Europe, and other regions where it is much colder in winter. In ancient civilizations, heat preservation measures could be roughly classified into the following three categories.

One measure was to enhance the body's own metabolic speed in cold weather. It depends on the person's physical condition and food supply.

The second measure was to build a small environment with a suitable temperature. It referred to trying to adjust the temperature of the living place to the appropriate level. The main ways were as follows. In winter, burning fires increased the heat release of the living place, such as heating with a fireplace, fire pit, ondol, or brazier. Reducing the speed of heat exchange with the outside world, such as setting up dwellings in caves or building the walls of houses to be thick, formed a small environment that was warm in winter and cool in summer. In the hot summer, creating a cool environment, such as by making the house permeable from north to south to form a passing breeze and by sprinkling cool well water in the house to create evaporative heat absorption. However, due to the level of technology and the ability to create wealth, people often had to make do with the living conditions, such as the walls of houses often not being thick enough for heat preservation. In the era of ancient civilization, most people still had to experience the baptism of cold and heat every year, and they could not live lives like modern people who use air conditioning to adjust room temperature. For example, before the Industrial Revolution, the main fuel of the United Kingdom was coal and firewood, and it required a lot of money to buy fuel. The poor sometimes had to reduce the number of times they cooked hot meals every day in order to save money. In winter, they naturally had to endure the torture of the cold environment.

The third measure was to build a suitable microenvironment. For example, in cold weather, one should wear enough warm clothes during the day and sleep under a warm quilt at night. If a person feels too cold, he or she could also use heating methods such as a hand stove or soup pot. In the hot summer, people could wipe their bodies with cool water to cool down, use a fan to speed up heat dissipation, and soak their bodies or parts of their limbs in cold water to cool down.

For humans in ancient civilizations, in general, the heat of summer was more tolerable than the cold weather in winter. After all, generally speaking, the total time when the temperature exceeds the comfortable ambient temperature of about 25°C to 27°C is not too much, and when it is hot, people can stay in the shade of trees or in houses, and they can also use cool water, which is an almost cost-free cooling measure. In cold weather, heat preservation requires enough food, warm clothing and bedding, heaters, fuel, shelter, etc., all of which require a lot of labor to create and obtain. In view of factors such as science and technology, production capacity, and natural and man-made disasters in the ancient civilization era, there were many people who lacked warm equipment in many cases. The following is a discussion on clothing and bedding in ancient civilizations.

In pastoral areas, animal fur was easy to obtain, and there were many items such as clothing and bedding made from animal fur, and their warmth performance was relatively good. However, pastoralists tended to experience colder weather, and the production of fur was quite time-consuming and labor-intensive, so it had historically been common for livestock and people to freeze to death due to extreme weather.

In the majority of the world's agricultural areas, where the land was heavily used for cultivation, livestock and other animals were usually less abundant, and the population was more populous. So warmer fur bedding and clothes were used at a low rate among the population, and they were generally only owned by the wealthier population. For example, in the Yellow River Basin and the Yangtze River Basin in China, ordinary people had few warm items such as fur clothes and bedding, and people usually used cloth spun from fibers to make warm items such as clothes and bedding. Before the Song Dynasty, people mainly used hemp and silk for weaving, and the rich would use the down from ducks and other animal plush with good thermal insulation performance as the filler to make warm clothes, jackets, and quilts, while ordinary people could only use rags, poplar catkins, reeds, etc., which had poor thermal insulation performance, as the filler to make jackets and quilts. From the Song Dynasty, cotton gradually became the main textile material, and cotton has good thermal insulation performance. Jackets and quilts with cotton filler became the warm items that ordinary people could have.

In the era of ancient civilization, due to the limitations of raw material production capacity and textile technology, textiles were basically very time-consuming work, and making clothes was also time-consuming and labor-intensive. So ordinary people usually did not have many clothes, which was completely different from the situation of modern people often thinking that their wardrobe was too small to fit their clothes. Moreover, the flat-headed people usually wore coarse linen clothes. After all, comfortable silk clothes were much more expensive.

In ancient times, the production of linen and silk products was physically intensive and time-consuming. The production of linen products had to go through more than ten very labor-intensive processes: planting flax → harvesting flax stalks → drying flax stalks → soaking flax stalks → peeling flax skins → drying flax skins → tearing twine → rubbing twine → soaking twine in water → … → weaving linen → cutting → sewing clothes. As a modern person, just imagining the work of peeling flax skins, tearing twine, and rubbing twine makes one feel numb. As for raising silkworms, it has been very hard work since ancient times. Regardless of day and night, people had to feed silkworms 6 to 10 times every day. Picking mulberry leaves was very time-consuming and laborious. Transporting mulberry leaves home was physical work, and picking up silkworm cocoons required patience, and there was much work to reel silk from cocoons…

People worked so hard in ancient times, but what was the yield? The "Book of Agriculture," written by Chen Fu in the Song Dynasty, recorded that "Some people in the countryside only use silkworms to make a living. A family of ten raises ten trays of silkworms, and each tray gets twelve catties of cocoons. It can take 1.03 taels of silk from each catty of cocoons. Every five taels of silk can be used to weave a small piece of spun silk." In the Song Dynasty, one catty was equivalent to about 625 grams, and one tael was about 40 grams. 1.03 taels were about 41.2 grams. Thus, about 4,900 grams of silk could be obtained from the 120 catties of cocoons. According to relevant estimates, each mu of mulberry field could produce about two kilograms of silk historically. As for the yield of hemp fiber, the "Encyclopedia of Agriculture," written by Xu Guangqi of the Ming Dynasty, contains "this hemp is harvested three times annually, and each mu gets 30 catties of hemp, and even if the yield is low, it should not be less than 20 catties." Converted to the current measurement system, each mu of hemp field can yield about 39 catties of hemp; that is, the yield of hemp field per mu is about 19,750 grams. However, one person could cultivate only several mu of hemp fields with crude tools in ancient times, and the annual output of hemp fibers per capita was naturally extremely limited. The article "Did Ancient Women Only Assist the Husband and Teach the Children? Their Contribution to the Family's Economy is Beyond Your Imagination" (https://m.163.com/dy/article/EFVV559K05438UAR.html) estimates that spun silk weighs about 60 grams per square meter, and linen weighs about 500 grams per square meter. There are many types of clothing, and the required fabrics are different for different types of clothing. Here, calculated at 2.5 square meters per piece of clothing, making silk clothes requires about 150 grams of silk, and making linen clothes requires about 1,250 grams of hemp fibers. The silk produced by a family of ten could only make about thirty-two pieces of clothing, and the hemp fibers produced in one mu of hemp field could only be used to make sixteen pieces of clothing.

As for the labor productivity of ancient weaving, the Han Yuefu poem "Go Up the Mountain to Pick Miwu" stated that "A new woman wove a type of cloth called Jian. An old woman wove another type called Su. One piece of Jian a day. Five Zhang of Su a day." The poem "Peacock Flying Southeast" mentioned that "Began to weave as soon as the cock crowed, night after night. Finished five pieces of cloth in three days; the monsignor still gave a disgusted look for weaving slowly." In the Ming and Qing dynasties, "the women of the southeast township weave three horses a day, but small and thick, not a patch on Songjiang." It is said that Songjiang's skilled weavers can weave seven to eight meters of homespun cloth a day. In the Han Dynasty, one "zhang" is equivalent to about 2.3 meters, and a piece of cloth is about 0.5 meters wide and more than 9 meters long. In the Ming and Qing dynasties, one "zhang" is equivalent to about 3.2 meters, and a Songjiang wide cloth is about 0.8 meters wide and 13 meters long. For an ordinary farmer family, there was a lot of housework and farm work to be done, so it often took many days of labor to weave a piece of cloth.

Although there were commercial exchanges in the era of ancient civilization, due to the limitations of production capacity and wealth, and the relatively high cost of logistics, ordinary people were more inclined to save if they could and did it themselves if they could. It was generally a self-sufficient small-scale peasant economy. People made clothes by hand, and women were responsible for sewing clothes in addition to housework. It was difficult for a housewife to be as skilled as a specialized sewing craftsman because housewives were often interrupted by household activities such as cooking and taking care of children. It is not uncommon for making clothes to take three to five days or even longer.

The high cost of making clothes led to the fact that ordinary civilian families in the ancient civilization era usually did not have many clothes. Because of the preciousness of clothing, the custom of adding new clothes and shoes for the New Year was even formed in China, and buying new clothes for the family became the highlight of the New Year.

Fig. 1.4.1 Part of "Ten Thousand Flowers Sleeping in Spring" Song Dynasty

In the state of sleep, the metabolic rate of a person will decrease compared to the wake state, and the decline rate is said to be up to 10% to 15%. That is to say, the rate at which the human body produces heat during sleep will be reduced. Many people have had the feeling that "it is not cold when awake, cold when asleep," which is caused by the decrease in the metabolic rate during sleep. Furthermore, the temperature at night is generally lower than that during the day, which means that in cold weather, the temperature difference between the human body and the outside world at night is greater than that during the day. This means that under the same insulation conditions, the human body usually dissipates heat faster at night. Therefore, in order to keep warm, it is necessary to reduce the heat exchange rate with the outside atmosphere during sleep; that is, more warmth measures are needed. If you wear a lot of clothes to sleep, it will be difficult to toss and turn and adjust your posture during sleep, and it is easy for people to feel uncomfortable while sleeping, which will affect the quality of sleep. Therefore, a quilt that does not restrict the body and allows the body to maintain a relaxed state has become the best choice. Sometimes, a family of several people can share a quilt and use the heat emitted by each person's body to create a suitable small environment. This contributes to achieving real huddling for warmth and spending the cold winter together. Fig. 1.4.1 is a part of the painting "Ten Thousand Flowers Sleeping in Spring" from the Song Dynasty, where the person lying on the bed is covered with a quilt.

The history of quilts is very long. For example, "the Analects of Confucius · Township Party," which was written more than 2,000 years ago, mentions that "there must be bedclothes, one and a half body long." In ancient China, quilts, with the exception of a few large quilts made directly from fur, were mainly made by stuffing wool-like items into quilt

55

covers sewn from cloth. The different economic circumstances of each family determine the types of flocculent that they use as fillers. Families with good economic conditions may fill quilts with silk, cashmere, duck down, etc. Before the Song and Ming dynasties, those families with poor conditions might fill quilts with rags, reed flowers, poplar catkins, or kapok, and even some people said that there were poor people who used straw as filling. Cashmere, duck down, or silk-filled quilts are very warm and comfortable, and to this day, they are still relatively high-end quilts. The property of keeping warm of the reed flowers-filled quilts is poor. For example, there is an allusion in Chinese history about Confucius's student Min Zi, in which Min Zi wore a thick "cotton-padded jacket" filled with reeds in a cold winter when he was young, but he was still shivering from the cold. As for the cotton with better thermal insulation performance, it was not until the Song Dynasty that it was widely popularized in the Yellow River Basin and the Yangtze River Basin. Especially after the first founder of the Ming Dynasty stipulated that "all people who have five to ten mu of land should plant half a mu of mulberry, hemp, and cotton respectively, and more than ten mu should be doubled," cotton had become the most important textile raw material and the main filler of quilts.

In the Yellow River Basin and the Yangtze River Basin, the situation of winter cotton jackets is similar to that of quilts. Families with good conditions filled cotton-padded jackets with silk, cashmere, or duck down, while poor families filled cotton-padded jackets with catkins and rags. Until the last thousand years, cotton, which had good performance in keeping warm, eventually became the main filler.

In general, the ancient civilization lacked strong technical means to regulate the temperature of the small environment. The ordinary people lacked the ability to effectively regulate the temperature of the small environment or even the microenvironment. In winter, ordinary people often suffered from cold weather. In the hot summer, ordinary people were often exposed to the scorching sun, especially the large number of farmers who were engaged in farming, when the hottest time was often the busy season. Therefore, in the ancient civilization era, the satisfaction of human heat preservation needs was not good, and the satisfaction level needed to be further improved.

1.4.6 The Satisfaction of "Health" Needs

After entering the era of civilization, human beings in various places also summed up a lot of medical and health technologies and established a supply of medicinal materials based on plants, animals, and minerals.

Although many human cognitions were mixed with obscurantism, witchcraft, and superstition due to limited technical means and scientific understanding, human beings around the world have gradually developed some relatively scientific health methods based on experience. Ancient doctors summed up a lot of medical knowledge through observation and practice, and some of the content even has a certain learning reference value in today's era of relatively developed medicine. For example, some medical students in China also have to study the ancient Chinese medical book

"Treatise on Typhoid Fever and Miscellaneous Diseases," which was written in the Han dynasty.

For disease prevention, the ancients also summed up a lot of experience and measures based on observation and practice.

The ancients also paid a lot of attention to drinking water that is related to health. For thousands of years, many people in China have been drinking water from wells. In ancient Chinese mainland, wells often had a wellhead above the ground to prevent sewage from entering when it rained. Compared with rivers, ditches, lakes, and marsh water, the well water isolated from them is naturally cleaner, which can greatly reduce the chance of various parasites harming human health. With the exception of a very small number of well waters with excessive levels of certain minerals, it is clear that drinking well water is more beneficial to human health. Historically, the Chinese began to drink hot water and boiled cold water very early. Especially since the Song Dynasty, China even formed a popular tea house culture, and a large number of Chinese used to go to the tea house in town in the morning, brew a cup of hot tea, and talk about the world. This habit had not changed until recent decades. In ancient China, herbal tea, i.e., boiled cold water, was also given to travelers as a good deed to accumulate merit. In the absence of modern water purification technology in ancient times, boiling water can effectively kill parasites, germs, and viruses in the water, which can also be said to be a major advance in preventive hygiene.

People had developed some measures for dental health protection in ancient times. As we all know, dental health is a major guarantee of good health. As we age, food becomes more and more likely to get embedded between our teeth, affecting the health of our teeth. People tend to feel very uncomfortable if food is embedded between their teeth, so they will naturally try to remove food debris. In the early stages, people mainly cleaned their teeth by rinsing their mouths with water, picking their teeth with small branches or toothpicks, and brushing their teeth with their fingers. As for the toothbrush, the most important tool for modern daily dental care, it is rumored that it was not until the Tang Dynasty that a tooth care tool similar to a modern toothbrush appeared, and its bristles were made of pig bristles. It is also said that in 1498, Emperor Xiaozong of the Ming Dynasty invented a toothbrush that used pig bristles. However, it was not until the thirties of the nineteenth century that DuPont manufactured synthetic fibers and used synthetic fibers to make bristles, which gave birth to a new generation of cheap toothbrushes and contributed to the popularity of toothbrushes. Toothpicks might have appeared before human beings entered the era of civilization. It is more certain that people have been using toothpicks for more than 2,000 years, and the Jin Dynasty document "The Letters to Brother Lu Ji" mentioned toothpicks. It's just that in ancient times, it was the upper-class people who could pay more attention to protecting their teeth, and the tooth protection behavior of the people at the bottom was likely to be: when there was food residue on the teeth and it was uncomfortable, they just used a finger or found a small branch or a relatively hard, thin grass stalk to remove the food residue.

The ancients had recognized that rats may bring diseases; for example, Wang Chong of the Eastern Han Dynasty

57

mentioned in "Lun Heng" that "if rats acted in the cooked rice, throw it away but do not eat." In ancient China, due to the difficulty of obtaining food, the people in the south of the Yangtze River would put the leftover rice into a bamboo rice basket, hang it in the air with a string, and place the leftovers in a specially closed-off vegetable cabinet. These measures could effectively avoid gnawing by mice and insects. Thus, they reduced the probability of disease occurrence.

For annoying mosquitoes, human beings have developed a variety of countermeasures such as mosquito nets and mosquito coils. They have reduced mosquito bites to a certain extent and have played a role in inhibiting mosquito-borne diseases. They have also increased the comfort of people's lives. After all, if people are bitten by mosquitoes, they will experience uncomfortable symptoms such as itching. The history of mosquito nets can be traced back to the Spring and Autumn Period and the Warring States Period more than 2,000 years ago. There is a legend that the mesh mosquito net was invented by Mrs. Zhao, the concubine of Emperor Wu of the Eastern Wu Kingdom during the Three Kingdoms period about 1,800 years ago. "Gleanings · Wu," written by Wang Jia in the Eastern Jin Dynasty, mentioned, "The concubine of Emperor Wu cut off many hairs, then connected them with god glue. The god glue came from the Yuyi country, and it could connect the broken string of the bow and crossbow, cutting and connecting at will. Hairs were woven into a thin and loose fabric, working for months. Then cut the fabric into a curtain. Seen from the outside, it was fluttering like smoke moving lightly. The inner room was cool." The invention of mosquito coils might be related to the hygienic customs of avoiding poisonous gases and burning incense during the Dragon Boat Festival in ancient China. It is said that early mosquito coils were used in the Song Dynasty.

In view of the high risk of childbirth in ancient times, ancient Chinese midwives usually prepared scissors and hot water, among which the scissors used to cut the umbilical cord were usually scalded with boiling water or roasted on the fire in advance. The newborns would be scrubbed clean with warm water. These measures could reduce the occurrence of infection and inflammation to a certain extent and helped reduce the mortality rate of mothers and infants. However, due to the low level of overall medical and health knowledge, the extreme lack of effective means to deal with the problem, and the lack of systematic education and training for midwives, the personal midwifery skills and literacy of midwives were usually poor, and the maternal and infant mortality rates were still very high.

Plague has always been the great enemy of mankind. It is well known that even in modern times, serious epidemic events still occur from time to time. In response to a vicious epidemic, many of the measures taken by the ancients seem to be very reasonable even today. The measures they had taken include prevention, isolation, medicine, and the disposal of dead bodies, etc. The "Sealed Diagnosis" unearthed from the Qin tomb more than 2,000 years ago mentions cases involving prevention and isolation: "… 'It is said that C has a highly contagious disease in his mouth and tongue, A and others cannot eat with him. Therefore, come and report it to you.' Recorded A and others names, occupations, and native places on the back of the document immediately … 'If there is a sacrifice in the village, C, the people in the same village, and A hold a party and dine together, they are all unwilling to share the eating utensils with C.' …". After the outbreak of an epidemic, in addition to self-help, the government often sent doctors to participate in the treatment and formulate countermeasures. For example, in the Song Dynasty, the government sent many imperial doctors to participate in the diagnosis and treatment when an epidemic happened in Kaifeng.

It's just that ancient people lacked modern physical and chemical knowledge and also lacked microscopic observation methods. The training and education of doctors were often not systematic. People's cognition of diseases and their causes was very limited, and it was often difficult to make accurate diagnoses of diseases. The proportions of active ingredients in medicinal materials were often very low. Anti-inflammatory measures and antibiotics were also missing, and various treatment methods were generally inferior. So many people in ancient times had to resign themselves to fate when they were sick. In ancient civilizations, an average life expectancy of about twenty to thirty years was common around the world, which strongly reflected that the health needs of human beings at that time were still far from being basically satisfied.

1.4.7 Overview of the Satisfaction of Human Needs Before Modern Industrialization

With the accumulation of knowledge and the development of scientific and technological civilization, on the eve of the industrial revolution or at the end of the development of ancient civilization, the living standards of the people in some countries and regions had been greatly improved compared with before. For example, in the western part of Europe, the land itself was relatively fertile, the climate was pleasant, and the density of people was not too high, so it could be said that the population had not reached the limit of the land's carrying capacity under the technical conditions at that time. Furthermore, the residents had obtained huge profits through colonization and commercial activities. Thus, the people in the western part of Europe had basically solved the problem of food and clothing, and many people had lived a relatively rich life. The satisfaction of the needs of people in these regions was probably at the top of the level of satisfaction outlined above.

However, there were also some places on the earth where the residents lived difficult lives on the eve of the Industrial Revolution. There were many reasons for this phenomenon. For example, in order to maintain their rule, the rulers engaged in the policy of keeping the people in ignorance and exploiting them heavily, coupled with repeated wars, huge war reparations, and other man-made disasters. Compared with their ancestors hundreds or thousands of years ago, the wealth that each ordinary person could have had decreased significantly, and the average level of scientific and cultural literacy of ordinary people had not only not improved but could even be said to have declined. The people had become extremely poor, just as in China for the last few hundred years. The following is an example of China, which outlines another type of human needs satisfaction situation on the eve of industrialization.

Taking China as an example, it can be said that before the reform and opening up, the vast number of rural residents carried out basically manual labor, living a life facing the loess with their backs to the sky. Their living conditions stayed the same as before the Industrial Revolution, and people's living needs could not be met, even the most basic needs for food and clothing. People's needs were in a state of complete dissatisfaction.

According to relevant research, during the Qianlong period of the 18th century, the annual income of a medium-sized peasant household with 50 mu of land in China was about 32 taels of silver. In the Qianlong period, one tael of silver could buy about 75 kilograms of rice. Since the families had about 5 to 6 people, the per capita annual income of medium farmers in the Qianlong period was only enough to buy about 400 to 500 kilograms of rice. This means that after subtracting various expenses, the annual income of a medium peasant household in the Qianlong period could only barely maintain the food and clothing of a family. It is said that in 1805, the average amount of land owned by a Chinese person dropped to only about 6.38 mu, which is equivalent to an average of 38 mu of land owned by a family of six members. From the Qianlong period of the 18th century to 1805, the development of China's production efficiency and scientific and technological level was stagnant. Thus, by 1805, the average household income of Chinese peasants was not higher than that of the average peasant household in the Qianlong period. In the more than 100 years since 1840, the Chinese people had been overwhelmed into a state of misery beyond words by nationwide social unrest, wars, and reparations that had occurred from time to time.

Even before the 1980s, rural China, which was largely pre-industrial, had large numbers of peasants struggling to get enough food to eat. Fig. 1.4.2 below is a few screenshots of the propaganda film "The Vast World," which was filmed by the Shanghai Revolutionary Committee during the Cultural Revolution in 1969 to beautify the so-called "intellectual youth going to the mountains and the countryside" movement. In picture (a), the girl was wearing pants with obvious patches, and the person in the back was walking barefoot on the road. In picture (b), the person was walking on the field path in rudimentary straw sandals. In picture (c), the young woman with glasses who was happily exchanging ideas had a large patch on the upper arm of her clothes. In a film that did beautification propaganda, it could still be seen that so many shots represented people who were still struggling to obtain food and clothing, which reflected how poor the real living standards of rural residents must have been at that time. People's basic needs were obviously far from being met.

(a) Picking up Buffalo Dung

(b) Walking on a Field Path

(c) Youth Exchanging Ideas

Fig. 1.4.2 Screenshots of the Film "The Vast World"

According to official data, 97.5 percent of rural residents in the Chinese mainland were still in poverty by 1978. Most of them were struggling to obtain adequate food and clothing, and 30.7 percent were in absolute poverty; that is, they had not even solved the problem of food and clothing. The article "60 Years of New China: Urban and Rural Residents Moving from Poverty to Moderate Prosperity in All Respects" (https://www.gov.cn/gzdt/2009-09/10/content_1413985.htm) mentioned, "by 1978, there were still 250 million rural residents in the country whose living standards were still below the absolute poverty line. On the whole, rural residents had not yet entered the stage of sufficient food and clothing." At that time, there were about 1.5 billion mu of cultivated land in the whole of the Chinese mainland. Because there were inaccurate factors in the measurement and statistics of cultivated land at that time, some said that the actual cultivated land area was about 18.9 billion mu at that time. There were about 800 million rural residents in 1978, which meant that peasants had, on average, only about two mu of cultivated land. According to the data from the statistics bureau, in 1978, China's total grain output was 304,750,000 tons. The average yield of a mu of cultivated land was about 200 kilograms. The average grain output per peasant was only close to 400 kilograms, which was completely incomparable with United States farmers, who produced 100 to 200 tons of grain per capita. Frankly speaking, with only about two mu of cultivated land per capita, it is impossible to make the peasants rich. In fact, after the great development of agricultural science and technology, the grain yield per mu still did not reach 400 kg, even though the seeds were optimized and the amount of chemical fertilizer increased from less than 6 kg per mu in 1978 to 21.9 kg in 2015. In 2015, the sown area of grain was about 1.7 billion mu, and the total grain output was about 620 million tons. Under such circumstances, it is necessary to introduce and use more advanced production technology and management technology, improve agricultural labor productivity, transfer a large number of labor forces that were originally engaged in agricultural production, and let them engage in industry and service industries. So, it is possible for the people to create more wealth and lift themselves out of poverty. Otherwise, there will be no chance that the needs of ordinary people in Chinese mainland can be met. In fact, since the reform and opening up of Chinese mainland, it is precisely more advanced technology and production modes that have provided the basic conditions for the improvement of people's living standards. It is precisely after 30 to 40 years of continuous improvement and expansion of modern production that the satisfaction of the needs of ordinary people in China has been greatly improved.

In fact, even in the early 1980s, there were still many rural dwellers living in extremely poor conditions. If you search for relevant documents, you can easily find many things that reflect the state of life at that time. For example, you can search for photos of poor rural villages in the 1980s published on the Internet by the author "History is Funny" (历史真好玩), which showed girls wearing pants that had been lengthened from old pants. At that time, there were still many people who usually wore patched clothes, especially the thrifty elderly, who had experienced difficult times and were reluctant to throw away their worn-out clothes. As an example, it is said that the photos on the web page https://www.163.com/dy/article/H7LSE7LO0543V970.html were taken in 1983, in which two old farmers in a very good mental state wore patched old clothes.

Before the reform and opening up, the Chinese people were mainly struggling to meet the most basic needs of food and clothing. The situation of satisfying other needs was naturally very poor.

For example, if we look at the demand for "housing" in a narrow sense, for the Chinese people before the reform and opening up, this demand was seriously unsatisfied, and the people basically lived helplessly in a cramped environment. According to relevant data, in 1978, the per capita living area of urban residents in China was only 3.6 square meters (https://www.sohu.com/a/159798557_594079), which was barely equivalent to the area of a small double bed with a width of 1.8 meters. Even if the area is converted into a concept that included a large amount of public land area that was later disregarded by ordinary Chinese people, the per capita residential "floor area" was only 6.7 square meters (https://baijiahao.baidu.com/s?id=1640081499170615524&wfr=spider&for=pc). The house area of rural residents was slightly larger, but the per capita residential area was still only 8.1 square meters, while rural residents had to place farm tools, grain storage cabinets, and other things in their homes. By the way, the vast majority of farmers in that period needed to save their own food, unlike urban residents who were issued food stamps and meat stamps every month and usually did not buy a lot of things at home at one time. So, the living space in the residence was basically very simple and narrow.

As for washing machines, refrigerators, televisions, and other daily necessities that facilitate life and meet the needs of "housing" in a broad sense, they were simply fantastical to Chinese farmers before the reform and opening up, and most people may have never heard of them.

As for the need for transportation, including the satisfaction of the need for communication and exchange, in China's rural areas before the reform and opening up, except for going out to the city by riding a bus without too many stops, the daily traffic could basically be described in this sentence: "The traffic basically depends on walking, and the communication basically depends on yelling." At that time, even the number of bicycles was very small. I vaguely remember that when I was very young, about the time when the reform and opening up began, there was only one or two bicycles in the village not far from Jinhua City, Zhejiang Province, where there were thirty to forty households. At that time, people urgently needed more convenient and labor-saving transportation and communication methods.

1.5 Discussion on the Satisfaction of Human Needs in the Current State of Development

Before the age of modern science and technology and modern machinery production, due to the relatively low level of science and technology and productivity, various human needs often went unsatisfied. For example, in the ancient hunting and gathering era, accidental factors and seasonal changes could all lead to starvation, and people's food needs could not always be satisfied. After entering the era of agricultural civilization, the occurrence of natural disasters such as floods, droughts, locusts, and man-made disasters such as wars might all lead to large-scale famine for human beings. Another example is the need for health; due to the lack of medical and health knowledge and hygiene methods, human beings lacked effective treatment methods for a considerable number of diseases that now seem very common, and patients were often forced to resign themselves to fate or engage in witchcraft and superstitious activities to make a prayer that was basically ineffective.

Since many scientists represented by Newton and others pioneered modern science and technology almost three to four hundred years ago, the level of human science and technology has developed rapidly. Especially in the past two hundred years, mankind has established a relatively comprehensive scientific system; scientific research and personnel education and training work have been systematized, and science and technology are accelerating development. Corresponding to it, mankind has experienced the First Industrial Revolution, the Second Industrial Revolution, the Third Industrial Revolution, and so forth, and the level of human productivity has been greatly improved. The improvement of the level of productivity has directly led to great changes in society and the improvement of human living standards.

Therefore, many people regard the First Industrial Revolution that began more than 200 years ago as a sign that mankind has entered modern society. For the societies that have entered industrialization one after another, with the improvement of the level of science and technology and the level of productivity, many of the needs of their people have been gradually satisfied.

Sure, because there are differences in the timetable and the degree of development of modern science and technology and productive forces in various parts of human society on the earth, there are naturally differences in the degree to which the needs of people in various places have been satisfied. In the regions that have entered developed society today, from the perspective of people's living conditions, many needs have been satisfied to very high levels. The living standards of the people in developed countries can well reveal the potential living conditions of the people if they stand at the forefront of science and technology and productive forces today. Referring to the current living conditions of the people in developed countries, if the science and technology and productive forces of a society are developed to the current front level, then many needs of the people in the world can be fully satisfied.

1.5.1 The Satisfaction of "Food" Needs

First of all, let's review the satisfaction of food needs. Today, human beings have basically realized the satisfaction of food needs. For example, the United States, Canada, Australia, the United Kingdom, and other countries have basically not had a large-scale famine for one to two hundred years. By the way, the author remembers that when he was young, he heard from his elders that one of the author's ancestors had lived in the United States for more than ten years at the end of the 19th century, and that his ancestor was very poor in the first few years in the United States and could only eat potatoes and chicken every day. According to historical data, the Chinese in that era were basically at the bottom of society in the United States, but they had already been able to fill their stomachs, although they probably ate the cheapest potatoes and chicken. As for the rest of the population in the United States at that time, whose economic status was much better than that of the Chinese, filling their stomachs was surely not a problem.

From the perspective of calorie intake and nutritional matching, the vast majority of people in the world have now met their food needs. In fact, people in many regions today are worried about overnutrition. Overweight and even obesity are not only problems faced by people in developed countries but also in many developing countries. The author has even heard a kind of self-motivated joke in the weight loss world: the poor are more likely to be obese, and the rich are more likely to be thin in the United States; it is because the rich are more likely to have good self-control and can often resist the temptation of food and pay attention to exercise, and the reason why the poor are poor is that they often lack self-control and have no control over their bodies. Through this joke, it can be seen that the poor in a country like the United States do not lack food and drink. As a fact, the adult overweight and obesity rate in Mexico, the United States, New

Zealand, Australia, the United Kingdom, Ireland, Iceland, Canada, Chile, Greece, and many other developed and developing countries has reached more than 50 percent. As is well known, today's China is still a developing country, and the poverty rate in its rural areas reached 97.5% in 1978 when the rural population accounted for 80% of the total population; the reform and opening-up has been carried out only for about 40 years. But by 2020, the adult overweight rate and obesity rate in China had reached 34.3% and 16.4% respectively, and these two proportions are in a rapidly upward channel. It is expected that by 2030, more than 60% of people in China will be overweight or obese. In the author's case, the current family income is in the lower reaches in Shanghai, but everyone in the family is overweight or obese. In recent years, people care more about maintaining good figures. In almost all countries with relatively normal development on the planet today, the daily problem faced by people is not finding food to fill their stomachs, but how to resist the appetite in the face of the temptation of food and how to avoid excessive calorie intake affecting their health.

According to the United Nations, less than 10% of the world's population is living in poverty today, and these poor people are mainly concentrated in a few countries and regions. Among these poor people, the poverty of some of them is caused by their society, which is still in a closed and semi-closed state, and they have not yet participated in modern production; the poverty of some of them is caused by the self-righteous foolishness of the local rulers, which limits the creativity of the people, or the poverty is the result of a small number of people in power carrying out certain policies for some extremely despicable and selfish reasons; the poverty of some people is caused by social turmoil or wars caused by factors such as ideological sectarian conflicts, tribal contradictions, and rampant gangs and banditry, which in turn leads to abnormal social production and abnormal wealth distribution. Of course, the poverty of some people is because they are unable to earn a living wage due to disability, and the local social welfare is not good enough. Basically, it can be said that the current poverty phenomenon in human society is caused by abnormal factors.

Taking a comprehensive look at the current state of human society on the planet, with today's advanced level of technology and productivity, the goal of zero hunger itself is feasible. The food supply and consumption situation in the developed world has proven that under the current level of advanced science, technology, and productivity, human needs for food can be relatively fully satisfied.

1.5.2 The Satisfaction of "Heat Preservation" Needs

Since ancient times, people have mainly met the "heat preservation" needs of the human body from the perspectives of creating a microenvironment or a small environment.

In cold or cool weather, clothing can be used to create a portable heat preservation microenvironment for the human body, and bedding can be used to create a comfortable microenvironment for sleep and rest. Therefore, since almost ancient times, clothing and bedding have been the two important heat preservation measures for human beings. Since entering the era of agricultural civilization, with the gradual scarcity and cost increase of animal fur resources and the development of the textile industry, the use of textiles to make clothes and bedding has become mainstream. Historically, the representative industrial aspect of the first industrial revolution, which began more than 200 years ago, is the revolution of the textile industry. The textile industry has evolved from manual labor to machine production, and in just a few decades, the labor productivity of the textile industry has increased dozens of times. As a result, the cost of obtaining clothing and bedding has been greatly reduced. With the global embrace of modern technology and production, the textile industry has been comprehensively developed. With the progress of science and technology, the materials used for textiles are no longer limited to natural fibers such as cotton, wool, linen, and silk; synthetic fibers have become a very important source of textiles. At present, the production of synthetic fibers has accounted for more than 50 percent of the total fiber output. For example, the production of synthetic fibers in China reached 56.338 million tons in 2020, and even if two-thirds of them are used in the textile industry, China's synthetic fiber industry can already contribute about 4.7 kilograms of textiles to everyone on the planet today. Coupled with traditional cotton, linen, wool, and silk, and considering the fact that so many countries in the world have contributed to the textile industry, it is conceivable how many textiles are produced for everyone in the world today. Statistically, in 2021, the world's per capita textile consumption reached 15.2 kg (reported by Sun Ruizhe, President of the China National Textile and Apparel Council, http://www.ctei.cn/jq/gzdt/202312/t20231220_4335850.html). At present, human society produces more than 100 billion new pieces of clothing every year, with more than a dozen pieces per capita. Nowadays, even in China, which is still far from the standards of the developed world, a large number of families are facing such problems: there are too many clothes and bedding at home, the places where clothes and bedding can be put are full, and finding a place to put newly bought clothes has become a headache. A lot of clothes are only worn with a fresh feeling when they are first bought, and then they are put at the bottom of the box and forgotten. For today's normal society, which accounts for the vast majority of human society, people need to spend at most one to two days' salary to buy a piece of ordinary clothing. For people in developed countries, many ordinary clothes are even worth only a few dozen minutes of labor salary. This means that people only need to spend a few days of work to achieve the freedom to buy their clothes for heat preservation. In addition, over the past 200 years, many textiles with excellent thermal insulation properties have been developed. Therefore, it can be said that the needs of human beings have been met in terms of "heat preservation" by creating a heat preservation microenvironment.

Creating a small environment with a suitable temperature for residences, offices, shops, leisure, and entertainment venues, etc., is also an important heat preservation solution for human beings today. In ancient times, people mainly used fire, ventilation, water evaporation regulation, and other basically open-loop methods to create a comfortable small environment, and the temperature control effect was not ideal in many cases, especially in hot weather. After entering the modern era, humans have invented modern air conditioners, combined with sensing technology. Humans can accurately adjust the temperature and other parameters of small environments. People can create a small environment that is as warm as spring in cold weather or a small environment that is like a cool autumn in hot weather. We often see in videos reflecting the daily lives of people around the world that people living in cold regions of the United States wear only thin clothes in winter. It is not that people in the United States are not afraid of the cold, but it is because their homes, cars, stores, etc., are air-conditioned. In fact, all over the world outside the United States, a variety of temperature control equipment is also very popular. Even in China, which is relatively not rich and has a per capita GDP only at the world average, except for those places where the climate is pleasant and does not need an air conditioner, air conditioning is already the standard equipment of every family. Human beings today have done a good job of meeting the needs of heat preservation by creating a pleasant small environment.

To sum up, this paper argues that on Earth today, for the vast majority of people, the needs for heat preservation have been well met already. There are a lot of concerns that the living conditions are too comfortable and that people have become too vulnerable. Now, there are also many people who are worried that people are too greedy for comfort and consume too much energy. Excessive energy consumption will result in excessive carbon emissions, affect the stability of the Earth's climate, and bring serious environmental disasters. As for the problem of excessive energy consumption, measures such as continuing to develop relevant science and technology can be taken to alleviate it.

1.5.3 The Satisfaction of "Housing" Needs

A comfortable house is an important condition for creating a warm and secure home. Comfortable housing needs to have a certain amount of space, a reasonable functional configuration, household appliances that meet the owner's wishes, and convenient surrounding living facilities.

Let's look at the space of the house first. Is the bigger the space in the house, the better? Obviously, no. The key is to be suitable. The size should match the number and characteristics of the residents; too small and too big are both unsuitable.

If the space of the house is too small, including the total area and the parameters of length, width, and height, it will make people feel psychologically cramped and depressed, and will lead to nowhere to put daily household items. In this way, life will naturally be very inconvenient. Therefore, a house that is too small cannot meet the needs of the people living in it.

Too large a house space is a kind of waste. After all, limited by energy and exercise ability, people's range of activities is actually very limited. If the house is too large, many places in the house will be vacant and may be left unvisited for a long time. Places rarely visited by humans are easy breeding grounds for insects and ants, and they are easy to spoil. Costs are needed to build and maintain a house. If it is only giving without income, then the cost expenditure may be classified as a waste of resources. Secondly, if the house is too big, it will take too much time and energy to clean the rooms. The maintenance cost will be too high, and the burden will be heavy. It is easy to make people feel unhappy. In addition, due to the emptiness and coldness, people who live in a house that is too large are prone to experiencing negative emotions such as loneliness, desolation, and fear.

According to the opinions of "Feng Shui (geomantic)" (although Feng Shui has been made into superstitious metaphysics by people who use it to make money, its origin itself has a certain scientific component), a house should be the right size. A house can accumulate vital energy only with a suitable size. The size should correspond to the scale of a family. The more people, the bigger; the fewer, the smaller. If there are few people and the house size is too large, then the vital energy will be more easily dissipated, and it is inauspicious. If the house is too small, occupants are prone to experiencing stale air, poor breathing, and depression, which will cause harm to the physical and mental health of the residents in the house. For example, Dong Zhongshu, a famous figure in the Western Han Dynasty more than 2,000 years ago, mentioned in "Spring and Autumn Dew • Following the Tao of Heaven" that "the too high platform is full of yang, the too wide room is full of yin, and they are far away from the harmony of heaven and earth. Therefore, sages did not pursue luxury and were just moderate." In Europe and the United States today, one family usually lives in a house of several hundred square meters. It is spacious but not empty, and the living conditions are relatively suitable. In the United States, there are often courtyards, lawns, and green trees in front and back of houses, and the living environment is really fine.

The basic function of housing is to provide services for daily life, including preparing meals, dining, bathing, convenient hygiene, sleep, and rest, etc. In addition, reasonable housing function configuration should also include emotional exchanges among family members, leisure and entertainment, and knowledge learning. Nowadays, housing for people in developed and moderately developed countries has basically become a complete set, generally including kitchens, dining rooms, living rooms, bedrooms, bathrooms, etc., and families with children going to school or intellectual families are likely to have study rooms. Like most United States citizens and Australians, people who live in single-family houses often have storage rooms, tool rooms, garages, home theaters, and entertainment gyms, etc., and many of them even have a small swimming pool at home. The above function configuration of housing naturally meets people's needs. Compared with the citizens of developed countries such as the United States, the vast majority of urban residents in China, people who live in apartment buildings, generally have a smaller housing area and usually live in apartments with two or three bedrooms. An apartment usually contains kitchens, bathrooms, dining rooms, and bedrooms. They basically satisfy the needs of contemporary Chinese families, since the sizes of Chinese families are usually very small. People can watch TV and chat in the living room. Some families will also transform a room into a study or computer room. Most of China's urban residential apartment buildings are divided into communities, and the residential communities usually have small squares and activity centers, equipped with simple fitness equipment for residents to carry out fitness, entertainment, and social activities. As for private cars, they are generally parked in public areas such as roadside parking lots in communities. It is equivalent to shifting some functions in the housing for American and Australian families to the public areas, which effectively reduces people's requirements for the size of the house.

With the development of science and technology, human beings have developed a wide range of household appliances to meet their needs, which greatly reduce the amount of housework and make it easier for ordinary people in contemporary society to create a comfortable home environment.

People's dietary life has been greatly facilitated and enriched by the improvement of kitchenware. With electric cookers and gas cookers, people need not prepare firewood and tend the kitchen fire as they did in the past. Moreover, many electric cookers have functions such as temperature control and time control, making it easier and more convenient to prepare meals. People who eat rice as their staple food can now easily prepare the main dish by mixing rice and water and pressing the "start" button. Cheap, small but powerful, easy-to-use modern household baking equipment has greatly facilitated the preparation of staple foods and dishes for many people. Cheap but excellent household food mincers and dough-kneading machines have greatly reduced the amount of labor and time required to prepare food. The popularity of refrigerators has made it possible for people to purchase or prepare fresh ingredients for several days or even longer. People need not prepare fresh ingredients every day, and each family directly reduces the labor time by half an hour, an hour, or even more per day. Dishwashers greatly reduce the amount of labor that people have to do to clean their dishes. The popularization of sterilizers has ensured the hygiene of tableware. The widespread use of tap water directly exempts people from the daily workload of fetching water.

Modern bathroom equipment makes people's lives more comfortable. Modern homes are almost always equipped with convenient facilities, such as flush toilets, which eliminate the trouble of ordinary people cleaning up feces in the past and help keep the air in the home fresh. The widespread use of gas, electric heating, solar energy, and other hot water equipment makes it possible for people to maintain comfortable personal hygiene at home at any time. The widespread use of washing machines has also freed people from the tedious and unpleasant work of washing clothes.

Creating a small environment with a suitable temperature and humidity to meet the heat preservation needs is also a reflection of housing comfort. The vast majority of ordinary people's homes around the world, such as those of United States residents and Chinese urban residents, are equipped with air conditioning or heating, so that people can avoid the torture of the harsh winter and the scorching summer. Especially for residents in developed areas like the United States, the air temperatures in houses are often regulated to be the most comfortable for the occupants.

Today, people produce a variety of comfortable bedding, fabric sofas, plush toys, and other living supplies in large quantities at low prices. Ordinary people can easily create a warm and comfortable living environment for sleep and leisure.

Modern family houses basically have living rooms. Living rooms are usually equipped with TVs, sofas, tables, chairs, etc. People can have leisure and entertainment in living rooms. Family members also communicate information and emotions in living rooms. Many families will also prepare study rooms or the like. Coupled with modern network communication technology, today's people can know about the world's major events without leaving home. Nowadays, people can better carry out activities such as knowledge learning and working from home.

Families in developed countries, such as the United States, often have special entertainment and fitness rooms at home. There are even many families who have swimming pools or playgrounds in their yards. It is easier to create laughter and shape the body in a home environment.

People have convenient living facilities in many countries. Now the urbanization rate in many countries is very high. For example, the urbanization rates of Europe and the United States have basically reached more than 70 percent, and most people live in large or small towns. Counting the population in the suburbs of the towns, it accounts for the vast majority of the population. Nowadays, in developed countries, convenient means of travel, such as cars, are primarily used for daily travel. Shopping, leisure, and entertainment are very accessible.

From the perspective of income and expenditure, under today's level of science and technology and productivity, can ordinary people have a warm and comfortable living home? Judging from the house-price-to-income ratio, ordinary people can actually afford to have their own warm and comfortable living house. For example, in 2024, the house-price-to-income ratio in the United States is about 4.0 times. In 2023, the house-price-to-income ratio in Australia is about 7.0 times, the house-price-to-income ratio in the United Kingdom is about 8.0 times, and the house-price-to-income ratios in many rich countries such as Canada, Italy, Switzerland, Germany, Japan, and France are around 10 times. In some countries, such as China, the house-price-to-income ratios are more than 20 times. But in fact, most Chinese have purchased their houses at prices much lower than the current housing prices. The urban residents' home ownership rate in China reaches 96%. Excluding factors such as commercial speculation and taxation, just from the construction cost of housing, ordinary people can easily have their own warm and comfortable living houses. The cost of construction and installation is generally not higher than the housing price. Since the housing price-to-income ratios in many countries, such as the United States, are about three to four times, the real housing construction cost-to-income ratio will not be higher than the above value. Thus, an ordinary family today is able to live in a warm and comfortable house. Therefore, under modern productivity, ordinary people can easily have a warm and comfortable living home.

To sum up, under the current level of human productivity, the needs of human beings for housing can be relatively well satisfied. In fact, whether from the size of the house or from household equipment and the convenience of life, the housing needs of ordinary people in many countries and regions have been well met.

1.5.4 The Satisfaction of "Health" Needs and "Life Continuity" Needs

With the development of modern science and technology, people have an increasingly scientific understanding of biology, disease, and hygiene, and their health knowledge is becoming richer and more reasonable. Especially in the last one to two hundred years, people's health has improved dramatically.

The invention and widespread use of modern water purification technology have contributed to the use of tap water and other clean water. Today, people can easily obtain healthy and safe drinking water without heating and sanitizing, effectively protecting their daily health. After all, for people, many diseases come from the mouth.

Since the nineteenth century, the widespread promotion of toothbrushes and toothpaste has greatly reduced the occurrence of tooth and mouth pain and effectively defended the oral health and physical health of human beings. Modern families are generally equipped with bathroom equipment and personal hygiene materials such as soap, shower gel, and skincare products. People can easily achieve personal hygiene and cleanliness, keep the human body comfortable, reduce the chance of skin infection by fungi, and reduce the occurrence of skin itching and uncomfortable lesions. Nowadays, human beings have more daily health knowledge and technical means, which ensure the good maintenance of their daily health status.

Since bleaching powder was invented in 1820 for the treatment of infectious wounds and the disinfection of drinking water, a variety of disinfection and sterilization technologies have been developed and popularized, such as iodine tincture disinfection, phenol disinfection, and 75% alcohol disinfection. With the above disinfection and sterilization methods, people can reduce the risk of wound infection and greatly avoid the occurrence of life-threatening phenomena caused by daily wound breakage and infection.

In the twentieth century, the discovery and use of antibiotics made it easier for humans to recover from bacterial infections, alleviating people's suffering and giving them more opportunities for health and longevity. Along with the development of modern medical diagnosis and treatment technology and pharmaceutical technology, the diagnosis and treatment methods and accuracy of human beings have been greatly improved, and more and more types of diseases can be treated. Nowadays, human beings can basically treat ordinary daily diseases. Even if some diseases cannot be completely cured, there are often solutions to alleviate pain and prolong life. For example, in the case of the malignant infectious disease AIDS, although infected human beings are basically not completely cured at present, there are already means to continue the survival of people living with HIV for decades. Compared with the human lifespan of only about 100 years, the survival of a few decades is a relatively long time.

Compared with the past, since the middle of the 19th century, the risk to human fertility has been greatly reduced. The maternal mortality rate in the First Obstetrics Department of the Vienna General Hospital was as high as about 30 percent in the early 19th century. Now, the maternal mortality rate in most countries has dropped to less than 2 or 3 per

71

10,000. The neonatal mortality rate has also dropped from 10 to 20 percent to a few thousandths now. The mortality rate of young children has also been greatly reduced. About half of the people did not live to adulthood in ancient times, and almost all people can live to adulthood now. People have also successfully developed assisted reproductive technologies, such as artificial insemination and test-tube baby technology. The advancement of modern science and technology greatly promotes the fulfillment of life continuity needs.

The average life expectancy has also increased significantly. The average life expectancy was about 30 to 40 years two or three hundred years ago, and it has increased to the 70s and 80s in most normal societies today. Now, the vast majority of people can live to an old age with a serious and natural decline in physical function.

Judging from the fact that the life expectancy of human beings in various places today is generally 70 to 80 years, which is the most important health achievement, the health needs of human beings have been met to a considerable extent. Of course, we humans must continue to develop health and medical technologies so we can maintain our youthful vitality for a long time, obtain a longer lifespan, and live a healthier, happier life.

1.5.5 The Satisfaction of "Rest" Needs and "Neuropsychological" Needs

With the development of the productive forces and the struggle of the workers, the working hours of ordinary workers have been reduced from more than ten hours a day to eight hours, and the current five-day workweek has evolved from only a few rest days a year, with some countries and regions even trying a four-day workweek now. At present, relatively formal large enterprises often provide paid annual leave, which can reach 20, 30, or even 40 days. In addition, there are many countries where the statutory holidays have reached more than 10 days. According to online information, the median number of working hours in the United States is about 1,791 hours. The average annual working hours of Canadians is about 1,685 hours. Germans have 178 days off and 187 days of work per year, and the annual working hours are about 1,496 hours. France basically works seven hours a day, and the working hours in a year are about 1,505 hours. The average working hours in the United Kingdom are about 1,677 hours. The average annual working hours in Sweden are about 1,420 hours. Greece is said to work four to five hours a day, with an average annual working hours of about 1,255 hours. Since there are a total of 8,760 hours in a year, the people of these European countries and the United States spend less than 20% of their total time at work. Compared to hundreds of years ago, ordinary workers have much more time to rest.

In recent centuries, with the advancement of science and technology and the improvement of production capacity, human beings have developed many different forms of leisure and entertainment. There are many kinds of leisure and entertainment that can help eliminate the physical and mental fatigue of the participants, allowing people to achieve psychological relaxation, emotional happiness, knowledge, and physical health. What types of entertainment and leisure are available today?

One type of leisure and entertainment is related to physical activities, including people's own participation in physical activities and watching and appreciating the physical activities of others. Nowadays, there are many types of sports and fitness activities. Among these activities, there are a large number of activities that are not high-cost for ordinary people to participate in, for example, entertainment and social activities such as dance; track and field sports such as running to train physical fitness; ball sports such as basketball, football, and table tennis; swimming, rowing, and other water-related sports; martial arts, boxing, and other sports related to individual force; archery, firearms, and other shooting sports related to hunting activities, and so on.

Film and television art performances are important means of leisure and entertainment. People can go to the theater to enjoy movies and theater performances. They can also enjoy films, television dramas, and other performances through TV or the Internet at home. People can even form interest groups with like-minded individuals to perform art together.

One type of leisure and entertainment is game activities, such as knowledge quizzes, chess, military flags, checkers, flying chess, and other chess games, poker, mahjong, and other card games.

Tourism is an important form of leisure and entertainment. It helps to broaden your horizons, understand the customs of various places, experience the lives of people everywhere, enjoy the food of different regions, and meet the needs of people's souls.

One type of recreational activity is participating in religious activities moderately. Regardless of whether the teachings of each religion are true or not, most religious sects teach people to be nice. People can often gain the identity of like-minded individuals by participating in them moderately and obtain a sense of spiritual security or peace through psychological activities such as brainwashing and self-brainwashing. Of course, a small number of people who regularly participate in the activities of certain religious sects are prone to gradually becoming extreme, and they may even engage in acts that endanger innocent people in society who hold different views from theirs. This requires our society's vigilance.

With the development of computer technology and the introduction of computers into thousands of households, people have developed computer virtual games. Computer games, combined with network communication technology, are characterized by allowing participants to quickly find game partners or opponents, who are either real people or computer simulations, relaxing the trouble of finding partners and opponents that often occurs in offline games. Today's computer games include games that run on personal computers and games that can be played on smart terminals, such as mobile phones. There are many types of computer games, such as role-playing games, real-time strategy games, fighting games, simulation games, and adventure games. Computer games are a form of entertainment and leisure, which can often give people a strong sense of participation and substitution. The rhythm of the game can be designed to be very fast, which can easily make gamers nervous and excited. This characteristic of computer games leads to the fact that people are prone to becoming addicted, especially teenagers, and often makes players forget the time spent playing, and even forget to sleep and eat, staying up all night for the game. It may not only waste people's studies and careers, but also affect sleep, physical exercise, and damage human health. The author's point of view is that for teenagers and people who are easily addicted, computer games are not a healthy form of recreation, but they are indeed a form of recreation in which many people participate today.

With the development of chip technology and computer technology, and the rise and popularization of network technology, people can easily use their mobile phones to obtain information, read online books, enjoy films and television works, play online games, browse, and select a variety of goods, and so on. Nowadays, human beings tend to have a full schedule of leisure and entertainment time. In fact, in recent decades, along with the popularization of televisions and the introduction of personal computers into millions of households, the average sleep time of human beings has been continuously shortened, especially after entering the era of smartphones. Today's leisure and entertainment time has been crowding out sleep and rest, and more and more people's sleep and rest time has become insufficient.

1.5.6 The Satisfaction of " Transportation" Needs

Since the Industrial Revolution, people have invented many mechanically powered vehicles: first steam-powered trains and steam-powered ships, hot air balloons, airships, etc.; and then electric locomotives, internal combustion engine-powered trains and automobiles, airplanes, and launch vehicles. Contemporary human society has many convenient and high-speed means of transportation, such as short- and medium-distance travel represented by automobiles, medium- and long-distance travel represented by trains and high-speed trains, and long-distance travel represented by airplanes. Mankind has built quite well-developed transportation facilities on the earth, such as railways and high-speed railways, roads and highways, and airports all over the inhabited continents, as well as ports and safe shipping lanes around the world. Nowadays, people's needs for transportation have been satisfied to a large extent.

Ordinary people no longer rely on two legs to travel but travel by car, subway, train, plane, and ship. The speed at which people move in space has been dramatically enhanced. For example, by taking the high-speed train, people can travel from Shanghai to Beijing in just four to five hours; by plane, you can fly from Beijing to London and from Beijing to New York in one day. In terms of travel, human beings can really be said to have realized the dream of the ancients to "travel to the North Sea in the morning, visit Cangwu at dusk." In addition, mankind is currently developing relatively cheap space transportation tools, and humanity is approaching the era of space.

As for the transportation of goods, people have developed powerful means of transportation, such as freight cars, trains, and freight ships. There are also a large number of machines for loading and unloading goods. People can transport goods from one place to another on the earth easily and quickly. For example, Americans can quickly receive customized clothes, shoes, and hats made in China; Chinese people can eat fresh fruits from Chile, which is half a world away; and

Israeli flowers can quickly appear in Western European markets.

As for the transportation of information and data, the current global high-speed communication network has been built and is developing rapidly, including optical fiber communication, satellite wireless communication, and so on. Real-time calls across continents are no longer a problem, and video chatting is no longer an issue. At present, people can know about the events happening on the other side of the world in real time. Live video reproduction with sound and light is no longer a problem. For example, on June 7, 2024, an expert who was in Rome successfully completed radical prostatectomy surgery for a patient in Beijing by controlling a remote surgical robot. According to the above-mentioned evidences, the data and information transportation capacity has been able to meet people's daily needs.

1.5.7 Brief Summary

The human body is limited. The weight of a person ranges from several kilograms to a few hundred kilograms. As well known, the quantity of food that a person can eat at once is much less than his or her weight. Therefore, the amount of food a person consumes in a day is also limited. An adult usually eats one to three kilograms of food a day, and the author has never seen a person who can eat hundreds of kilograms of food a day. Even if someone can eat hundreds of kilograms of food a day, such eating will be a great torture for him, not his food enjoyment.

The space occupied by a human body is usually a few tens of cubic decimeters, and the super big guy merely occupies a space of a few hundred cubic decimeters. The living space that most people really need is not very large. For example, if a person lives in a building like the Shanghai Tower, such a large house may not bring convenience and spiritual happiness to the person; on the contrary, such a huge residence is likely to bring a strong sense of loneliness and panic to them. Naturally, a person does not need a large temperature-controlled space. The idea of adjusting the temperature of the entire atmosphere to a level at which the human body feels comfortable is not a real human need; it is just a boring and unrealistic desire.

There is a limit to how much time each person can use. Under today's levels of science and technology, people usually can live for 30,000 days in their lifetime, and those who are particularly lucky can have about 40,000 days of life. Everybody has 24 hours a day. Therefore, the time that people can spend on food enjoyment, study, exercise, work, leisure and entertainment, rest, and other activities every day is limited. Moreover, the time resources that need to be invested in a certain activity and those actually needed for the activity are often limited; for example, non-stop entertainment 24 hours a day can make people lose their interest in entertainment, and sleeping 24 hours a day is often uncomfortable.

Therefore, in principle, though human desires can be infinite and difficult to satisfy, people's real needs are often limited and can be satisfied to a large extent. In fact, under the modern levels of science and technology and productive forces, many human needs have been satisfied to a very high degree. For many ordinary people on the earth, especially ordinary people in developed and moderately developed countries, the needs for food, heat preservation, rest, health, housing, transportation, and so on have been relatively well satisfied.

As a fact, with the exception of a small number of countries and regions that are ruled and controlled by some bad people, and those that are affected by certain historical realities, based on per capita GDP values and commodity prices, today's human society has generally solved the problem of food and clothing and entered the stage of a moderately prosperous or affluent life. For example, wheat is about 200 US dollars per ton, and corn is cheaper than wheat. In 2023, the world's annual per capita GDP is 12,894 US dollars, wherein the per capita GDP of South America is 9,099 US dollars, the annual per capita GDP of developing countries is 6,326 US dollars, and the annual per capita GDP of Southeast Asia is 5,441 US dollars. The poorest countries in South Asia and Africa have annual GDP per capita of $2,310 and $2,178, respectively. Thus, even in South Asia and Africa, where people have the lowest per capita GDP, they have enough per capita GDP to buy more than 10 tons of food per person. The expenditure on insulated clothing and fuel is generally less than the expenditure on food, and a person only needs a few hundred kilograms of food a year. Today, most people have solved the problem of food and heat preservation. There is an important conclusion on China's social development that "a per capita GDP of more than 3,000 US dollars is the fundamental sign of building a moderately prosperous society in an all-round way". Today's human society has generally entered the stage of being moderately prosperous or affluent.

Today, many of the needs of mankind have been well met, and it is believed that with the continuous development of science and technology and productive forces, the various needs of mankind can be better satisfied.

Since the universality of human basic needs is well met now, our human society actually does not need to rush to develop artificial intelligence technology, and there is no need to rush to indiscriminately apply artificial intelligence technology in various industries.

1.6 Review and Discussion

From the mechanical perspective, some important human beings' needs have been analyzed in this chapter. There are food needs, heat preservation needs, rest needs, housing needs, health needs, life continuity needs, transportation needs, neuropsychological needs, knowledge and skills needs, etc. Human individuals rush to do things, basically to meet these needs.

Human beings possess advanced intelligence, robust bodies, and flexible hands. Humans are capable of manufacturing tools and developing science and technology. These have freed humans from the fate in which animals can only pursue a few basic needs, such as food and survival. With the development and accumulation of scientific and technological knowledge, human beings are gradually able to pursue and control the satisfaction of their various important needs.

In this chapter, the author analyzes the degree of satisfaction of people's needs during the ancient Paleolithic and Neolithic eras, analyzes the degree of satisfaction of human needs in the era before the Industrial Revolution after entering the civilization era, and analyzes and discusses the satisfaction of human needs after several modern industrial revolutions. Through these analyses and discussions, for three hundred and sixty professions, each profession has its own insights and contributions. With the development of various scientific and technological fields, human beings have gradually improved their satisfaction of needs, although the process may be complicated for some groups of people. Especially in modern times, many people's needs have been met well. It can be said that a solid foundation for meeting various important human needs has been laid by the development of science and technology. Therefore, we humans cannot be hostile to science and technology, and we humans need to continue developing a wide variety of scientific and technological advancements.

It is precisely because people's living standards have greatly improved with the advancement of science and technology that most people today have a very good impression of science and technology, and even a certain degree of worship. Certain degrees of worship of science and technology are good for the development of society and the satisfaction of human needs. However, if the degree of worship is at a blind level, it is not a good thing. After all, science and technology are double-edged swords. Some science and technology will be the great scourge of humanity if they are not used well or are controlled by malicious individuals.

Artificial intelligence technology or robot technology is exactly the technology that has the potential to be a double-edged sword. AI technology is developing at a high speed, and it is changing our society rapidly. Most of us can only say "Ah … Ah … Ah" when facing AI and AI applications. Most people will be amazed by the incredible impact it brings. People only fantasize about the scenarios that "If I have intelligent robots in the future, I will be much more comfortable." People tend to neglect the crisis of social unrest caused by artificial intelligence. Perhaps the next catastrophic social turbulence may be caused by the unrestricted use of AI. What could this catastrophic turbulence be? Perhaps it's war; perhaps it's slaughter. Turbulence is likely to result in unfortunate outcomes for ordinary people. Ordinary people may become dispensable, captive, and live in a state similar to that of slaves.

2 Overview of Robotics and Artificial Intelligence Technologies

2.1 Overview of Robots

2.1.1 What Are Robots

People often had to do a lot of hard work in order to reap the meager wealth, especially in the time before the Industrial Revolution. When a person is fatigued and exhausted, naturally, he may fantasize about how good it would be if pies could fall from the sky and there was ready-made wealth to pick up. The fantasy mentality should be very common. For example, there are many stories about secret treasures in literature; the lottery business is booming in many parts of the world today. In order to have ready-made wealth to enjoy, someone may raise the idea of using other means to work for him. Theft and robbery, ancient wars and plunder, and slave exploitation are probably all products of the unearned mind. But theft, robbery, plunder, and slave oppression are sinful. They are all not in line with modern ethical and moral standards. The person who carries out sinful behaviors will face the risk of being punished by the pushback. Therefore, some people raise the idea of using a machine that can work like a human or an animal and has the characteristics of being obedient, not resisting, tireless, and so on. Perhaps this is the simplest starting point of human beings' dream of robots. For example, as the Honda website (https://www.honda.com.cn/honda/news/voice/HondaStories_20230118.html) states, the Honda robotics team is based on the development of entourage robots as a foothold to develop the famous robot ASIMO.

After the Industrial Revolution, large-scale machine production brought great changes to human society, changed people's lives, and gave people a deep perceptual understanding of the power of machines. As a result, there are a lot of science fiction works related to robots. In 1920, the Czech writer Karel Čapek named the robot for the first time based on the Czech word for slave (robota), which is the official origin of the name robot. In 1940, the writer Asimov gave the robot an ethical qualification: the famous Three Laws of Robotics.

(1) A robot may not injure a human being or, through inaction, allow a human being to come to harm.

(2) A robot must obey the orders given to it by human beings, except where such orders would conflict with the First Law.

(3) A robot must protect its own existence as long as such protection does not conflict with the First or Second Law.

Asimov's Three Laws of Robotics can only be regarded as a beautiful vision and expectation of human beings for robots. In reality, so far, the vast majority of robots classified as robots do not possess any advanced intelligence and are basically aimed at a relatively specific single application environment. In principle, today's robots are basically incapable of identifying whether humans are being harmed, let alone following the Three Laws of Robotics. Until now, robots have been basically automated machines. Of course, it may be that in the near future, humans will develop robots that follow the ethical norms set by humans.

Before the invention of computers, it was difficult to simulate humans or livestock to have the ability to perceive, make decisions, and execute behaviors. Thus, robots before the invention of computers could not be regarded as modern robots with basic characteristics such as perception, decision-making, and execution. Therefore, both the legendary southward-pointing cart and the puppet made by a clever artisan in Emperor Sui that could perform actions such as sitting, rising, worshipping, and prostrating, strictly speaking, cannot be regarded as robots in the true sense.

Since the famous electronic computer ENIAC was created in the United States in 1946, robots have the foundation of having a brain. After decades of continuous investment in manpower and resources, people have developed a large number of robots. These bots are divided into many categories. There are many ways to classify robots based on the different focuses of various research areas; for example, dividing them based on developmental stages, dividing them based on control modes, dividing them based on application environments, dividing them based on modes of movement, and so on.

In practical applications, robots are often divided into two categories: industrial robots and intelligent robots. For example, the United States Robotics Association (RIA) once defined a robot as "A robot is a reprogrammable, multifunctional manipulator designed to move material, parts, tools or specialized devices through variable programmed motions for the performance of a variety of tasks," which is actually a definition of industrial robots. The Japan Industrial Robot Association (JIRA) once defined a robot as "a general-purpose machine that is equipped with a memory device or end effector and can turn and automatically complete various movements to replace human labor." In general, an industrial robot is a multifunctional machine capable of performing actions similar to those of a person's upper limbs (hands and arms); an intelligent robot is a machine that has the ability to feel, recognize, and control its own behavior. Note: Refer to Cai Zixing's "Robotics."

2.1.2 Industrial Robots

The most common industrial robots are a variety of manipulators, commonly used in contemporary manufacturing plants, such as spot-welding manipulators in automobile manufacturing plants that often appear on TV news. In addition to advantages such as speed and tirelessness, a great advantage of a spot-welding manipulator is that it avoids the issue of bright light burning the human eye during manual welding. Manipulators are relatively simple, mainly imitating the function of the upper limbs of the human body, generally having multiple degrees of freedom, and there are many specific forms. Fig. 2.1.1 shows two types of industrial robots: a manipulator-type industrial robot on the left and a multi-degree-of-freedom robot with a guide rail on the right. A large number of videos and images of various industrial robot applications can be easily found on the web.

In the early days, industrial robots were mainly used in the automobile manufacturing industry and the electronic product production industry. With the development of digital technology, a variety of machinery used in many industries has been automated, such as machine tool automation, pharmacy dispensing machinery automation, and warehouse machinery automation. From the characteristics of industrial robots, these automated machines are the same as traditional industrial robot manipulators. They are all programmable and can automatically complete a series of operations. From the definition of robots, today's automated CNC machine tools, automatic placement machines widely used in the electronics manufacturing industry, and dispensing machinery for pharmacy automation can all be regarded as robots, and because they are used in production, the author believes that they should actually be classified as industrial robots.

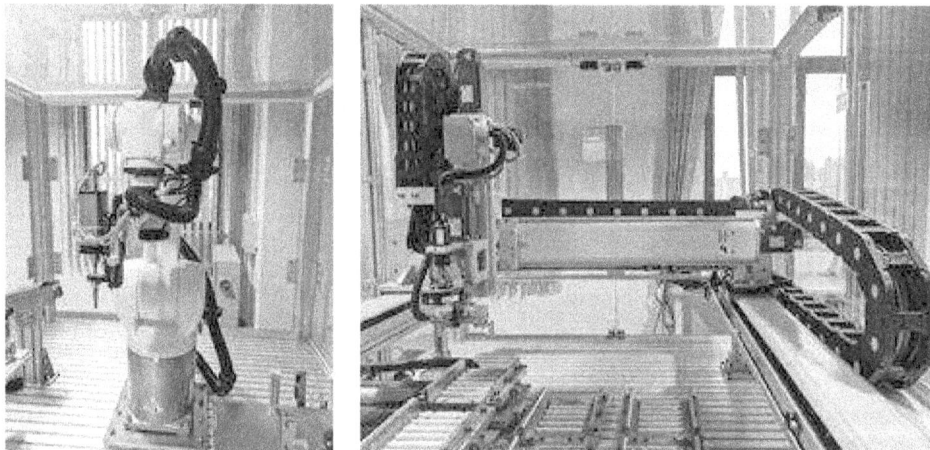

Fig. 2.1.1 Examples of Industrial Robots

In the twentieth century, the country with the best application of industrial robot technology was almost Japan. With the development and change of industries in various countries, now the highest average density of industrial robots is in Korea. Up to 2020, the density of industrial robots in Korea's manufacturing industry reached 932 per 10,000 people, which far exceeds that of other countries, including Japan. China's development is fast, and the sales of industrial robots reached 303,000 units in 2022. Figure 2.1.2 shows the average density of manufacturing industrial robots in some countries and regions searched on the Internet.

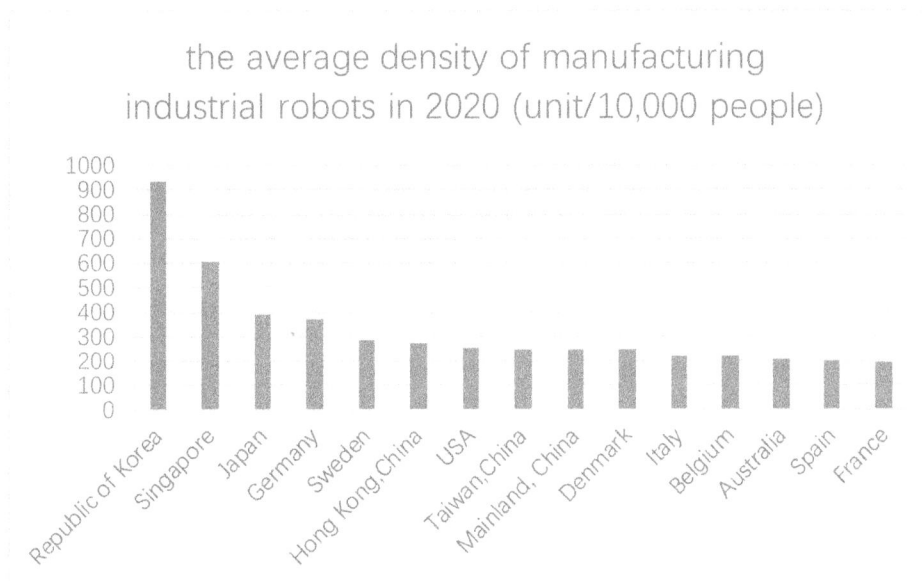

the average density of manufacturing industrial robots in 2020 (unit/10,000 people)

Fig. 2.1.2 Densities of Manufacturing Industrial Robots in Some Major Countries and Regions in 2020

Due to the issue of statistical caliber, some automated CNC machines are not classified as industrial robots in the above statistics. The author believes that the actual number of robots used in the industrial production process is greater than the figure above.

2.1.3 Intelligent Robots

Industrial robots usually do not have the ability to perceive the external environment in the early days. Industrial robots are basically not intelligent, and they perform the established series of actions in turn according to the pre-designed sequence. For the robots that do not have the ability to perceive the external environment, they do not know whether the workpiece exists or not, do not know whether the amount of operating force is suitable, and do not know whether the result is good or bad. In order to make up for the shortcomings, people began to study sensory robots in the late 1970s based on the development of sensing technology and computer technology. The sensory robot is usually equipped with certain kinds of sensors that perceive the external environment, such as force sensors, vision sensors, and auditory sensors. The sensory robot can obtain and analyze the position and shape of the workpiece. It should be said that sensory robots already have a certain amount of intelligence.

Intelligent robots often have a variety of sensors, which can make certain judgments and decisions, and can make behavioral decisions autonomously according to their own state and perceived external environment.

From robot bionics, vision is the most important source of environmental information for humans and higher animals. For human beings, who are the objects of imitation in developing intelligent robots, more than 70 to 80 percent of the information is obtained through vision. Visual images can provide detailed environmental information, which is far

81

beyond the reach of sensing methods such as ultrasound and LiDAR ranging. The daily environment we are in is often very messy and complex, and intelligent robots need to be applied in chaotic and complex environments, so they need to have a sufficiently fine source of environmental information and establish a sufficiently fine environmental information model. Therefore, visual information is simply the best choice for the development of highly intelligent robots.

The feature of visual information is that the real-time data size is very huge. Assume the resolution of a camera's visual image is 640×480; each frame of the image contains 307,200 pixels, each pixel uses 3 bytes of RGB data, and there are 10 frames of images per second. Then the amount of data generated by the camera per second is up to 9.216 MB. By the way, the resolution of about 300,000 pixels is much lower than the resolution of about 13 million pixels of the cameras in today's entry-level smartphones.

It requires that, on the one hand, the communication rate between the sensor and the brain of the intelligent robot - the computer should be fast enough, and on the other hand, the computer should be able to process visual image data quickly enough. Computers' speeds were too slow in the early stages. For example, the computing speed of the early microprocessor 8080 was 290,000 instructions per second, and the microprocessor 8086 could run 330,000 instructions per second. These processors could not support the real-time data processing of visual images required by intelligent robots. With the rapid development of chip technology and computer technology, the computing speed of computers has been getting faster and faster, and the real-time processing of visual image information has gradually become feasible. In particular, the fifth-generation Intel microprocessor 586 was introduced to the market in March 1993, marking that the computing power of the PC had entered a new level and begun to enter the multimedia era more formally. In 1996, the introduction of the USB interface made it very convenient for peripherals to connect to PCs, which was very important for developers of intelligent mobile robots who were generally not experts in computer systems. This directly cleared a major technical barrier and allowed them to focus on the research of robotics. In addition, the USB 2.0 interface standard launched in 2000 increased the theoretical data transmission rate to 480 Mbps. Thus, the visual image data collected by the digital camera can be transmitted to the computer in time for real-time analysis and processing. After all, the transmission rate of the earlier serial interface and other interface standards was too low, such as the baud rate of the early RS-232 serial interface, which was only tens of kbps, and was not enough to transmit visual image data. USB 2.0 has a transfer rate of up to 480 Mbps and can transfer up to 60 MB of data per second, which is six or seven times the 9.216 MB mentioned in the last paragraph.

While the computing speed of microprocessors is increasing rapidly, digital camera technology and products are also developing and maturing quickly, providing a hardware foundation for intelligent robots to have "eye" vision capabilities.

Therefore, since the foundation of computer software and hardware technology was established in the late nineties of the twentieth century, intelligent robot technology has entered a path of rapid development.

Fig. 2.1.3 shows the medium-sized autonomous soccer robot developed and produced by the research team in which the author participated around 2002. At that time, researchers of intelligent robots from various countries wanted to promote the exchange and development of intelligent robot technology through the project platform of football robots. Under this background, the Institute of Robotics and the School of Automation of Shanghai Jiao Tong University organized a joint research group on intelligent mobile robots to conduct academic research and talent training. At that time, the author's joint research team developed some autonomous soccer robots, as shown in Fig. 2.1.3, and participated in a series of national and international competitions. The research work of the author's research team should be regarded as standing at the forefront of the international frontier (here is a self-boast to illustrate that the author is not ignorant of the field of artificial intelligence). The robot uses a laptop computer to make reasonable behavioral decisions and process sensing information, such as visual images, to establish detailed and accurate environmental models. Several robots in a team work together to complete the football match confrontation. The robot is equipped with a panoramic camera, a front-facing camera, several ultrasonic sensors, and a laser rangefinder. At that time, everyone was exploring technologies such as image visual information processing, multi-sensor information environment modeling, and multi-robot collaboration. In the author's vague memory, limited by the computing power of the laptop and the limited technical accumulation of the developers at that time, the refined real-time processing of image and visual information was not done well, and there were many problems with the accuracy of the built environment model.

Fig. 2.1.3 Medium-sized Soccer Robots in Commissioning (Took photo in 2003)

Around that time, the author was also involved in a mobile robot project for Omron in his laboratory. When the robot showed up at the 2004 Shanghai International Industry Fair, it amazed many people: the head of the robot was equipped with a camera, and the computer used as the brain could relatively accurately determine the gender and age of the person standing in front of the robot by processing the image data obtained by the camera. Then the robot told the judgment result to the people by voice. As far as the author can remember, the accuracy of judgment at that time was eight or nine times out of ten. Since the focus of the project at that time was not on the accuracy of image processing judgment, there was no accurate value of judgment accuracy based on large samples. But in any case, the judgment accuracy rate of nine times out of ten should be regarded as the cutting-edge level at that time.

There are many types of research involved in intelligent robot technology. For example, in the author's research group in the 2000s, some people studied using vision to identify the quality of fruits and vegetables and how to control the sorting machine to grade fruits and vegetables; some people tried to develop glass curtain wall cleaning robots; and there were people who studied humanoid bipedal upright robots, and so on.

Aerospace exploration is an important application field for mobile robots. It is well known that current space exploration is fraught with risks. Many places in space are not suitable for human survival. If we humans were to explore space directly, we would have to carry a great deal of necessary materials and equipment for survival. This would directly lead to a sharp increase in exploration costs and even fundamentally make exploration unfeasible. As a result, people have developed many robots for space exploration. Various models of Mars rovers and lunar rovers have been applied to actual space exploration, contributing to humankind's understanding of our universe.

2.1.4 Smart Cars

Around 2000, car autonomous driving was also a hot field of research, and the level of car autonomy at that time was such that the car could successfully drive several kilometers on relatively simple roads. In fact, no team finished the race in the first self-driving car race, the DARPA Grand Challenge, in the Mojave Desert in the United States in 2004, and the farthest any team traveled was only about 7.4 miles, less than 5% of the entire race.

Only about 20 years have passed, and the media and the market have been hyping cars equipped with autonomous driving systems. Up to now many motor corporations and software companies, including Tesla, Google, Baidu, Huawei, and so on, have developed their own advanced driver assistance systems or self-driving systems. Self-driving cars are now one of the most common types of intelligent robots. There are many self-driving cars being tested on the roads now. People can often see unmanned test cars driving in some sections of Pudong, Shanghai. Nowadays, many cars on the market are equipped with car-assisted driving systems or automatic driving systems, and some car owners privately enable the car's automatic driving system to act as the absentee driver while driving. The driverless taxi company Carrot Run, Baidu's subsidiary, is now operating in many cities in China, such as Wuhan, Shenzhen, and Shanghai. Thousands of driverless taxis have been introduced in Wuhan, causing a lot of social welcome, concern, complaints, and backlash recently.

Fig. 2.1.4 Operating Cities of Baidu Carrot Run

2.1.5 Humanoid Robots

Usually, when people think of intelligent mobile robots, the first thing that comes to mind is humanoid robots. Restricted by the level of technological development, the first problem encountered in the research of humanoid robots a few decades ago was how to make humanoid robots stably carry out the basic movement of upright walking. Moreover, at that time, because the road to industrialization was still relatively far away, the resources invested for research teams in various places were often very limited, and they were often unable to obtain comprehensive investment in the fields of motor ability, sensing and perception ability, and intelligent technology. In addition, the ability of computer computing had yet to be broken through, and it was difficult for microcomputers at that time to support real-time intelligent analysis and decision-making. Pattern recognition technology and machine decision-making technology had yet to be developed at that time. Therefore, in the early days, people focused on the standing and walking ability of bipedal robots and paid more attention to the development of humanoid robots' locomotion capabilities, such as standing, walking, running, jumping, and other motor abilities. For example, Honda established a robot research team in 1986, and the first work was to conduct dynamic analysis, imitating human lower limbs, focusing on the ability to stand and walk from the perspective of motion control to make robots with similar degrees of freedom to human legs. The team at Honda had developed E-series and P-series robots one after another. They launched the cute bipedal robot ASIMO in 2000, which can be regarded

85

as a milestone success. The bipedal robot ASIMO amazed the world at the time, and Japan once regarded it as a national treasure, performing in front of many VIPs and in many parts of the world. At that time, ASIMO was a world leader in being able to not only walk quickly, trot, and jump, but also to climb and descend stairs, stand on one foot, and pour water from a soft paper cup. It wasn't until later that Boston Dynamics launched the Atlas, a bipedal upright robot with super athletic abilities that created a stronger visual impact on people. If you're interested in it, you can surf the web and find a lot of videos and images. Many research units and enterprises have developed humanoid robot kinematics systems to a very high standard. Among them, the Boston Dynamics Atlas of the United States ranks among the most prominent performers, can walk, run, and jump, and its athletic ability has even far exceeded that of untrained ordinary people.

Although the intelligence level of independent humanoid intelligent robots is still not high, many investors have begun to focus their investment in humanoid robots on robot intelligence over the past two years. With the current development status of speech recognition technology, face recognition technology, and other types of artificial intelligence technology, and with a technical basis for the implementation of intelligent systems provided by the currently relatively powerful microcomputers, the intelligence of humanoid robots will soon be improved to a level comparable to that of humans. Robots will even far surpass humans in terms of reaction speed, judgment accuracy, and coordination among multiple individuals. Many investors have now realized that humanoid intelligent robots may have great market potential and have begun to invest more capital in humanoid intelligent robots. The so-called humanoid robot concept has even taken shape in the Chinese stock market. We really don't know whether it is good news or bad news for human beings, especially ordinary people.

In fact, humanoid robots are already being used in production. According to online news, Mercedes-Benz announced in March 2024 that it will cooperate with the American robotics company Apptronik to use the humanoid robot Apollo in automobile manufacturing production lines, mainly for completing so-called low-skilled labor such as handling and assembling parts. It is said that the Apollo robot had been tested at Mercedes-Benz's Hungarian factory before.

2.1.6 Virtual Robots

People have extended the concept definition of robots, and robots in people's minds today do not necessarily have a mechanical entity. A robot may only be a software system; for example, a network robot for network data mining, a network customer service robot for Internet telephone customer service, etc. They are just software entities. A robot is a virtual artificial intelligence entity in this case. They are virtual robots.

2.1.7 The Three Laws of Robotics

Go back to the famous Three Laws of Robotics proposed by Asimov. The Three Laws of Robotics are a beautiful dream of human beings for robots, just as outlined in the development of entourage robots at Honda in 1986. But in fact, AI technology itself is just a cold technology. AI can be used to help and harm people, and in many cases, it both assists and harms humans. Today's robots also include a variety of military robots, such as drones that have directly affected the outcome of battles in wars such as the Armenian-Azerbaijani War and the Russian-Ukrainian conflict in recent years. Military robots are used in military confrontations, and robots that carry offensive weapons to attack are obviously beneficial to one side and disadvantageous to the other. Even the big dog robots that are only used to carry goods and are not used for attacking in war will impact the outcome of a war. Obviously, military robots no longer meet the Three Laws of Robotics.

Looking at it from another perspective, if it is defined according to the Three Laws of Robotics, then today's military robots cannot be called robots anymore but should be called machine devils or something similar. It's just that whether they are called "robots" or "machine devils," they are essentially the same from a technical point of view. All of them are based on robotic technologies. It doesn't make much sense to call this a robot and that a machine devil just from an ethical point of view according to the Three Laws of Robotics.

In fact, one of the most important areas for the application of robotics is the military field. People have developed all kinds of unmanned aerial vehicles, some for reconnaissance, some for electronic warfare, some for physical attacks, some rotary, some fixed-wing, and even some flapping. People have also developed a variety of unmanned combat vehicles, robotic mules and horses, robot warriors, skeletal robots, etc. A wide variety of unmanned surface ships and unmanned underwater robots have also been developed. The actual use of military robots has brought many casualties. Since they don't know when they are targeted and attacked by drones, the soldiers on the battlefield in Russia and Ukraine often feel terrified.

Due to the fact that robots are widely used in the military field, we come to the conclusion that the technology itself is cold and often has two sides; that is, it may benefit humanity or harm it.

Moreover, ethical issues are complex, and there are multiple ethical systems around the world. It is even difficult for individual human beings to discern whether the results of certain actions are good or bad. So far, no robot has been able to make ethical judgments. Giving robots the ability to comply with ethical norms requires very strong environmental information recognition capabilities, object analysis capabilities, etc., which are likely to be much more difficult than endowing robots with the intelligence needed to solve problems in their application fields.

Therefore, for today's human society, the Three Laws of Robotics are more like the beautiful dreams of human beings than the constraints of reality.

2.2 Overview of Artificial Intelligence

Since the epoch-making computer ENIAC was invented in the United States in 1946, computer technology has developed rapidly. The advanced computer software and hardware have provided a solid foundation for artificial intelligence technology.

Speaking of artificial intelligence, we have to mention Turing. In 1950, Turing published the famous paper "Computing Machinery and Intelligence." In this paper, Turing raised and explored the question of "whether machines can think" and gave an operational definition of artificial intelligence: if a machine and a human give the same answer to a question, there is no reason not to think that the machine is thinking.

In 1956, scientists such as John McCarthy, Marvin Minsky, Claude Shannon, Allen Newell, and Herbert Simon met at Dartmouth College to discuss the use of machines to mimic human learning and other aspects of intelligence. The term "artificial intelligence" was proposed for the first time at this meeting. Thus, some people called 1956 the first year of artificial intelligence.

Artificial intelligence attempts to study and explore the nature of intelligence. Its goal is to develop intelligent machines that can make judgments, decisions, and reactions in the same way as human intelligence. Artificial intelligence covers robotics, speech recognition, natural language processing, image recognition, computer vision, expert systems, neural networks, machine learning, and more.

Thanks to the rapid development of computer technology and other scientific and technological fields, artificial intelligence technology has developed rapidly since its birth. Since 1970, IBM has set up a speech recognition research team. Only about 20 years passed; its ViaVoice speech recognition system was commercialized in the 1990s. Today, the accuracy of speech recognition has reached a very high level. Now voice input has developed into a standard input method for many handheld intelligent terminal devices. Nowadays, many smart devices, including certain models of mobile phones and some new models of cars, allow people to use their voices to give specific commands. In daily life, ordinary people have often come into contact with intelligent voice customer service assistants used by banks and communication companies. These intelligent voice customer service assistants must first identify the questions raised by our human voices and then find out the corresponding answers and play them with a voice, forming a human-machine dialogue between customers and service providers.

The development of image recognition technology started in about 1950 with the research on text recognition. Text recognition includes the recognition of letters, numbers, symbols, etc. The research fields on text recognition cover printed text recognition and handwritten text recognition. Due to the relatively simple and regular recognition objects, especially for the printed text, the technical requirements for text recognition are relatively simple. After decades of development, today's text recognition technology can be said to have developed quite maturely. An obvious proof of maturity is that today's smart terminals, such as smartphones, are generally configured with handwriting input modes.

As for the general image processing and recognition technology, due to the wide variety of recognition objects and the wide range of fields involved in the content, the technical requirements are relatively high. The research of digital image processing and recognition technology began in 1965. People have developed the technology of digital image processing and recognition very rapidly. By the late 10s of the 21st century, image processing technologies such as face recognition have been rapidly and widely used in high-standard and high-demand fields such as security, banking transactions, and identity authentication for collection and payment. Carrying out facial authentication and facial payments is a routine operation now. All this means that people have developed facial recognition technology to a very high level. In fact, the accuracy of computer facial recognition has surpassed that of ordinary people a few years ago. Furthermore, the carrier computer for running artificial intelligence has the characteristic of reliable storage, and memories do not fade slowly over time like those of the human brain. Computer memory can be made very large, and it can store much more massive facial images than ordinary people can remember. Based on certain relevant research, the speed at which the human eye processes visual images is approximately equivalent to the processing speed of Nvidia GeForce RTX 3090, while the computation speed of the RTX 3090 is approximately 36 TFLOPS and some chips now have a computing speed of over 4,000 TFLOPS, far faster than that of the human brain. Moreover, many times the pixel resolution of the camera is much lower than that of the human eye, which can still meet the technical requirements. As a result, facial recognition technology now can be more reliable and have a faster response time than that of ordinary people.

Image recognition also includes the recognition of objects, which mainly refers to the recognition and perception of objects in the three-dimensional world of our space. Object recognition has very important uses in the field of industrial and detection robots, and it is also a key issue for intelligent service robots in the future. The current object recognition technology should be said to have reached a certain height. As evidence, automotive automatic driving systems or assisted driving systems, which are based on an accurate perception of the road environment, have been taken as selling points by many automobile companies, though the intelligent car environment modeling also uses a lot of LiDAR-type sensing information.

Strategic planning and adversarial skills are often used to detect and measure whether someone is smart or good at solving certain problems. For example, people usually think that those with high levels of chess and other games are smart. A considerable number of AI experts have devoted their energy to the study of strategic planning with computers and often use chess confrontations as the entry point for strategic planning research in the last century. The rules of chess confrontation are clear, the types and number of chess pieces are limited, and the timeliness requirement for decision-making is not high. Therefore, even if the computing power of a computer is at a low point, the computer can also be used for practical testing of AI adversarial strategies and ideas. Machine-versus-strategy planning technology developed rapidly. Chess computer players had begun to reach the master level by the 1980s. In May 1997, Deep Blue defeated the world chess champion Garry Kasparov. It is a milestone incident; i.e., machines have surpassed humans in certain strategic response planning aspects.

Strategic planning techniques in the AI field are often used in computer games, such as chess, Chinese chess, Go, and some standalone versions of military confrontation simulation games. Intelligent confrontation strategy planning has been applied in the military field. Intelligent simulation has certain value in the military. The use of AI technology to assist in strategic and tactical planning has become an important option for military powers.

Expert system is also a very active application area of AI technology, and it was an important branch of AI technology in the early days. The expert system simulates the process of human experts in a certain field to solve problems and usually has multiple constituent modules, such as an expert knowledge base, knowledge reasoning mechanism, knowledge acquisition, human-computer interaction interface, interpreter, and comprehensive database. In 1965, there was an expert system that could infer the structure of chemical molecules. Since then, a variety of expert systems have been developed in many fields, such as medical diagnosis, geological exploration, commerce, and agriculture.

Artificial intelligence technology has invaded many aspects of various industries, and its impact is becoming increasingly profound. For example, the use of artificial intelligence technology is becoming increasingly prevalent in the financial industry. Recently, we have even heard the concerns of international financial industry regulators: everyone uses artificial intelligence technology in the transaction process, and due to the monopoly of artificial intelligence technology, the unification of the decision-making model may lead to everyone making exactly the same decisions with the same limited data, limited decision-making mechanisms, and decision-making models, superimposing and amplifying the fluctuations of market transactions, resulting in a financial crisis. There are also many applications of AI in software design. For example, some software integrated development environments can provide a lot of prompts in real time, such as syntax prompts, variable prompts, code logic prompts, and even include the software writing itself. Some people even think that there will be no programmers in the future; i.e., programs will be automatically written by machines in the near future.

On November 30, 2022, OpenAI released the chatbot program ChatGPT, which shocked the world. ChatGPT has been able to truly chat like a human, and it has become difficult for ordinary people to distinguish whether they are talking to a chatbot or a human on the internet. ChatGPT can perform tasks such as language translation, essay writing, news reporting, and even writing code, checking for program errors, and correcting bugs and errors. Compared with the human body, the computer has the advantages of huge information storage, an extremely low storage error rate, fast input and output, etc., which makes ChatGPT show the advantages of erudition and accurate memory far beyond human individuals. ChatGPT has directly smashed the intelligence advantage of humans over traditional machines. Ordinary human beings are really very weak.

Optimistic estimates suggest that artificial intelligence will fully rival and surpass human intelligence around 2030.

For individual intelligent robots, their superintelligence can be provided by the computer system located in them, namely their built-in brain, and can also be provided by a superintelligent center that has high-speed communication with them, as shown in Fig. 2.2.1. Thus, along with the emergence of artificial intelligence systems that can rival and surpass human intelligence, highly intelligent robots will also appear soon. Ordinary human individuals will have to face challenges on many occasions.

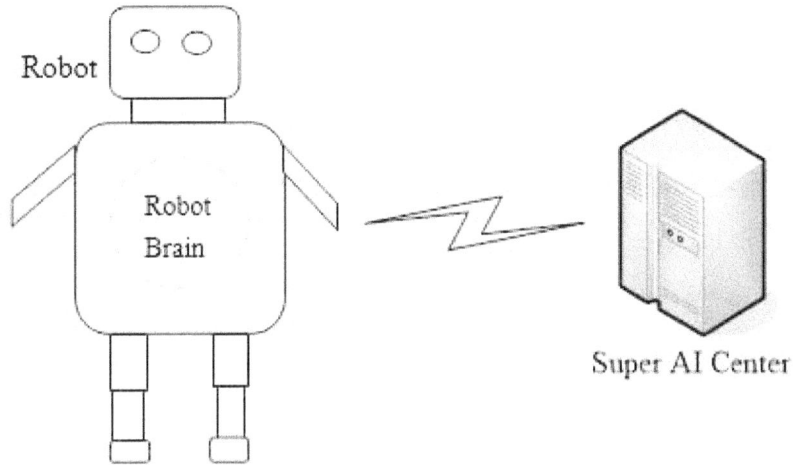

Fig. 2.2.1 The Intelligence Source of Intelligent Robots

Not to mention, in recent years, a huge amount of capital and resources have been rapidly invested in all aspects of the field of artificial intelligence technology, and artificial intelligence technology is developing rapidly at an unimaginable speed. The unlimited use of AI is constantly squeezing ordinary people in various industries out of the wealth chain. Combined with the various conditions of today's human society, human society is approaching the edge of the cliff. If it is not dealt with well, human society will be pushed into a situation of no return by artificial intelligence technology.

3 Speculation on the Social Organization Structure after Using Artificial Intelligence in All Aspects

Along with the rapid development of artificial intelligence technology, it is highly likely that artificial intelligence or robots will be able to completely replace human workers in a few years. Here, the complete replacement of human workers by artificial intelligence or robots is referred to as "comprehensive artificial intelligence."

At a time when artificial intelligence technology is in full swing, everyone will be very concerned about what will happen to human society in the future. In modern human society, the vast majority of individuals rely on their contributions in social cooperation to obtain all kinds of wealth needed for life. There are very few human individuals who are completely isolated; that is to say, the vast majority of human individuals are members of society. Therefore, the social organization structure and social operation mechanism directly affect the lives of everyone in society. In this chapter, the potential social organization structure and social operation mechanism in the era of comprehensive AI are discussed.

3.1 Introduction to the Organizational Structure of Human Society

3.1.1 Differences between Individuals Lead to Different Sparks of Thought

Physically speaking, at a certain moment, each person is in a different position in physical space, and the collision and interaction between each person and the material particles in the external environment, as well as the interaction of electromagnetic radiation, etc., will be different. Each person is made up of a staggering number of atoms and molecules, so in a sense, everyone is unique and different.

With the perspective of the microscopic composition of human beings, the DNA structure of each person's genetic material is different for the vast majority of people. The gene expression of life will be different in each person's life process. Even if the material conditions are exactly the same from a "microscopic" perspective, the work and production of human cells and the like will be different under the control of genetic materials such as DNA, which have different structures. Even if the DNA of two people is identical, such as in identical twins, the genetic characterization of their DNA will be somewhat different due to different environments and ingested substances. Over time, the differences will accumulate and tend to grow larger. In fact, for so many identical twins, we have never seen twins who can answer all the questions exactly the same in mental exams, such as the high school entrance examination and the college entrance examination. All this also illustrates the diversity of human ideas from one perspective.

From the perspective of the body's material metabolism, the amounts of various food components consumed by each person differ. Even if the amounts of substances ingested are the same each time, it is difficult for each person's physical state to be accurate and the same when ingesting, such as exercise status, heart rate, and fatigue level. This means that the body will be different in absorbing and utilizing the ingested substances. As a result, even if two human individuals grow up on macroscopically "identical" foods from the same fertilized egg, they will grow differently over time.

The world is complex and has many fields of knowledge. From the perspective of human brain development and knowledge growth, each person's growth environment, the things they are exposed to, and the training they receive will be different, so each person's response to the same problem encountered is often different. For example, the feeling of pain is different; the fear of injections is not the same; the sensitivity to odor is not the same; the content field and degree of knowledge mastered are different; the importance of family affection is not the same; and the feeling of friendship is not the same. The list goes on and on.

Moreover, everyone has a different starting point in life; that is, at the same moment, everyone is at a different stage of life's growth, and naturally, the reaction to the same thing will be different…

All these differences between people have created colorful and complex sparks and behaviors in human beings.

Fig. 3.1.1 Diagram of Conflicts of Different Ideas

3.1.2 Different Sparks of Thought, Conflicts, and Coordination

In the face of the same thing, human beings often produce colorful and complex sparks of thought. This characteristic of human beings often makes it difficult for many people to cooperate in the process of carrying out a task, and there will often be disagreements and contradictions between individuals in terms of program ideas, as well as differences and conflicts in the evaluation of contributions and gains and losses. In the case of conflicts in the evaluation of contributions and gains and losses, it is more common for individuals to overestimate their own contributions, which leads to conflicts between individuals, and of course, it is not excluded that some individuals may underestimate their own contributions.

In human society, it is difficult to accurately measure and evaluate different kinds of things and resources.

For example, the issue of how to confirm the contributions of capital investment and labor investment in enterprises is significant. After all, the way of resource input, the distribution of remuneration, and the degree of risk are different between these two. This is also the crux of why serious labor conflicts erupt from time to time. In fact, if we pay attention, we can see news about strikes and demonstrations around the world every other day or so.

For example, it is often difficult to accurately determine the contributions among inventors, creators, and the workers who produce inventions.

For example, it is sometimes difficult to determine how the contributions of different types of work are measured. As you can see, for the question of how to evaluate the contribution between teachers and farmers, teachers and farmers consume different human abilities; one mainly consumes brain power and vocal cords, and the other mainly consumes limbs and physical strength. The fruits of the above two labors are also different: one is mainly training and educating people, and the other is the production of agricultural products, which are the materials for human survival.

Moreover, even contributions to the same thing can sometimes be difficult to measure. For example, in the evaluation of the contribution of the army, some people may say that if they do not fight, soldiers have no contribution in peacetime; some people may say that there are some countries that exist normally without an army in the world, so the army is dispensable; there are many more people who will say that, except for a few countries with special surrounding environments, without the existence of the army, the security of the country and society cannot be guaranteed, and the deterrent effect of the army in peacetime is the greatest contribution to society, and fighting a war is actually the last resort.

As we all know, there are often many ways to solve a problem, and everyone may have their own way. When many people cooperate to do something, they can often choose only one method to execute it. Therefore, it is likely that conflicts will arise between individuals when it comes to choosing a solution to a problem. The conflict here doesn't have to be a quarrel. :)

When the solution to a problem is determined, there are often contradictions due to the division of responsibilities of each person in the process of collaboration; after all, people may be rushed to occupy some positions, while some other positions that people do not want to occupy.

In this way, the sparks of people's diverse thoughts, concepts, ideas, etc., will bring about all kinds of complex contradictions and conflicts. When we are executing a task that requires the collaboration of multiple people, and because the resources that can be invested in the process of executing the task are basically limited, we generally need to determine the execution plan of the task first, including how to subdivide the task and assign subtasks to the determined executors,

94

etc. As mentioned earlier, because the sparks of human thought are free, diverse, and even bizarre, it is difficult to achieve the level of collaboration by allowing each individual involved in the task to do what they want. In addition to the tasks that themselves allow everyone to follow their own thoughts, it is necessary for the task participants to choose or discuss a spark of thought among the various sparks of thought and use it as an implementation plan and code of conduct.

Therefore, in order to resolve contradictions, complete collaborative tasks, and achieve social harmony, society needs to have rules to constrain, arbitrators to give evaluations, and organizers to coordinate. For example, under the market economy system, money is used as a medium to measure the contribution of each person to social production by determining the respective prices of different commodities and formulating rules for commercial competition, and to constrain and determine the distribution of wealth and results. This, in turn, gives rise to the issue of constructing an organizational structure, including who leads, who executes, how to lead, how to execute, how to distribute and enjoy the fruits of wealth, how to coordinate and restrain contradictions, and so on. For example, in the primitive tribal era, the position of tribal chief was created to coordinate and manage the internal and external affairs of the tribe. Another example is that in today's society, government agencies coordinate and manage many public and foreign affairs related to the country.

3.1.3 Large Organizations Need a Hierarchical Organizational Structure to Reduce Coordination Costs

The choice of the spark of thought can be determined by the participants in negotiations, quarrels, or by people in certain positions.

For a task organization with a large number of members, it is not practical for everyone to come together to agree on a plan or rules. This is because when there are many people, to a certain extent, the cost of bringing everyone together, the cost of negotiation, and so on, will add up to a suffocating and unbearable amount.

For example, let's say a small city has tens of thousands of people and needs to address the city's public spending for the next year. If all residents are absolutely equal in decision-making power over urban public affairs, and everyone expresses their own ideas, bringing together tens of thousands of people to discuss the issue, then the residents of the city must first solve the problems of gathering places and gathering times. Assuming that everyone spends a few minutes talking about their own opinions, it will take tens of thousands of minutes or even hundreds of thousands of minutes for tens of thousands of people to express their ideas once. As we all know, an eight-hour working day is only 480 minutes, and a month's working time is only about 10,000 minutes. It is conceivable that with such a flat social organization mode, the final cost of human and material resources will be huge, and it is even likely to far exceed the scope of public expenditure itself. Obviously, a more reasonable way is for the city to elect a small team as the task organizer for the corresponding issue. The organizers will organize personnel to conduct investigations and research, put forward one or several alternative plans, publicize them, and allow citizens to propose amendments or new plans within a specified period of time. Then, all citizens or citizen representatives will vote on the final implementation of the plan, and finally implement the relevant content according to the final plan.

This is still the case for small cities with tens of thousands of people, and even more so for organizations with larger populations, where not everyone can speak freely and completely equally. Large organizations with large numbers of members need dedicated teams of organizers or representatives. These organizers or representatives will inevitably have more voice and decision-making power than ordinary people in the process of carrying out tasks, and even the organization has to give some organizers and executors certain rights to command ordinary people. In this way, in a sense, it is natural to form a hierarchy of the members of the organization in a certain matter. Suffice it to say, the vast majority of large organizations have some hierarchical organizational structure.

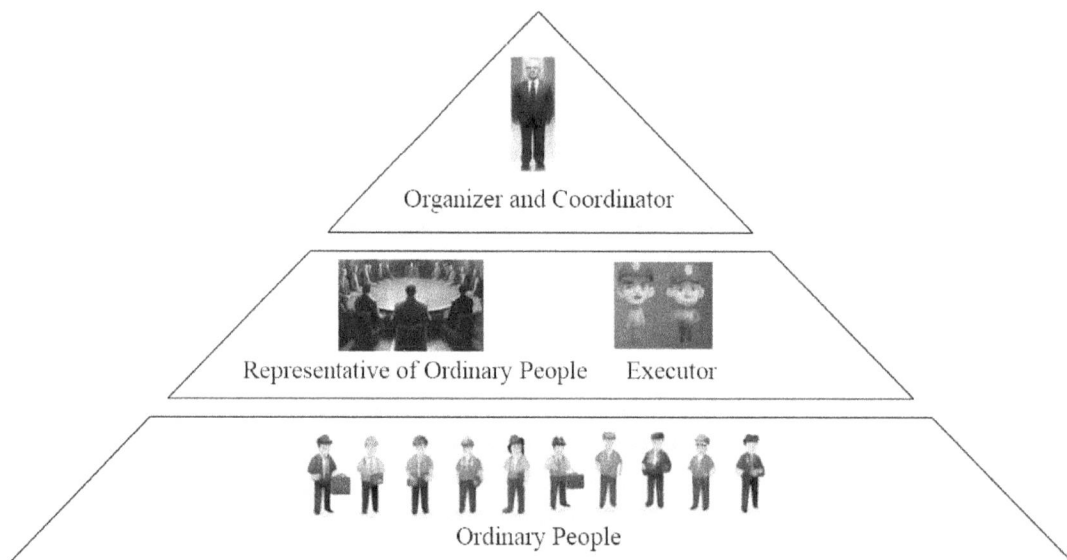

Fig. 3.1.2 Schematic Diagram of the Hierarchical Structure of a Large Organization

3.1.4 Real-time Missions Require a Dedicated Commander

The rate at which people communicate information is relatively slow. The rate of information exchange is limited by the specific form of communication and is basically subject to the slowest link contained in that form of communication, such as the slowest writing speed in written communication and the slowest speaking speed in spoken communication. At the normal speed of speech, people speak with about three syllables per second. If they make five to seven syllables per second, the speed of speech is already quite fast. If someone pronounces ten sounds per second, it not only tires the person who speaks but also makes it more difficult for others to hear clearly. The normal speed at which a person can

96

read a text is slightly faster than the speed at which he can speak, but the reading speed is still very limited, and two to three times is almost the limit. The so-called "speed reading" of ten lines at a glance is actually no longer normal reading, but more like a quick search for image information, because it misses a lot of things, and it is difficult to remember what the eye has scanned. On the other hand, a message often needs to be conveyed through multiple sounds or words. From this, you can intuitively feel that the speed of human information exchange is not fast. Compared with the current computer network communication, which can transmit hundreds of millions or tens of thousands of text contents per second, the speed of human information exchange and transmission is simply slower than that of a snail.

Limited by the extremely limited rate of information exchange, for multi-person collaborative tasks that require immediate and rapid responses in a complex and ever-changing environment, it is often inappropriate for all participants to unify their thoughts and make action decisions through communication, discussion, and quarrels, which can lead to mission failure. After all, by the time everyone finishes discussing, the daylily may get cold. In this case, the most reasonable response is to set up a task leader, and the leader will do the on-the-spot decision-making and on-the-spot assignment of tasks. In military operations, this kind of task force is organized by a team leader to organize, assign, and manage the implementation of the task, which is the most common way.

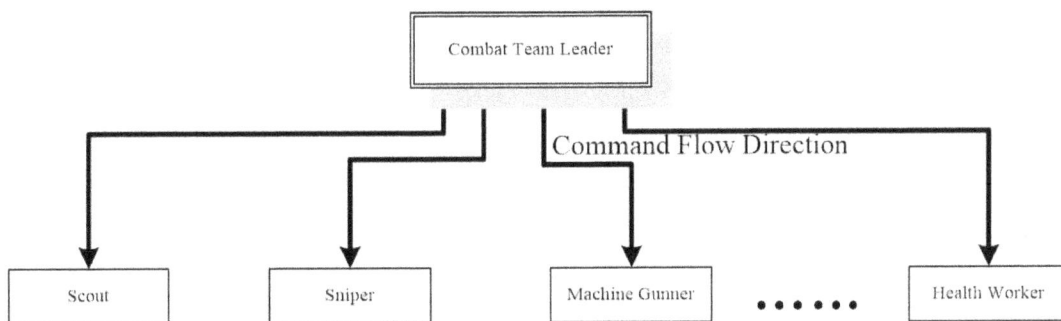

Fig. 3.1.3 Schematic Diagram of the Composition of a Combat Team

3.1.5 Hierarchical Structure of Brotherhood and Religious Organizations

The form of the organizational structure is governed by the agreement of the founders of the organization and often evolves with changes in the size and status of the organization.

For example, the Heaven and Earth Society, a Chinese brotherhood organization created hundreds of years ago, is said to have been originally established by six people, including a man named Falong Wan, to swear blood as an alliance and become sworn brothers with different surnames. When it was first established, due to the small number of members and few internal matters to deal with, the Heaven and Earth Society was more like a level-level organization without a hierarchy. Later, with the growth of the organization's members, the organizational structure gradually evolved due to the needs of the organization's internal management and external affairs. Many functions were set up, which gradually evolved into an organization with a hierarchical structure; along with the historical evolution, many independent organizations evolved. Fig. 3.1.4 is a rumored organizational chart of the Hung Men organization (the Heaven and Earth Society) in Hong Kong today ("Chang Luowen: Why was this famous Hong Kong triad once able to cover the sky with only one hand?" https://k.sina.com.cn/article_1887344341_707e96d5020014z57.html). The mountain master or dragon head is responsible for the entire gang organization. Vanguards, deputy mountain masters, and incense masters carry out activities under the leadership of the leading boss, and there are red poles, straw sandals, and other posts in the next layer. In fact, there are many more types of functions in some Hung Men organizations than in the figure below, and the hierarchical relationship may be more complex.

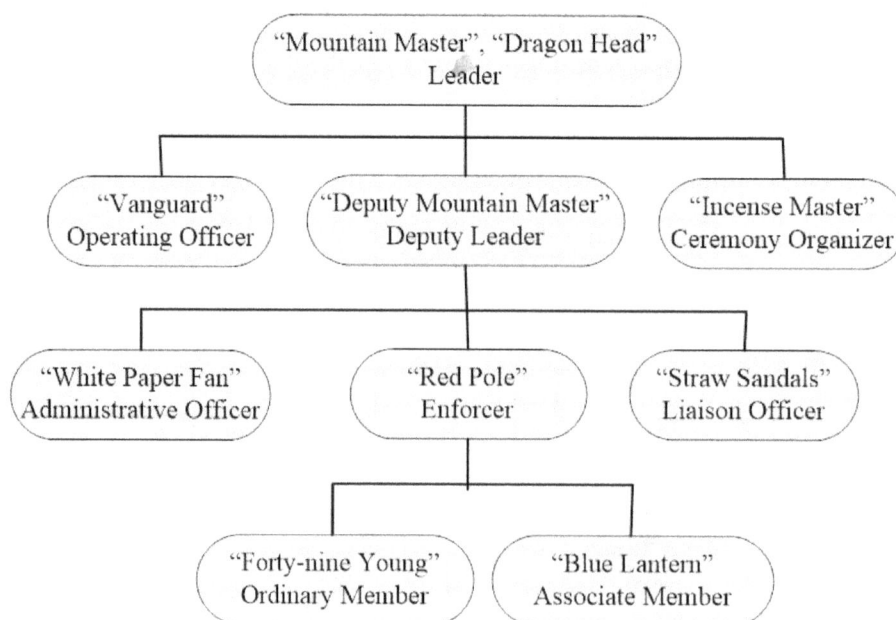

Fig. 3.1.4 An Organizational Structure of the Hung Men Organization in Hong Kong

The same is true for religious organizations. In the initial stage, the founders of the religion spread their teachings openly or covertly, absorbing believers. There are relatively few internal issues, and the organizational structure is generally simple in form and without hierarchy. When it reaches a certain scale along with development, the various internal and external matters of the organization increase, and they begin to need to be handled by specialized personnel. Thus, there will be a division of labor, and different positions will have different responsibilities regarding these matters, leading to a hierarchical structure of rights and status. For example, for a temple that is a gathering place for Buddhist practitioners, when it has only a few practitioners, it may simply exist in the form of a condisciple relationship or a master-disciple relationship. When the number of practitioners in a temple reaches hundreds or thousands, in order to coordinate and deal with the internal and external affairs of the temple, it is necessary to arrange a division of labor at the level of functions. Fig. 3.1.5 below shows a type of organizational structure of large temples in mainland China (Refer to "Organizational Structure of Buddhist Temples."

https://www.douban.com/group/topic/186062996/?_i=2343323QYjqFMx). Among them, the abbot is the highest, and below him is the prime inspector. The first seat, hall master, etc., is on the third layer. There is a yard inspector, karma, assigner of seats, head of huts, etc., on the fourth layer. These positions are each responsible for managing certain tasks; for example, the assigner of seats is responsible for managing the practitioners who are responsible for the functions of burning fire, preparing water, cooking, carrying, and so on. Buddhism itself advocates the equality of all beings, and it can be said that it is a religion without a hierarchical concept. However, after the scale of the temple becomes large, there will be a division of duties and responsibilities and a hierarchical division of temple management.

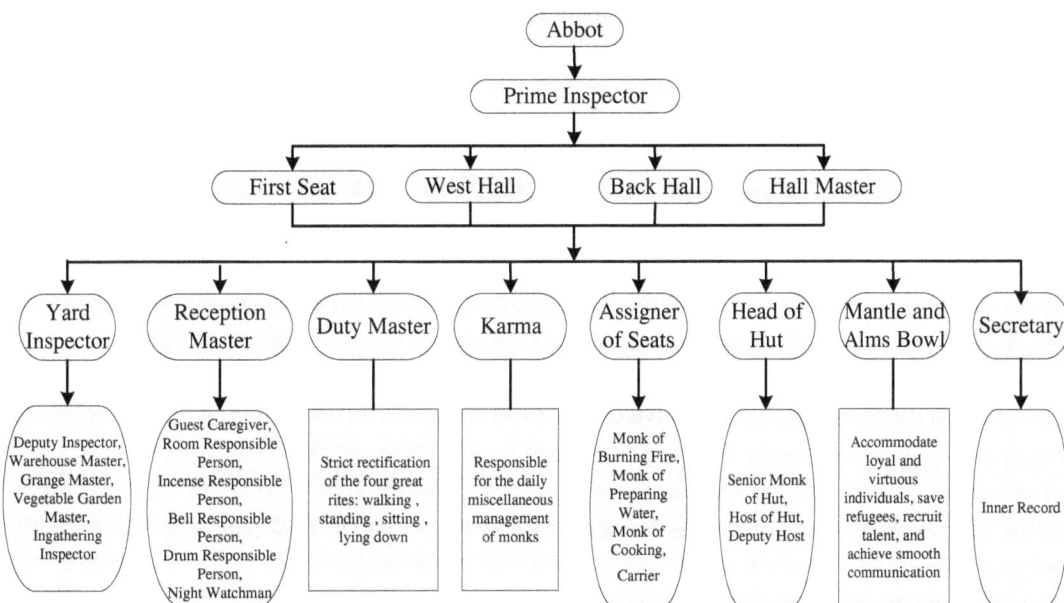

Fig. 3.1.5 An Organizational Structure of a Large Buddhist Temple

Catholicism says that everyone is brothers or sisters. Because of the large number of believers, there are also many hierarchical divisions, such as the Pope, cardinals, archbishops, bishops, priests, and friars. Because different levels of function have different divisions of power, the operation of Catholic organizations has certain characteristics of a hierarchical structure. Islam is a religious sect that holds a knife in one hand and scriptures in the other. Throughout history, in areas dominated by Islam, Islamic organizations are often religious organizations integrating religion, military, and politics, and clerical groups hold military and political power. Naturally, everyone's voice in society will be very different; that is to say, there is a de facto hierarchical difference in the decision-making power regarding certain affairs.

3.1.6 Ethics Affects Organizational Structure

The form of organizational structure is constrained by social ethics and morality. An organization can function only if the members of the organization act according to their assigned roles. Human behavior is governed by mental activity, and only by psychologically acknowledging and accepting the roles and tasks assigned to them can a person perform their duties well. Ethics and morality delineate the code of conduct that can be widely accepted by a society, constrain people's psychology and behavior, and directly affect what rules and constraints they can accept when participating in an organization. Thus, the ethics of a society affect the structure and functioning of the organizations in that society.

For example, in a market economy, an employer and an employee enter into an employment transaction, and the employer pays a salary to buy the employee's labor, including the employee's working time, physical or mental power, etc. According to the ethical and moral constraints of the market economy system, within the framework of legal rules, employees must obey the employer's work arrangements and work hard to complete their tasks. This means that the employer has the right to arrange work for the employee, which naturally creates a hierarchical structure of rights in the work arrangement. The business owner determines the purpose of the enterprise's operation, and under the social and legal framework, the ideological spark determined by the enterprise owner is the ideological spark that the enterprise should comply with and implement. Fig. 3.1.6 below illustrates the hierarchical structure of the rights of a micro-enterprise with only a few employees, which is divided into two levels of rights in terms of work arrangements. According to the ethics of the market economy system, the owner of the enterprise directly determines the job responsibilities and work content of each employee and arranges for their employees to work, and each employee should follow the employer's orders.

According to the ethical norms under the market economy system, the business owner can designate other people to decide on employees' job responsibilities and work tasks. For example, with the expansion of the scale of the enterprise and the increase in employees, the enterprise has to divide into more levels and will create a variety of departments, sub-departments, project teams, etc., according to the characteristics of the work tasks and other factors. At this time, under the constraints of market economy ethics and morality, enterprise investors do not need to directly face each employee. Enterprise investors can appoint responsible persons at all levels, give responsible persons at all levels the power to determine the job responsibilities of employees and arrange the work content of employees, and form a hierarchical structure of a certain right in the enterprise, such as the president in charge of the director, the director in charge of the department manager, and the department manager in charge of the grassroots employees in the department, so that the enterprise becomes a dynamic operation as a whole.

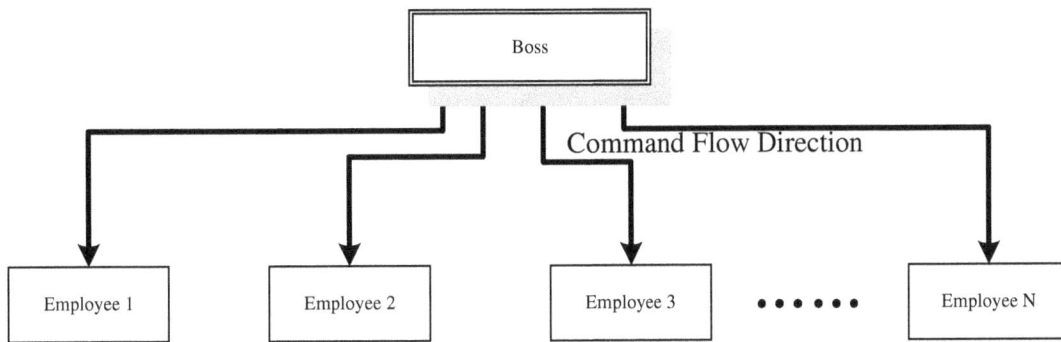

Fig. 3.1.6 An Organizational Structure of Microenterprises

3.1.7 Equality in Legal Status Does Not Mean the Same Discourse Power

In terms of legal theory, the mainstream societies on the earth today pursue equality for all; that is, the legal status of each citizen is the same, and the legal provisions that adult normal people need to follow and apply are the same, regardless of whether they are a cabinet minister or a person who is responsible for maintaining a public toilet.

However, equality in legal status does not mean that everyone has the same voice in everything. As we all know, in a professional field, the words of experts are generally more credible, the answers to professional questions are generally more reasonable, and the experts' voices are generally correspondingly louder. Due to the division of labor, a person in a managerial position has the authority to assign work tasks and supervise the progress of tasks, and he or she will have a greater voice in a task than ordinary employees who only accept work tasks and supervision. Although industry experts are equal to ordinary people, managers, and ordinary employees in terms of legal personality, their voices on some specific matters are different and unequal.

Analyzing the organizations existing in today's human society, it can be found that large-scale organizations usually have a division of labor, not only a division of labor among parallel and equal jobs but also a division of labor between the regulator and the regulated. The division of labor in function means the division of rights. The division of labor between the regulator and the regulated means that there is a hierarchical structure of rights in dealing with something, which in turn means that there will be a hierarchical organizational structure in large organizations when dealing with something. In particular, today's government organizations and military organizations all have obvious hierarchical structures.

The author believes that most ordinary members at the bottom of an organization naturally dislike this kind of hierarchy of rights and that accepting the hierarchy of power and the regulated situation is basically out of a kind of helplessness, as well as ethical, moral, and legal regulatory constraints.

Equality is the universal pursuit of the human public. Is it possible for human society to form a structure similar to the World Wide Web and blockchain, where there is no relationship of leadership and obedience among the members of the organization during normal operation? Here, the administrator who does configuration management work is not counted because he is not a node in the network.

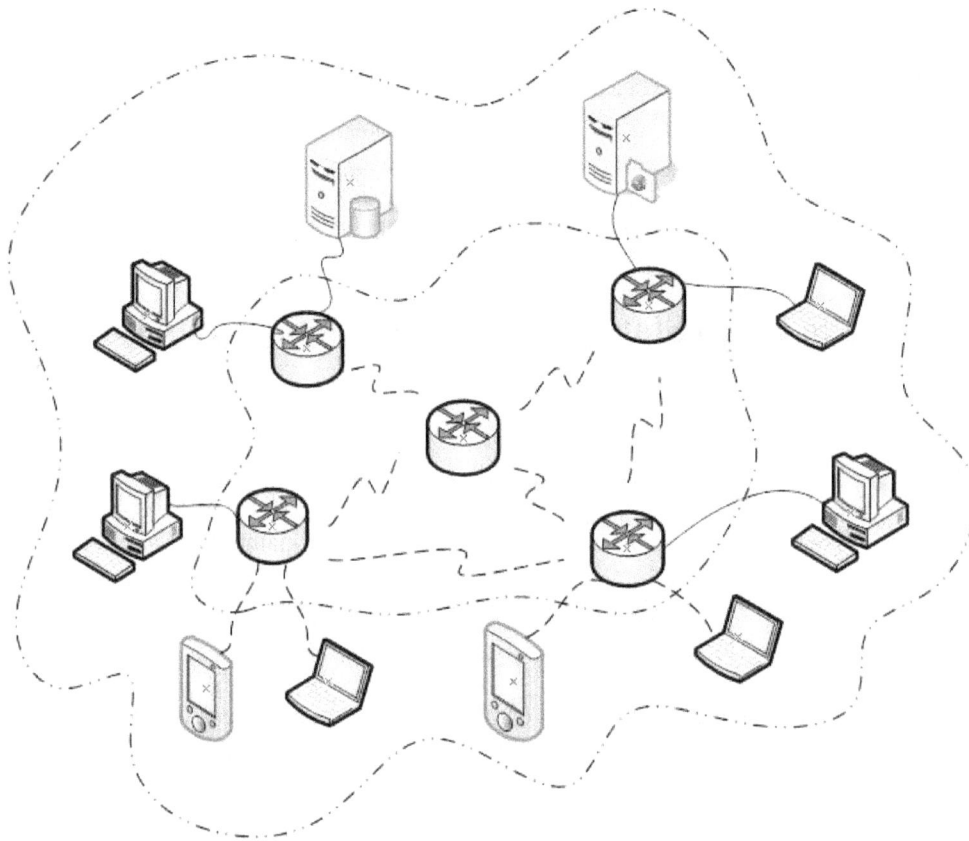

Fig. 3.1.7 Schematic Diagram of the Structure of the World Wide Web

Like the World Wide Web, the members of the organization follow the established protocol to perform their own actions. In a sense, the nodes in the network are self-managed and work according to the protocol, not at the mercy of other nodes, and there are no variables, so the nodes can be regarded as completely equal.

Human society is much more complex; there are many variables. It is difficult to make detailed agreements and plans for many things in advance, and it is also difficult to make accurate judgments, such as the determination of responsibility, the judgment of violations and crimes, etc. Sometimes it is even difficult to make judgments directly based on the existing legal provisions, and it is often necessary to refer to whether there are similar judgments. It is difficult to achieve clear legal provisions like those in computer networks. Therefore, there is often a need for arbitrators and facilitators who have more power than ordinary members. As mentioned above, many task organizations need leaders to coordinate and select the appropriate spark of ideas. Leaders are needed to divide tasks and supervise the progress of tasks, and there will naturally be a hierarchy of power among the members of the organization.

Due to the vast scale of human society, there are always many public affairs to handle. Therefore, even after the production and life of human society fully use AI, there will still be a hierarchical structure in human society, and people in different public affairs positions will have different rights of decision-making, even if, legally speaking, all people are equal in legal personality.

3.2 Speculation on the Organizational Structure in the AI Era

3.2.1 A Potential Social Organization Architecture After Using AI in All Aspects

Whether it is ChatGPT, which was released in 2022, or Deep Blue, which defeated the chess champion more than 20 years ago, or Atlas, a bipedal humanoid robot with strong athletic ability, or the intelligent face recognition technology that has surpassed the face recognition accuracy of ordinary people, such examples have proved that human beings are not unsurpassable from the perspective of various capabilities. With the rapid development of artificial intelligence and robotics, it is inevitable that they will surpass humans across the board in the near future.

Looking at the attitudes of the people and governments of various countries towards artificial intelligence technology or robot technology, there is generally a little bit of "worship of mystery," and they generally feel that artificial intelligence technology is advanced. They welcome or even encourage it indiscriminately, and there are few opposing voices. Therefore, at present, robot technology is being developed more and more maturely; there are more and more applications in the field of wealth creation, and human workers are constantly being squeezed out of various industries.

Assuming that AI continues to develop in this way until it matures to the point where it fully surpasses human beings and completely replaces humans in areas such as wealth production, what will the social organizational structure look like? You may have many beautiful dreams about the social organizational structure after artificial intelligence has completely replaced human beings in wealth production and other areas. However, the author worries that the future structure of human society will take on a form, as shown in Fig. 3.2.1 below. Based on speculation, it is a highly probable form. As shown in Fig. 3.2.1, a human society at the national level is likely to be composed of three parts:

One part is made up of human beings, which is called the "Human Section" in this paper. A large number of idle, ordinary people form the basis of the "Human Section." Due to the large number of ordinary people, it is difficult to avoid conflicts among them. Therefore, it is necessary to set up job positions such as formulating norms, coordinating contradictions, arbitrating, and executing punishments. People are all human beings with the same needs and common interests, so there is a need for positions that express, plan, and implement the public interest of the people. Some of these responsibilities may be fulfilled by intelligent robots. However, due to the pursuit of some elites in the human race to control their own destiny and out of concerns about the potential problems and dependability of artificial intelligence systems, the author believes that the top positions and a considerable number of middle-level positions should still be filled by humans.

The second part is an unmanned intelligent wealth creation and distribution system composed of intelligent robots, automated machines, non-automated machines, network communication equipment, etc., which is called the "Wealth Section" here. In the early stages, there may have been some human beings who were engaged in product design. However, with the highly developed artificial intelligence in the future, product design, scientific exploration, equipment production and maintenance, equipment operation, human demand information collection, task decomposition, and execution of human top-level commands, etc., will all be handled by artificial intelligence and automation. So, in the end, it may be a completely unmanned intelligent wealth creation and distribution system.

The third part is an unmanned intelligent military force system composed of intelligent robots, network communication equipment, unmanned intelligent weapons, non-intelligent weapons, etc., which is called the "Military Affairs Section" here. It is assumed that AI technology has developed so advanced that the interpretation of military orders and the determination of detailed tasks, the formulation and execution of tactics, the management and maintenance of weapons, and so on have been completed by intelligent robots.

The possible mode of operation is that the top leader of the "Human Section" or the person with the highest rank issues relevant orders to the Wealth Section or the Military Affairs Section. The intelligent robots of the Wealth Section and the Military Affairs Section interpret the relevant orders, carry out task decomposition and task planning, and report the relevant information, especially the key part information, to the person who gave the order. According to the ratification status, the intelligent robots then modify the task planning and report back to the person who gave the order or perform the tasks. The Wealth Section distributes the wealth created to the members of the Human Section on time, following certain rules.

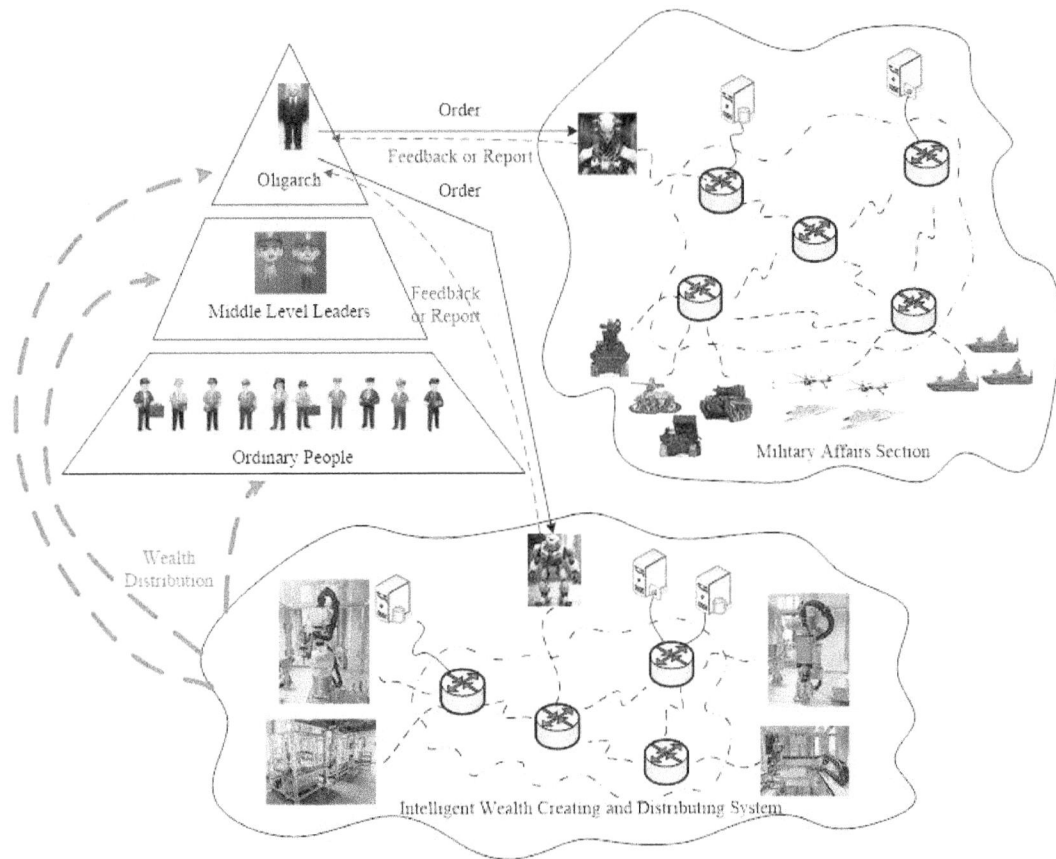

Fig. 3.2.1 A Potential Societal Structure in the Era of Comprehensive AI

3.2.2 Why

Question one. Why is the "Human Section" a hierarchical structure?

Answer. Human society has a large population, and the populations of most countries are quite large. With the exception of the Vatican, the Holy See State, other countries all have more than 10,000 people, even if they are small. Large countries even have hundreds of millions to more than one billion people. In fact, the countries in today's world have an average population of about 40 million. As can be seen from the realities of the planet today, the number of people in the world is too large for the negotiation of all adults on an equal footing at an acceptable cost. Therefore, because social organizations at the level of the state all have large populations on Earth today, in order to ensure the normal operation of society and reduce the cost of negotiation, it is necessary to adopt a certain hierarchical organizational structure in dealing with public affairs. In fact, regardless of whether the principle of "human beings are equal" is followed in legal theory, human societies in various countries today have adopted hierarchical social organization structures for dealing with public affairs.

Today's countries basically have heads of state, heads of government, and other positions with greater decision-making power in public affairs in the administrative and military fields. From the perspective of human individuals in society, these positions are at the peak of the power hierarchy, which can be called "oligarchs." In the vast majority of countries, there are still various management positions and various grassroots personnel in society.

Therefore, this paper speculates that the human section is a hierarchical organizational structure in the era of comprehensive AI.

Question two. Why should the supreme dominance right of the unmanned intelligent wealth creation and distribution system and the unmanned intelligent military force system be retained in the hands of human beings?

Answer. After all, this is a human society, not a robotic society. Controlling one's own destiny and dominating the world is a relatively common psychological demand of human beings. Some people are forced to give up this kind of psychological demand out of desperation, and some people forget that they have such a psychological demand simply because they have given it up for a long time. The big people in real human society are often keen to impose their ideals on society and to control the fate of themselves and others. Therefore, when designing an artificial intelligence system that will take over social wealth creation and military activities, the big shots will basically demand that this supreme decision-making power and dominance be retained.

Events such as war are major events related to the rise or fall of a country, so not everyone is qualified to directly direct the military and intervene, and it is natural that the most trusted person of the people should hold command. Obviously, it is the most acceptable to the people that the national leader is the commander of the intelligent combat robot system. For example, in the United States, the commander-in-chief of the Army is the president, and the commander-in-chief of the armed forces of China is the chairman of the Central Military Commission.

Throughout history, human thought and culture have developed and changed. If you hand over all control to AI, it may not be able to understand human changes and meet human needs very well.

Moreover, software tends to be flawed, and we cannot guarantee that AI systems are free of flaws. Defects may be introduced by the negligence of the original designer, or they may be introduced due to the lack of understanding and ability of the initial designer. They may also be introduced in the process of iteration of the AI itself, in the process of writing software by the AI, and may be caused by changes in applicable environmental conditions that the software does not keep up with, etc. If the decision-making power is left to the AI system, there is a risk that there will be an irreparable situation when human society encounters the outbreak of AI defects.

Therefore, it is a more reasonable choice for human beings to retain the supreme decision-making power, the right to dominate, and the power to interfere with and amend.

Question three. Why is the unmanned intelligent wealth creation and distribution system ordered by the oligarchs?

Answer. As for the production and distribution of wealth, the historical and present situation is that the vast majority of people are ordinary individuals who can only obtain the material wealth needed for life by selling their physical or mental labor, and that only a very small number of people in society can become high-ranking government officials or capitalists. Therefore, the vast majority of people will have nothing to do in the era of comprehensive AI; that is, the vast majority of people will lose the ways they used to obtain wealth for living and may lose the sources of wealth for living that people used to have. In this situation, in order to avoid a tragic event, society can only adopt a comprehensive welfare distribution system. By the way, in this situation, the traditional marketing economic system and the private property rights system will lose their value.

In order to cope with the comprehensive artificial intelligence of society, people have to implement a comprehensive welfare distribution system. Thus, the existing private ownership of property will collapse, and private business owners will most likely be squeezed out of the fields of wealth creation and distribution due to the loss of the market. Since the production and distribution of wealth cannot be stopped, there is a very high probability that the production and distribution of wealth will be led and decided by the leaders of public affairs in human society. In this case, the supreme decision-making power and directive power over the production and distribution of wealth will naturally be in the hands of the oligarchs. In fact, only the people who are in control of the decision-making power are the oligarchs. After the powerful person issues an order for the production and distribution of wealth, the AI system automatically formulates a task plan and executes the relevant tasks according to certain rules.

Question four. Why do the oligarchs directly give orders to the unmanned intelligent wealth creation and distribution system and the unmanned intelligent military system?

Answer. Due to the high development of artificial intelligence technology, intelligent robot assistants should be able to easily understand the requirements of the command issuer, make a task decomposition plan according to the command, and then formulate a reasonable task execution plan and implement it. Increasing the intermediate layers through which task commands are delivered in human organizations will only slow the speed at which commands are delivered and implemented.

Moreover, for task organization, it generally should not have too many bosses. If anyone can give an order or something, and each order is of the same level, there will inevitably be confusion. Therefore, unmanned intelligent systems, such as an intelligent robot army, must be set with the highest command authority. Whoever controls the highest command authority can control everything, and whoever has the greatest power. For unmanned intelligent systems, generally speaking, the person who controls the interface that gives orders to them is the master. And for the powerful, giving up their control means that they no longer have power.

Therefore, it is very likely that the oligarchs will directly order the mission themselves.

Question five. Why is there an unmanned intelligent military force system?

Answer. Judging from the current state of human society, there will be a long period of existing social organizations at the national level, and the Earth will not be unified into a country in the near future. For example, it is likely that people in rich areas do not want to live in the same country as people in poor areas, and they may be afraid that welfare will be shared. The leader of an authoritarian monarchy may be reluctant to unite with a democratic state in one country, fearing losing his voice, losing his position, and losing everything.

At present, the development status and resource status of various parts of the earth are different; there are certain differences in culture, ideological sects, ethics, and morality in various places, and many resources are limited, so contradictions and conflicts are bound to exist.

Since there are all kinds of sovereign countries and competition for resources, cultural and ideological competition, and so on, it is very difficult to avoid the existence of international contradictions. In order to cope with violent international contradictions that may arise, the establishment of armed forces has become the only choice for many countries.

To welcome the era of comprehensive artificial intelligence, the current military force system will naturally evolve into an unmanned intelligent military force system. In fact, in the military force system of developed countries today, automated weapon systems such as unmanned combat vehicles and unmanned fighters are occupying an increasingly important share and position, and artificial intelligence technology is constantly being introduced and applied in war simulation and decision-making planning at all levels, including strategy and tactics.

Question six. Is it possible for a dictatorship to emerge after comprehensive artificial intelligence?

Answer. This article argues that a dictatorship is very likely in the era of comprehensive AI.

The reason why a country with a democratic republic can be a democratic republic lies in the checks and balances among all parties. Under the influence of laws, regulations, and education, the citizens of a democratic republic have formed a set of value systems suitable for the democratic republic, and many times have formed a relationship of both obedience and checks and balances, such as the relationship between the commander-in-chief and the army. On the surface, the army must obey the president's orders, but in potential situations, if the president's orders violate the president's professional ethics and undermine the democratic republic, the army no longer needs to obey the president's orders.

After all, the human brain is not like a computer hard disk that can read each byte of content. A president usually cannot trust his generals to obey his chaotic orders to do mischief, and he naturally suspects that his generals will not rise up and rebel against him because of his violation of ethics. Shown as Fig. 3.2.2, in the organizational structures of human societies, when senior officials formulate a self-interested policy or decision, questions will almost inevitably arise either directly or potentially in their minds: "Are subordinates reliable?" "Will subordinates take the opportunity to counterattack?" "Will subordinates comply in appearance but oppose in heart while carrying out their duties?" "Will it touch the bottom line of society?" And doubts may arise in the minds of the middle-layer officials, such as, "Is the command reasonable and legal?" "Will subordinates resist it?" "Can we take advantage of the unreasonableness of the policy to overthrow the upper echelons?" Ordinary people at the lowest level may complain, "Is this policy reasonable and legal?" "Is it necessary to rise up and resist?" It is precisely because of the opacity and unpredictability of ideas existing among people that a balanced chain in the hierarchical structure of human society's organization forms. It can bring certain constraints on the senior officials of the organization.

In the era of comprehensive artificial intelligence, dictatorship is more likely to occur because intelligent robots may not be able to judge whether the orders from the top leader are "chaotic commands," and they are very likely to obey the words of those who have the power of the highest order, and there is no potential check and balance at all. If a president could command intelligent unmanned military forces at will, without fear of being resisted, his power would reach an incredible height, resulting in a dictatorship.

Artificial intelligence or robots are generally designed to have absolute obedience. In this way, the senior officials of the organization no longer have to worry about robot subordinates resisting or rebelling; that is, the chain of checks and balances, such as suspicion, resistance, and rebellion from the bottom to the top, will no longer exist. When the upper echelons of a society master the powerful capabilities of robots, do they still need to worry about the resistance of ordinary people who have no power to resist? Certainly not.

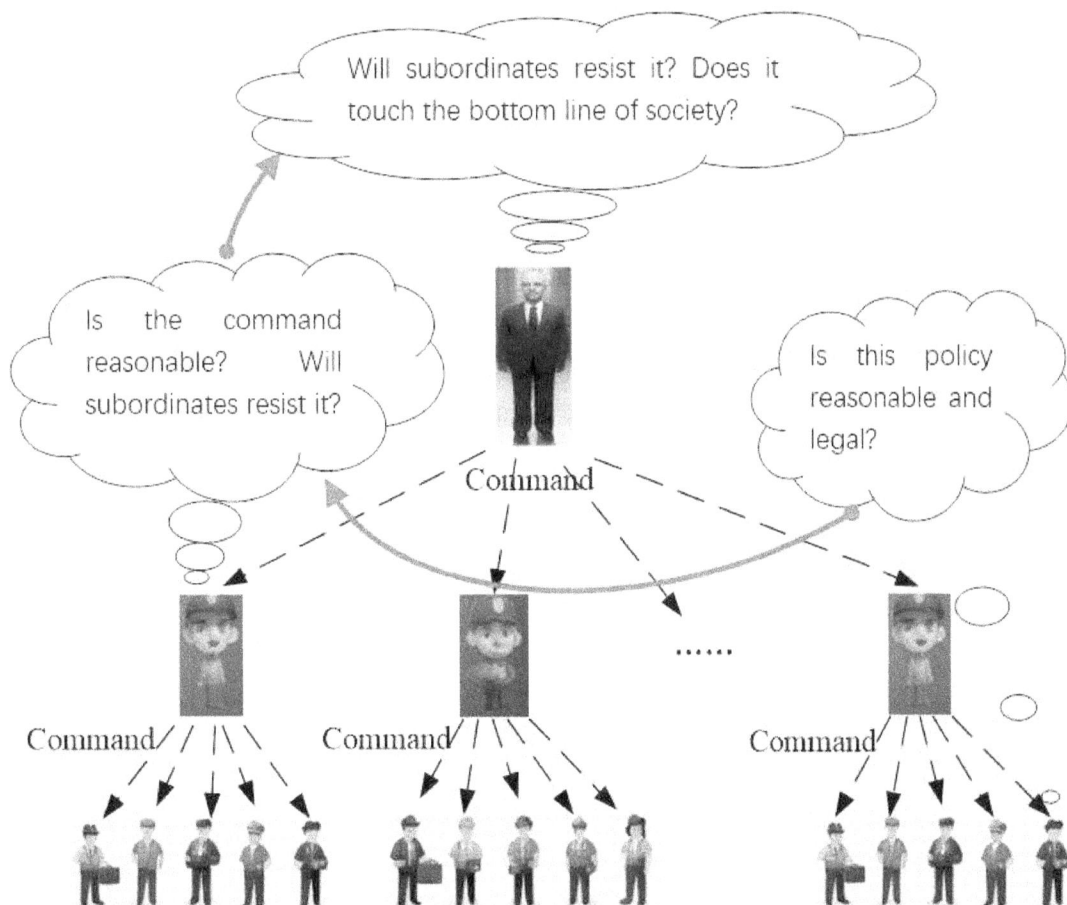

Fig. 3.2.2 Doubt and Checks and Balances Chain in the Hierarchical Structure of Human Social Organizations

Question seven. Will people be equal and happy in the era of comprehensive artificial intelligence?

Answer. If the organizational structure of human society presents a form of wealth production and distribution controlled by a few individuals in the era of comprehensive artificial intelligence, this article argues that ordinary people will not become much more equal and happier than in today's society.

Throughout the ages, in countries ruled by "saviors," the daily life of ordinary people is often very hard. Even today, as these words are written, there are several countries led by saviors on our planet, and the people in these countries are still struggling to meet their most basic needs for food and clothing. In the neighboring countries and regions, even if there is tension and constant fighting among heads of government and social and political leaders, ordinary people can generally live prosperous lives. As the Internationale sings, "No savior from on high delivers; no faith have we in prince or peer."

To be honest, the author, as an ordinary person, fears the oligarchic social system in which power lacks checks and balances.

The first, it is not possible to ensure that those who hold power are completely impartial, and the influence of the personal partiality of the oligarchs, who control the production and creation of wealth and the distribution of wealth in the era of comprehensive AI, can easily be magnified, causing a disastrous impact on ordinary people.

Second, it is difficult to guarantee whether the person in power suffers from mental problems, and the proportion of mental problems in the group of political leaders in history should be quite large. For example, it is said that the famous former British Prime Minister Winston Churchill spoke openly about his depression. A characteristic of a post-AI society is that the society lacks checks and balances on the power of oligarchs, and the mental problems of the oligarchs are likely to be greatly magnified.

Third, even if the power oligarchy has a pure and virtuous mind, due to cognitive reasons, they may naturally sacrifice the "current interests" of ordinary people or the legitimate interests of a considerable part of the population for the sake of the so-called "great ideals" and "long-term interests" in their minds. After all, human society is quite large and pluralistic today, and the power oligarchy itself is only one member of the human race, and in essence can only occupy the unity of its own place and tolerate the plurality of others. The ethical ideals of the power oligarchy are not necessarily the most in line with the needs of the general public.

Fourth, the Earth's resources are limited, and unless technologies other than AI have been greatly developed, today's human society cannot expand the scale of production at will. As evidence, the production and life of human beings have affected the Earth's climate and hydrology to a considerable extent. Nowadays, some countries and regions are suffering from serious air pollution, and the carbon emissions of human society can be compared to the total annual photosynthesis of the Earth. Human society has reached the point where it must control the total amount of carbon emissions. For example, in 2023, the total production of salmon in China was about 45,000 tons, and the per capita output was only about 32 grams. In such a situation of limited wealth, it will be difficult for the few powerful oligarchs to make decisions to achieve absolute fairness in the distribution of wealth in a comprehensive artificial intelligence society.

4 Analysis of Issues Related to the Use of Artificial Intelligence

As for the relationship between artificial intelligence and the satisfaction of human needs, it can't be expressed in a few words, and there is a great deal of uncertainty involved. If our society is in the era of comprehensive artificial intelligence, then social wealth production and distribution all depend on artificial intelligence. Naturally, the satisfaction of human beings' needs, such as clothing, food, housing, and transportation, is closely linked with artificial intelligence technology. It is just worth mentioning that even though human society has not yet developed artificial intelligence technology to maturity, human needs can be met quite sufficiently. In addition, the comprehensive use of artificial intelligence may deal a blow to the satisfaction of some human needs. Since ordinary people have nothing to do in the era of comprehensive AI, it is difficult to meet the spiritual needs of a sense of accomplishment based on wealth creation and to meet the spiritual needs of self-actualization.

With the current state of society, the use of artificial intelligence technology in certain fields or occasions is considered reasonable by the authors. There are also many occasions where AI technology should not be used or can only be used to a limited extent, given the current state of society. This chapter examines the question of whether "full-scale AI" or "comprehensive AI" is justified and briefly discusses in which fields AI can be used and in which fields AI should not be used.

4.1 Without Constraints on the Use of AI, Ordinary People will Lose Their Work

What were the characteristics of technology and industrial mass production decades ago?

One of the biggest features was that the machine amplifies the abilities of people's hands, feet, eyes, and ears, etc. For example, the crane can be said to amplify the ability of people to grasp things with their hands and carry things on their shoulders; cars, trains, airplanes, etc., can be said to amplify the mobility of people's feet and the ability of the human body to carry things; microscopes, telescopes, etc., can be said to magnify people's eyesight; and communication devices such as telephones can be said to amplify the power of people's mouths and ears.

The second feature was to maintain the use of environmental perception ability, thinking ability, and control ability of the human brain in production and scientific research. Therefore, in the entire process of wealth creation in daily life, including production, transportation, circulation, and distribution, there must be people participating.

What is the most significant feature of artificial intelligence? The most significant feature of artificial intelligence is that machines replace human brains, and machines make decisions autonomously.

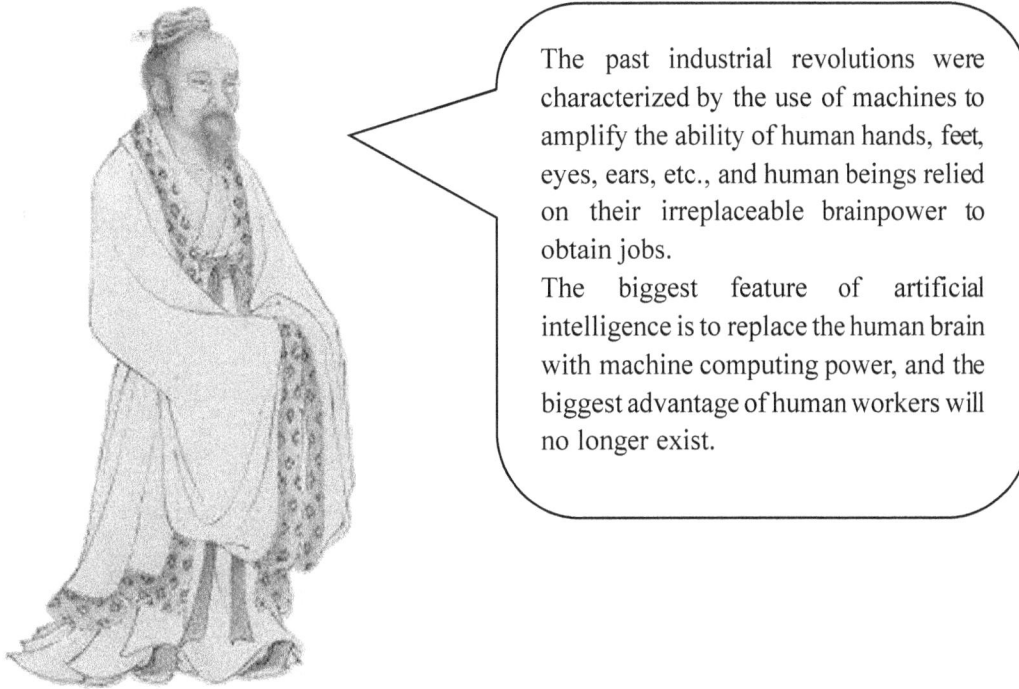

The past industrial revolutions were characterized by the use of machines to amplify the ability of human hands, feet, eyes, ears, etc., and human beings relied on their irreplaceable brainpower to obtain jobs.

The biggest feature of artificial intelligence is to replace the human brain with machine computing power, and the biggest advantage of human workers will no longer exist.

Fig. 4.1.1 Characteristics of Artificial Intelligence

For the majority of ordinary people in modern society, what is needed by the powerful and capitalists is that the human brain has the ability to make independent decisions that traditional machines do not have and can finish the work that traditional machines cannot do. Even manual workers fundamentally rely on the judgment and decision-making abilities of the human brain. For example, the value of a bricklayer is largely due to the fact that he knows how much mortar to use, where to place the bricks, what adjustments to make, and what standards the brick wall must meet to be qualified. You might as well imagine, for the work of building walls, what is the use of a strong gorilla that does not know how to build walls?

Compared with materials such as steel, the strength of human bones is negligible, and muscles and skin are even more fragile. If a large production machine is regarded as an elephant, in terms of strength, physical energy, and other abilities, a person is as weak as a kitten, a puppy, or even a small ant. Perhaps it is precisely because of the advantages of machines in terms of strength and physical energy that an important feature of the previous industrial revolutions was the replacement of human manual labor with machines, allowing human beings to withdraw from heavy and tiring physical labor and enabling people to engage in lighter physical work, which requires mental sensing, judgment, decision-making, and control.

For capitalist investors, what they want is to achieve their goals at the lowest possible cost. In the absence of constraints, if replacing workers with machines can reduce production costs, investors will definitely not hesitate to do so. If computers are used instead of the human brain to do the work of sensing, judging, decision-making, and control that traditional machines are not capable of doing, and this replacement can reduce business costs, capital investors will definitely not hesitate to use computers. Even if the business costs are equal, capital investors may still give priority to the use of computers because people will be tired, emotional, have ideas, and fight. Additionally, people will have higher autonomy, and there will be more uncontrollable and uncertain factors.

Looking at the computer market, the hardware performance of computers with the current price of several hundred dollars is quite good, and they have been able to provide extremely high computing power. At present, they have been able to give intelligent responses in real time for many relatively complex scenarios, such as the development level of the automotive unmanned intelligent system, which is good proof that computer hardware has been powerful enough to achieve a more ideal real-time artificial intelligence response. Moreover, with the development history of integrated circuits or chips in the past 50 years, it has been proven that the computing power of chips at the same price has become stronger along with the development of technology. With the passage of time and the development of artificial intelligence technology, coupled with some software and sensors, computers with more and more powerful computing power can complete the sensing, decision-making, and control work that is originally undertaken by the human brain.

Software is characterized by low replication costs, and in a sense, it can even be said that there are no replication costs. Therefore, in the near future, when AI technology is fully matured, AI systems with computer hardware to replace the human brain will be very inexpensive. This means that the cost of artificial brains (artificial intelligence systems) to replace human brains will be very low, and perhaps the entire AI system will be less than a month's salary of ordinary workers in developed countries in Europe and the United States today. In this case, one can imagine whether the investor will hire humans to complete the wealth creation work for him or use robots (artificial intelligence systems) to create wealth for him in a situation where society lacks corresponding laws and regulations.

In fact, there are already a large number of robots used in the field of wealth creation. Not to mention the many industrial robots, CNC machine tools, automated production machines for electronic products, cleaning robots, and other robots—even for lifting and assembly work—Mercedes-Benz and other companies have begun to use intelligent mobile humanoid robots. It is almost certain that the end of ordinary human labor is at hand, and idle days of unemployment are coming soon.

4.2 Investors or Powerful Individuals Account for only a Minority of the Population

Just as there is only one monkey king in a monkey group and only one wolf king in a wolf pack, in human society, the powerful people who control the operation and direction of human society account for only a very small number of human groups.

Taking the United States Civil Service field as an example, the most powerful people include 1 president, 1 vice president, 1 secretary of state, 2 speakers out of 538 members of the Senate and House of Representatives, 50 governors, 1 secretary of the Treasury, 7 members of the Board of Governors, 12 presidents of the Federal Reserve Bank, 94 federal prosecutors, 9 associate justices of the Supreme Court, 1 secretary of defense, 1 chairman of the Joint Chiefs of Staff, several commanders of various services, 6 theater commanders, about 600 to 700 generals, and so on. In the entire United States, there are only a few thousand people with great decision-making power in public affairs, and compared with the United States' 300 million citizens, the powerful can be said to be one in a hundred thousand. Moreover, the core public service decision-makers in the entire United States can be said to consist of only a handful of people. The situation is similar in other countries, where the share of the population with greater public decision-making power is extremely low as well.

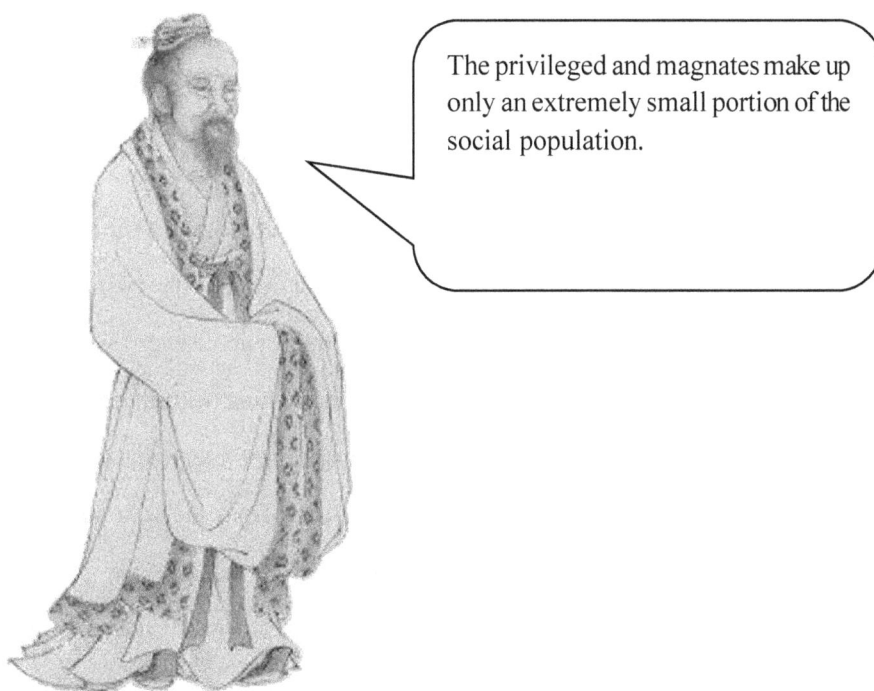

The privileged and magnates make up only an extremely small portion of the social population.

Fig. 4.2.1 The Social Elite Make up Only a Tiny Minority of the Population

The vast majority of people in today's human society are ordinary individuals who do not have great social influence. Especially in today's highly urbanized modern society, the vast majority of people are ordinary individuals who do not control the means of production and whose fate is bound by social trends. As an ordinary person today, the most important way to obtain the wealth needed for life is to sell one's brainpower, physical strength, time, and other resources related to human abilities.

For almost all countries, the vast majority of their citizens are ordinary workers who are at the bottom of the pyramid. In the citizen composition of the major countries in the world today, the number of capitalists and people living mainly on investments is a minority. For example, according to a variety of data sources, the proportion of people who currently have substantial means of production is extremely low in China.

On January 27, 2022, at a press conference held by the State Council Information Office, Yang Hongcan, director of the Registration Bureau of the State Administration for Market Regulation, said that by the end of 2021, there were 154 million registered market entities in the country, including 48.32 million enterprises and 103 million individual industrial and commercial households. The numbers may seem like a lot, but not many have enormous financial firepower. China has about 6.7 million factories in 2023, and there is a factory for about every 209 people. There are about 46 million enterprises, of which about 41.4 million are small and medium-sized enterprises, and there is an enterprise for about every 30 people. However, due to the relatively low cost of enterprise registration, many enterprises are actually only registered and do not operate much; in fact, many enterprises do not have employees who purchase social insurance. Therefore, the number of enterprises should be greatly exaggerated, and the actual number of enterprises is much smaller. Moreover, it is often the case that one boss registers many enterprises, so the number of real capitalists is much smaller than the number of enterprises.

Compared with the total number of enterprises, the data on the number of enterprises above designated size better reflect the situation of capitalists in a country. Let's take a look at the situation of enterprises of a certain scale in mainland China. At present, there are about 2 million small enterprises, 1.2 million medium-sized enterprises, and 500,000 large enterprises in mainland China. There is a large, medium, or small-scale enterprise for about every 380 people. By the end of 2021, there were about 400,000 industrial enterprises above designated size in China, with about every 3,500 citizens corresponding to each industrial enterprise. Industrial enterprises above designated size refer to industrial enterprises with annual main business income of more than 20 million RMB. As can be seen from the following criteria for the classification of small and medium-sized enterprises, the size of small businesses is actually very small. With the fact that "profits are generally much less than turnover," we can conclude that the owners of small businesses basically do not have much financial power. If we only consider medium and large enterprises, there is one enterprise corresponding to almost 820 people on average. Even if a company has one or two major shareholders or bosses on average, it is almost impossible for the bosses and their families to account for more than one percent of the country's population. In fact, according to relevant data, by the end of 2022, there were about 1.5 million households in the Chinese mainland with 6 million yuan of investable assets, accounting for only 3‰ of all households, and 67,000 households with 100 million yuan of investable assets, less than 0.14‰ of all households.

Table: Criteria for Classification of Small and Medium-sized Enterprises Categories

Category	Small Enterprises		Medium-sized Enterprises	
	Turnover (10,000 yuan)	Number of Employees	Turnover (10,000 yuan)	Number of Employees
Agriculture, Forestry, Animal Husbandry and Fishery	50~500		500~2000	
Industry	300~2000	>20	2000~4000	>30
Construction	300~6000 (and assets >300)		6000~8000 (and assets >5000)	
Wholesale	1000~5000	And >5	>5000	And >20

According to the above data on the number of Chinese enterprises, if the creation and circulation of wealth are fully reliant on artificial intelligence, under the market economy system, at most only several percent of people will be able to make money.

Considering the fierce competition and crowding out of enterprises in the era of comprehensive artificial intelligence: due to the disappearance of the "hard work" factor of people who are key to making money for traditional enterprises, the internal factors that have an impact on the competition between enterprises are likely to be only capital and channels. In this case, it is likely that the enterprises with insufficient capital strength will be quickly cleared out of the market, and the number of remaining enterprises is likely to be even more pitiful. It is even likely that people who are able to make money account for less than one percent of the population.

In one sentence, in the era of comprehensive AI, the vast majority of people will lose their traditional sources of wealth under the traditional market economy system.

4.3 Not Every Person Is Suitable for Research and Development

Similar to the development process of other scientific and technological advancements, artificial intelligence technology follows a development route from simple to complex, from fixed processes to highly varied, and from weak to powerful. History and reality have repeatedly confirmed that artificial intelligence technologies, including robots, first replace simpler labor and finally replace complex mental work. Therefore, we assume that artificial intelligence will first replace human manual labor with relatively low mental requirements, and then, after a long period of development, it can finally take over relatively complex scientific research.

Note: The author believes that since the research and development of science and technology should also follow the laws of nature, there are certain rules and routines; therefore, the research and development of science and technology should ultimately be taken over completely by artificial intelligence.

Although, in fact, some R&D-related work has been taken over by artificial intelligence, and there should be more R&D work taken over by artificial intelligence in the near future, what is being discussed now is the status before artificial intelligence takes over complex human R&D work, i.e., because creative R&D work is more complex and advanced, it has not been taken over by machines for the time being. In this case, how many people can rely on their mental work for wealth?

Although we often compare humans with animals and conclude that humans are smart, the difference in IQ between human individuals is not small; that is to say, the answer to whether they are suitable for R&D work is quite different. Anyone who has attended secondary school may notice that some people have poor comprehension and memory in learning; it is difficult for some people to focus their attention. In ordinary classes, the proportion of students with strong learning abilities is not very high. It is said that according to the Wechsler Intelligence Scale, only about 10% of the population has an IQ above 120, and only about 3% of the population has an IQ of 130 or more. In other words, the proportion of people who are smart enough to do research and development is not very high in the total population. The author does not deny that people may do research and development, even if they are not highly intelligent. Since today's science and technology have been quite developed, if someone wants to stand at the forefront of the trend to do research and development work, he or she needs to master a lot of basic knowledge, which further requires research and development personnel to have strong enough learning ability, comprehension ability, and exploration ability. Naturally, if the IQ is not high enough, he or she will encounter greater obstacles if he or she wants to enter the field of research and development.

In reality, by searching for relevant information, it is not difficult for us to find that, at present, scientific researchers account for a very small proportion of human society. Judging from the data, the number of R&D personnel in various countries today is basically less than 1% of the total population. For example, by 2021, the total number of R&D personnel in mainland China was 5.72 million, with an average of about 4 people per 1,000 conducting R&D work and about 7.7 R&D personnel per 1,000 employees. According to Russia's Kommersant data, there are 2.415 million researchers in the United States, 945,000 in Japan, 754,000 in Germany, and 669,900 in Russia, all of which do not exceed one percent of the total population. In Israel, which is famous for its scientific research, there were 8,250 R&D personnel per million people in 2012, which did not exceed 1 percent. Korea claimed in 2022 that it has 9.1 R&D personnel per 1,000 people, ranking first in the world in terms of R&D personnel; however, it still does not reach 1% of the population. According to the above data, it can be seen that R&D personnel account for only a very small minority of the entire human population.

Note, the above data source is from below.

人民日报，我国研发人员总量稳居世界首位，https://www.gov.cn/xinwen/2023-02/23/content_5742821.htm
程序员客栈，2023 年程序员数据报告：全球有 2690 万程序员，近一半不到 35 岁，
https://baijiahao.baidu.com/s?id=1761765212390537751&wfr=spider&for=pc

参考消息，俄机构公布科研人员数量排名，中美日德俄名列前五，

https://baijiahao.baidu.com/s?id=1782442419746528928&wfr=spider&for=pc

界面新闻，韩国 2021 年研发经费首破百万亿韩元，占 GDP 比例居全球第二，

https://baijiahao.baidu.com/s?id=1752806018871296835&wfr=spider&for=pc

亚太说事，研发人员比例世界第一！以色列为什么这么发达，

https://baijiahao.baidu.com/s?id=1642553897199145415&wfr=spider&for=pc

盘古论今 2021，以色列的九大最尖端科技，

https://baijiahao.baidu.com/s?id=1687053831728088211&wfr=spider&for=pc

In addition, from the perspective of R&D needs in another aspect, human society does not necessarily need too many R&D personnel. In fact, the types of products demanded by human society are very limited, and millions of people often use the same models of products, such as home appliances, automobiles, and other items. In particular, many daily necessities that have been developed and matured do not require much research and development any longer. In fact, there are not many projects for people to explore, and too many repetitive or overlapping R&D efforts are simply unnecessary.

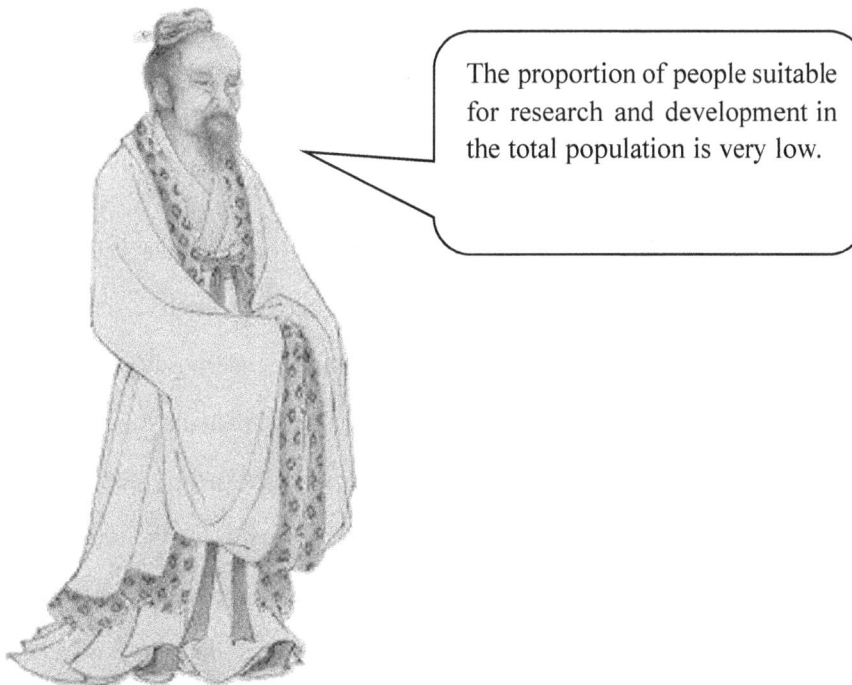

The proportion of people suitable for research and development in the total population is very low.

Fig. 4.3.1 Very Low Proportion of R&D Personnel in the Total Population

As we all know, in fact, many products are now being developed repeatedly by various enterprises or even many nations out of competition. If society still runs with the market economy system after it implements comprehensive artificial intelligence, the operating mechanism of enterprises will have changed, the human factor in the process of making money will be weakened or even disappear, a large number of enterprises will be squeezed out, and the number of enterprises in the market will be greatly reduced. In this case, will the same product need to be redeveloped too many times? The answer is obviously no; naturally, it also means a significant reduction in the demand for R&D work, which results in a reduction in the number of scientific researchers.

Moreover, R&D work often requires a significant amount of investment; wealth resources are limited; and society cannot afford for all employees to engage in R&D.

Therefore, human society fundamentally does not need to have a high proportion of R&D personnel. In other words, if the wealth creation and distribution model of the market economy continues, in the era of comprehensive artificial intelligence, not many people will be able to continue to earn the wealth they need to live by engaging in R&D work.

4.4 Mankind Is Not Ready for the AI Era

4.4.1 The Existence of Interest Groups Such as Countries

There are now about 200 countries and regions in the world. It has been some years since we entered the era of globalization, and the history of frequent material and human flows in human societies in various regions of the earth has been hundreds of years. There have been a lot of collisions and exchanges between human societies around the world, and human beings even established the United Nations, which has influenced the world after World War II. The United Nations has indeed made some contributions to the coordination of international relations and the balance of international development. However, the United Nations is a loose organization and has no strict constraints on each member. Based on the current international situation, there is still a long way to unify the earth into one country. At present, it is difficult to see the hope that people all over the world can live a harmonious, friendly, and prosperous life in one united country.

Today, the development of human society is uneven, with some regions being rich and others poor. This uneven development has hindered unifying all countries into one country throughout the world. In the process of their operations, human societies in various places often concentrate a certain amount of social wealth for the social welfare of their members, especially in developed regions, where social welfare is generally better. Moreover, developed regions tend to have an active economy, and there are more and better job opportunities. As a result, some people in the developed and wealthy regions are worried and afraid of the wealth and welfare divided away by the poorer regions. Perhaps it is precisely because of this concern that after World War II, some politicians in the former Western colonial overlords actively encouraged their former colonial areas to establish independent states, such as the Netherlands even paying money to "seek" Suriname's independence. Even within developed countries, there are people in some regions with better development who are seeking independence, such as Texas in the United States, where a few people want independence.

Therefore, based on the current situation of uneven global development, it is estimated that most of the people in developed and wealthy countries and regions will not be willing to eliminate interest groups at the "country" level, and their will to block global unification will be relatively strong. It is estimated that many people in poor or relatively less affluent countries and regions will want the "country" barrier to be removed globally, as evidenced by the fact that a significant number of people have fled to the United States and Western European countries in recent years, even after hardships and even if their lives are in danger during the trips. However, in today's human society, developed countries tend to have stronger strengths, greater discourse power, and greater influence on the international landscape. Eliminating the imbalance in the development of human society in all regions of the world is not an easy task. In fact, after World War II, only a handful of countries and regions on the entire planet have successfully stepped into the ranks of developed countries. Therefore, there is still a long way to go to eliminate the current situation of division of power among the countries around the world and to realize the reunification of human society in the world.

There are all kinds of interest groups and complex schools of thought and culture on the earth today, and there will be competition between interest groups and collisions between schools of thought, so that contradictions and conflicts will almost inevitably arise. In reality, there are many contradictions and conflicts in the world today, as the epitome of fierce conflicts, and even today, when the author knocks on the keyboard, there are at least three battlefields on the earth where the conflicts are extremely fierce and people are fighting for their lives: Russia and Ukraine, Hamas and Israel, and Myanmar. These various contradictions and conflicts hinder the harmony and unification of all human societies.

"Countries" will not disappear in a short period of time. AI may exacerbate the internal contradictions of some countries. AI is also likely to increase the squeeze of developed countries on poor and underdeveloped countries.

Fig. 4.4.1 The Existence of Interest Groups at the Country Level

The people in a modern democratic country often undertake and share the protection of the state, share the same social welfare, and it is easier for the people to form a community of interests. However, there are many contradictions within modern democracies. For example, the conflict between capital investors and employees; they often have their own standpoints and pursuits on the issue of "how to divide the profits of the enterprise in order to be reasonable." Another example is that there are contradictions between different industries: for example, there are often contradictions between importers of certain commodities and local suppliers; there may be a contradiction between civil servants and non-civil servants. After all, when the total cake of wealth created by society is fixed, the more government employees get, the less others get of the cake. When such internal contradictions become too serious, the people of the country may no longer be able to be said to be a community of interests because the common interests account for too little.

It is often difficult for people in authoritarian states to be truly grouped into a community of interests. In such a country, the so-called "aristocracy" often uses the so-called "bloodline" and other factors to "inherit" public rights, rules the country by means of deception, violence, and intimidation, and enslaves others to work for them. The idea that opposition to them is opposition to the whole people may have been fabricated and instilled. For example, there are still rulers of countries today who regard the state as their private property, describe the public wealth of all citizens as their private wealth, and then divide the lion's share of this wealth among themselves and their descendants. When they have to leak some of the wealth that should belong to the whole population to the ordinary people, they proclaim that it is their generous gift to the people. Filthy rulers like this will instinctively prevent the unification of the earth because once the earth is unified, their luxurious life or heavenly level of life will come to an end.

Against the backdrop of a world that is not unified and where there is non-interference between countries, the full use of artificial intelligence and robots in wealth creation is likely to cause serious problems. In those countries where state power is privatized, there is a high probability that intelligent systems or robotic systems will be controlled by those in power. For rulers who are accustomed to using deception, violence, and other means, and even rulers who have already thought that "it is natural to use deception, violence, and other means to treat ordinary citizens and plunder citizens," after they fully use robots to create wealth, because ordinary citizens have lost their use value, rulers are likely to have the idea that ordinary citizens have no right to live. In this case, the ordinary citizens in the country may be even more miserable.

In addition, against the backdrop of a world that is not unified, it is likely that the artificial intelligence or robotization of the social wealth creation process will be realized first in the technologically advanced countries. After the realization of comprehensive artificial intelligence in technologically advanced countries, the wealth creation process will not be limited by the labor force, including the limitation of the skill quality of the labor force population and the limitation of the number of labor force population, which is likely to greatly reduce the unit production cost of their national products, allowing them to achieve a more favorable position in international business competition. It will inevitably have a huge crowding-out effect on working people in poor countries and regions with backward technology, making their lives more difficult.

4.4.2 Unquiet International Community

Modern human society is not a calm society but a society full of violent contradictions. In the past 100 years, large-scale military conflicts in distant times, such as the two world wars, have caused casualties in the tens of millions. In recent years, fierce wars and conflicts have continued, including the Gulf War, the Kosovo War, the Afghanistan War, a series of wars in the Middle East after the Arab Spring, the war between Saudi Arabia and the Houthi armed forces in Yemen, and the war between Armenia and Azerbaijan. Even at the end of 2023, our world is still engaged in three wars of no small scale at the same time: the Russia-Ukraine war, the Hamas-Israeli conflict, and the intra-Myanmar conflict. It is said that so far, the Russian-Ukrainian war, which has lasted for more than two years, has caused a total of more than one million casualties on both sides; the Hamas-Israeli conflict may have killed tens of thousands of people; the conflict in northern Myanmar, which has received little media attention, is estimated to have killed and injured tens of thousands of people. The author argues that the causes of these war conflicts vary. The author's understanding of the causes of war is not necessarily reasonable due to his limited knowledge, but one thing the author thinks is certain: these war conflicts prove that there are too many factors that may cause brutal conflict in our world. The Russian-Ukrainian war may have originated from the contradictions between the Russian-concentrated areas in eastern Ukraine and the central government in Kiev, Ukraine, on issues such as policy direction and distribution of interests, mutual distrust between Russia and NATO, etc., and finally caused contradictions and conflicts that gradually amplified to the extent that the soldiers of the two countries are fighting for their lives. The Hamas-Israeli conflict involves many complex reasons, such as religious beliefs and historical entanglements. The root cause of the conflict in northern Myanmar lies in the fact that the central government of Myanmar continues to implement a national identity classification system, and it is said that there are as many as six types of identity cards, and the citizens are treated differently, resulting in the dissatisfaction of ethnic minorities in Myanmar, which has led to a military struggle against the junta. In addition, it is said that some local warlord forces in Myanmar and even some high-ranking officials of the Burmese military government have gotten involved in fraud, human organ trafficking, and other criminal acts. Some local armed forces, which are dissatisfied with the rule of the Burmese military government, grasp the opportunity, hold high the banner of justice, and crack down on the junta and those local warlord forces supporting wire fraud and other criminal acts.

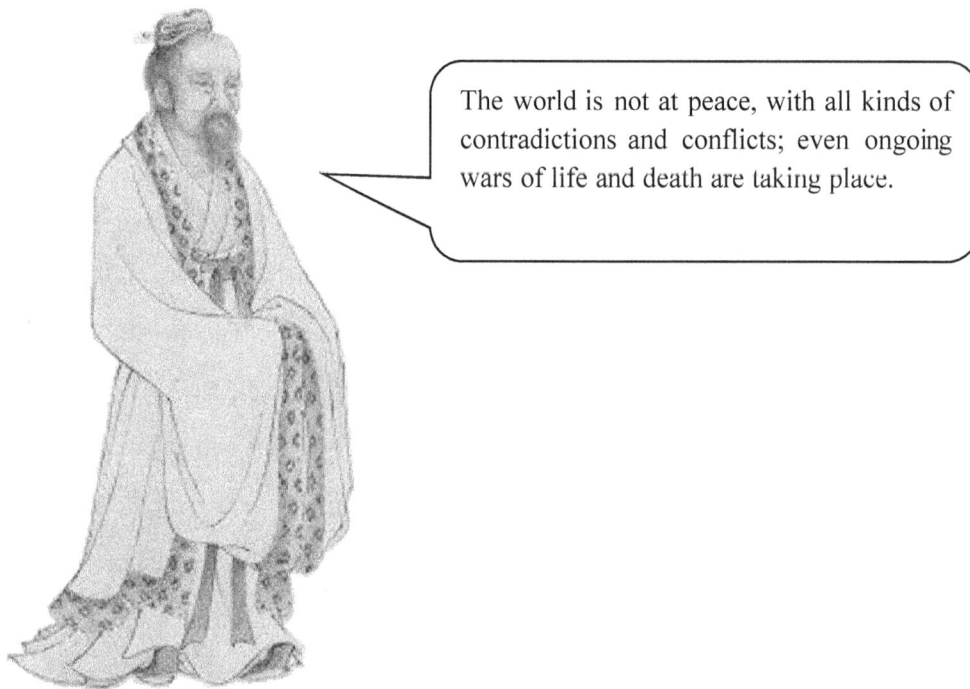

The world is not at peace, with all kinds of contradictions and conflicts; even ongoing wars of life and death are taking place.

Fig. 4.4.2 An Unrestful Human Society

There are various state systems in today's human society, including democratic republics, constitutional monarchies, autocracies and dictatorships, religious laws, capitalism, socialism, and so on. There are many potential contradictions between countries with these different systems.

For example, the rulers of authoritarian states may instinctively hate democratic republics, fearing that the winds of democracy will blow into their countries and affect their ruling authority. Some people in a democratic republic will be disgusted with an authoritarian dictatorship, including sympathizing with the oppressed ordinary people in an authoritarian dictatorship and fearing that the forces of the authoritarian dictatorship will undermine their democratic republic.

For example, some people in religious and religiously conservative countries may despise people in secularized countries, and they may inexplicably develop a sense of so-called superiority similar to "being a cut above others" because they are constantly bathed in the preaching of religious laws. Extremists of some sects may also be hostile to the people of secularized countries, believing that people who do not believe in their religion have "blasphemed" and "challenged" the gods in their minds, and even have thoughts and actions of "purifying" the world with things such as "stones," "knives," and "fire." The "9/11" incident in the United States might be said to be, in a sense, an example of some extremists carrying out the "purification" in their minds. It is natural that some people in secularized countries are afraid of being "purified" by certain extremists. At the same time, there are people who sympathize with certain groups in religious countries that are bound by religious laws and have difficult lives.

For example, some people in capitalist countries fear socialism, fearing that they will lose their right to freedom of wealth after entering socialism and that they will become "screws," as they are called in some propaganda. Some people in socialist countries are afraid of capitalism, afraid that after society is transformed into a capitalist society, they will become homeless at the bottom of society, and they are afraid that they will not have a sense of security.

Artificial intelligence will bring about major changes in the production capacity and military capabilities of various countries and will inevitably increase the possibility of reshuffling the international pattern, which is equivalent to increasing the contradictions in competition among countries that are already full of contradictions. It is likely to exacerbate international contradictions and even trigger more wars, sacrificing the lives of more ordinary people.

Finally, a word of caution: Along with the transition to the era of comprehensive artificial intelligence, robots will gradually become the core productive force of society. Assuming that in the era of comprehensive artificial intelligence, the Earth still maintains the current international pattern, will people paralyze or even destroy a country in one fell swoop by secretly arranging powerful intelligent robots in it, such as investing in or hacking the superficially friendly, internally hostile country, and ordering those robots to rebel within a specific time?

4.4.3 The Socio-cultural and Psychological Dimensions Are Not Ready

What is the current state of human society? Are humans ready for comprehensive artificial intelligence in the socio-cultural and psychological dimensions?

This paper argues that human society is not ready for comprehensive artificial intelligence.

Assuming that in the era of comprehensive artificial intelligence, the production and distribution of material wealth will be entirely taken over by artificial intelligence, and ordinary people have been completely decoupled from the creation of material wealth, then we only need to care about whether human beings are ready for comprehensive artificial intelligence in the spiritual realm or the spiritual world.

There are many, many sparks in the human psyche, either realistic or dreamlike, so there are many different schools of thought and religious sects in the world today. For example, in today's human society, some people believe in animistic primitive shamanism, some believe in the caste inequality of Hinduism, some believe in Buddhism, where all beings are equal, some believe in Christianity and Catholicism, some believe in Islam, some believe in aliens, some believe in science or Taoism, some believe in atheism, and so on. There are extremely diverse types.

It is natural and understandable for a school or sect to instill in its members a slight sense of spiritual superiority in order to spread and grow. However, there are some existing sects that go to extremes in this regard, adopting extremely discriminatory attitudes towards human beings who are not of their own sect, even to the point of arbitrarily enslaving and killing those who do not believe in the tenets of their faith. Just imagine, if such an extremist-minded madman holds the core command of the mature AI power, wouldn't it be a terrible catastrophe for a large number of people who do not believe in his school of thought? In this world, there are some schools that, if their believers hold the core power of AI, will even be a disaster for people who do believe in it, such as some "doomsday" cultists. After all, there are still many believers of extremist schools of thought on the earth today, and there are also many believers whose ideas derived from certain schools of thought have gone to extremes, and they have created many horrific anti-human incidents. Even in recent decades, there have been occasional killings led by extremist schools, such as the mass suicide of the "People's Temple" in the United States that killed more than 900 people about 40 years ago, the poison gas attack on the Tokyo subway carried out by "Aum Shinrikyo" in Tokyo, Japan, which caused more than 6,000 casualties about 30 years ago, and the ruthless killing of Yazidis by ISIS against Yazidis who do not believe in their religion about several years ago. As for other small influences, there are countless incidents that hurt people because of their thoughts. At present, due to the fragmentation of human society, it seems that civilized society does not have any effective strategies to prevent the emergence of extremists.

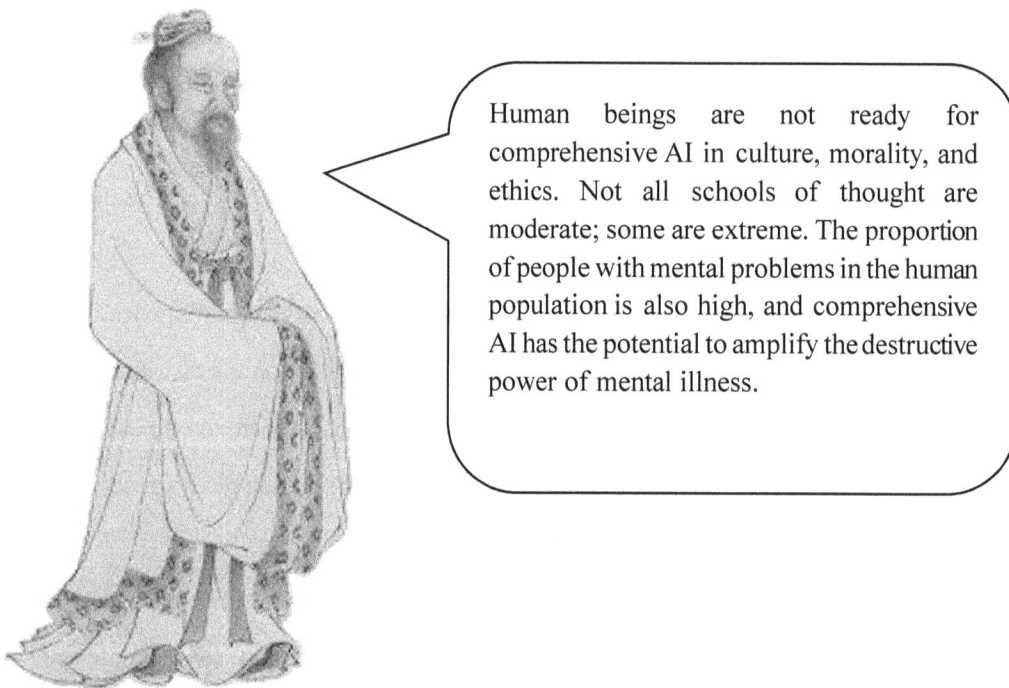

Human beings are not ready for comprehensive AI in culture, morality, and ethics. Not all schools of thought are moderate; some are extreme. The proportion of people with mental problems in the human population is also high, and comprehensive AI has the potential to amplify the destructive power of mental illness.

Fig. 4.4.3 Not Ready for Comprehensive AI in Socio-cultural and Psychological Aspects

Living in this world, it is natural for people to have labels such as gender, name, age, hometown, primary school, secondary school, university, ethnicity, and nationality. These labels themselves have nothing to do with a person's rights and wrongs, good or evil, or whether their behavior is illegal or criminal, and should not be used as a criterion for whether they should be punished. But in the real world, people often feel close to each other because they have a certain label, and they distance themselves from each other because of a certain label. For some personal purposes, some careerists often use people's sense of belonging to labels to manipulate society, thus committing unforgivable crimes, such as Hitler using the so-called racial and ethnic labels to manipulate the Germanic people to reject and kill the Jewish people after World War I. In 1994, certain politicians and careerists manipulated and instigated the massacre between Hutu and Tutsi in Rwanda. In 1998, certain Indonesian politicians and careerists manipulated Muslim thugs to rob, rape, and kill Chinese Indonesians…

In this world, there are many crimes that occur simply because of neuropsychological impulses. Some are just crimes committed by criminals who find a certain crime interesting and want to have fun; some of them just happen because criminals don't like each other, such as unpleasant tastes in clothing and speech; some crimes occur only because criminals want to establish authority and kill the chicken to scare the monkey; some criminal acts occur simply because the person committing the criminal act has a psychotic episode and falls into a state of fantasy; some criminal acts occur only because the criminal is caught in a certain superstitious idea and feels that some actions of others infringe on his potential rights and interests. For example, in some places, some people will feel that they have been violated by their neighbors because their neighbors' doors are a little higher than their own. It is very difficult to eradicate this kind of crime, which does not have a material conflict of interest and is caused only by neuropsychological impulses.

There are a lot of people with mental problems, and the wide range is that about 10% to 30% of the total population suffers from mental illness. People with severe mental disorders, such as schizophrenia, are said to be as high as 1%. According to data from the Chinese Health and Family Planning Commission in 2015, there are 4.297 million patients with severe mental disorders registered in China, and there is almost one registered person with severe mental disorders in about 300 people. Social leaders are not exempt from mental illness, and the proportion of people with mental problems is not low. Many political leaders often live in a state of heavy psychological pressure, and long-term psychological pressure can easily distort people's psychology, making them susceptible to anxiety, depression, and other symptoms. It is said on the Internet that ten to twenty percent of politicians may have mental problems. For example, it is rumored that many Northern Qi emperors during the Northern and Southern Dynasties in ancient China were psychologically abnormal.

After all, with the help of artificial intelligence or robots, the power of individual humans can be greatly amplified. Human behavior or power is controlled by people's mental activities. If there is a problem with an individual's mental and ideological activities, in the era of comprehensive artificial intelligence, his or her destructiveness may be magnified to an unimaginable degree.

If the post-AI society adopts the pessimistic organizational structure model mentioned in the previous chapter, and if dignitaries betray the people, the people will have no resistance to the dignitaries. For example, if a country's AI-powered army or robotic wealth creation and distribution system is controlled by an extreme figure, it would be a terrifying thing for the people who are not with him wholeheartedly. Or how terrifying it would be if a country's AI-powered army or robotic wealth creation and distribution system were somehow controlled by someone suffering from some kind of hidden mental illness.

4.4.4 Artificial Intelligence Weakens Human Friendships

In the era of comprehensive artificial intelligence, will artificial intelligence pets cause people to spend more and more time at home, minimize social activities, and weaken the friendships between people? If this is true, it is likely to lead to social problems.

In many countries today, families are small and have a limited number of family members, with a significant number of families even having only one member. In today's day and age, people from the same workplace live in different locations, and many city dwellers are completely unfamiliar with their neighbors, let alone neighbor-to-neighbor interactions. In today's world, there are many people whose emotional needs are often not met.

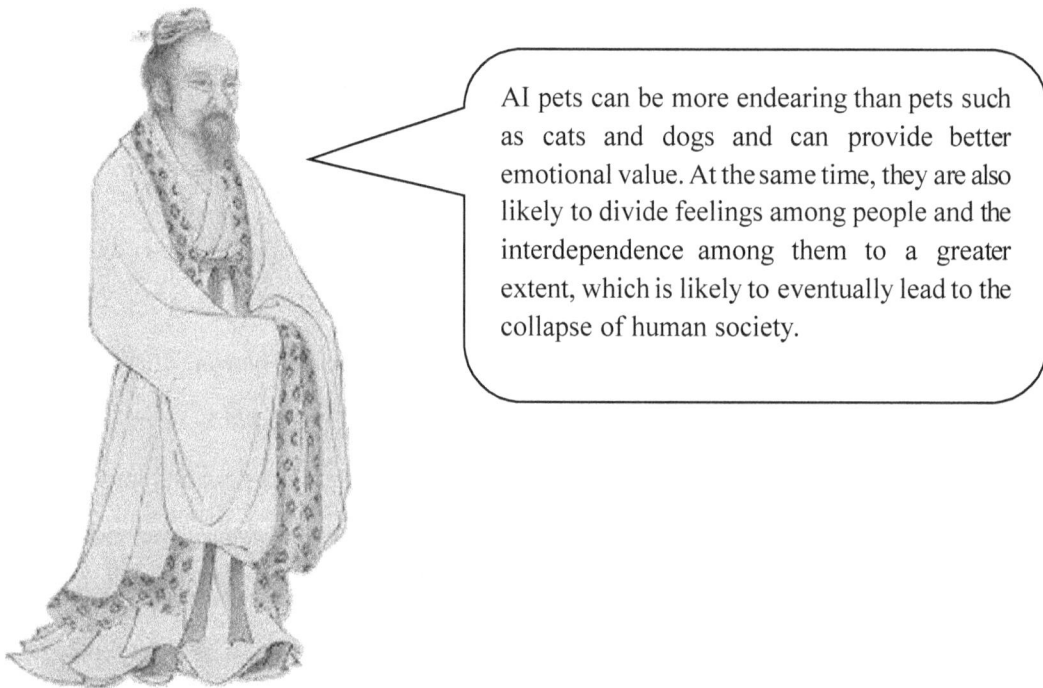

AI pets can be more endearing than pets such as cats and dogs and can provide better emotional value. At the same time, they are also likely to divide feelings among people and the interdependence among them to a greater extent, which is likely to eventually lead to the collapse of human society.

Fig. 4.4.4 AI May Destroy Friendships Among People

Nowadays, many people stay at home after work, just reading books, surfing the Internet, and keeping pets, rarely interacting with others and having relatively indifferent relationships with others. As a result, some people put their emotions into pets and regard pets as children or companions, far more than their feelings for other people. Especially, dogs generally show loyalty and obedience to their owners and will please them. Dogs often express their pitiful grievances through facial expressions and physical behaviors when the owner scolds them, and they usually shake their heads and tails to indicate intimacy when they welcome their owners, providing good emotional value for owners whose emotional needs are not met. It makes many people treat dogs and other pets as if they were their own lives. You can see a lot of incidents related to pets in the news media. For example, someone walking a dog stopped a car when the car honked and refused to let the car go, asking the car driver to apologize to the dog because the dog owner thinks the car driver scared the dog; someone felt that their own puppy had suffered a loss in a fight between his puppy and another person's puppy, and he beat the owner of the other dog; in 2018, there was such a vicious case in Qingpu, Shanghai: when a young lady was picking up the express, a dog jumped out and barked at her and showed an attacking state; the lady was scared and asked her father to escort her, the dog still barked at them, and the woman's father tried to scold the dog to drive it away; then the dog owner felt very unhappy, jumped out and made a noise, and beat the woman's father to death.

Technically speaking, artificial intelligence pets can be more loyal to their owners than puppies. Artificial intelligence pets can make the most suitable response to the owner's psychological needs by judging the owner's emotional state and providing better emotional value for the owner through language, expression simulation, and behavior simulation. In the case of AI pets, owners are likely to invest a lot more emotion than they would in an animal pet. The United States movie "Finch," starring the famous actor Tom Hanks, shows the possible love of human beings for robots, and the robots in the movie are not even as well-behaved as cats and dogs, nor do they have pitiful expressions.

Previously, we speculated on a social organizational structure after the full maturity and application of artificial intelligence. In the social organizational structure, the powerful are likely to directly control the armed forces composed of intelligent robots and manage the automatic wealth creation and distribution systems composed of intelligent robots. In this case, if those dignitaries have no direct interaction with ordinary people and are surrounded by a group of high-level intelligent machine pets, will the dignitaries have no feelings for ordinary people in society at all and regard ordinary people as mere mustard or little grass? In this situation, ordinary people cannot defeat the armed forces of intelligent robots, and since production resources are not in their hands, the outcome is predictable: they likely will not even be able to live a meager existence.

4.4.5 Energy Consumption Issues of AI

Human society on modern Earth is facing serious environmental problems such as energy consumption and carbon emissions. In the process of cosmic operation, the energy obtained by the Earth from the sun and the energy radiated by the Earth were originally in a state of dynamic equilibrium, which maintained a climate and environment that were more suitable for the survival of human beings. After the great development of modern human populations, people have developed and used a lot of mineral energy, and the carbon emissions produced by human activities every year have been comparable to the total amount of photosynthesis on the Earth. Many experts are worried about whether the Earth's climate will no longer be suitable for human survival in the future.

After the comprehensive development and application of artificial intelligence, will it greatly increase the energy consumption on the earth? A large number of artificial intelligence systems that replace humans, including intelligent robots, completely abandon the natural computing power of humans, which will superimpose energy consumption. Artificial intelligence relies on the powerful computing power of electronic computers, and every unit of computing power of electronic computers means energy consumption. The human brain should also be regarded as a kind of computing power resource, and abandoning the natural ready-made computing power of the human brain and using machine computing power on various occasions should be regarded as a serious waste of resources, right? After all, the human brain consumes energy whether it is used or not.

Using only the computing power of the machine will obviously increase energy consumption in terms of computing power. For example, the driverless cars that are popular in today's commercial society basically have an energy consumption power of the intelligent driving system on each car that will reach more than 100 watts and even several times more, while the normal energy consumption power of an adult is only about 100 watts. Even if human drivers do not drive, they will not save the 100 watts of energy consumption.

In fact, now Google and other companies that rely on computing power are very staggering in terms of energy consumption and water consumption. According to the data obtained from Internet searches, ChatGPT chatbots consume 500,000 kilowatt-hours of electricity per day, and Google's electricity consumption is even comparable to that of a country, which consumes tens of billions of kilowatt-hours of electricity a year.

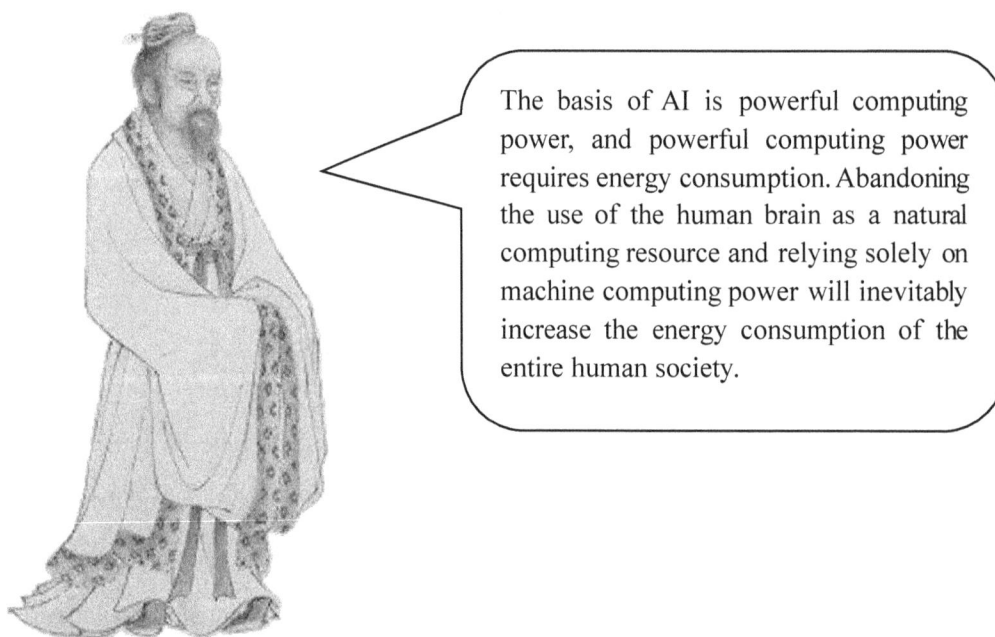

> The basis of AI is powerful computing power, and powerful computing power requires energy consumption. Abandoning the use of the human brain as a natural computing resource and relying solely on machine computing power will inevitably increase the energy consumption of the entire human society.

Fig. 4.4.5 AI Will Increase the Energy Consumption of Human Society

If we abandon human computing resources completely and only rely on machine computing power in the field of wealth production and distribution, will it cause serious global environmental and climate problems and make the Earth unlivable? It is also an issue that needs to be considered regarding whether to fully promote AI in the future.

4.4.6 Technology Issues of AI

Few experienced developers can claim to be able to guarantee that they will not make bugs or mistakes when developing and designing large, complex software. After all, man is not the all-powerful god of legend. In the development process, developers are likely to be inconsiderate and may overlook some potential threats that may be brought about by certain factors, and they may not take into account the particularities of certain situations.

Sometimes, limited by the developer's ability, the most correct solution for some problems may not be made, and the solution is only suitable for certain occasions or specific conditions. When the environment being applied has factors other than the specific conditions, it is likely to cause a big disaster.

In the era of comprehensive AI, including the development of the technology itself being taken over by AI, the mistakes introduced by the original developers in the development process are likely to be passed on. These errors, if triggered under certain conditions, are likely to cause serious disasters for humanity.

The AI program may be thrown into confusion after the intelligent robot is subjected to certain disturbances. For example, strong electromagnetic radiation interference may lead to the complete dysfunction of intelligent robots that rely on electronic computers as brains and may even cause them to fall into a state that seems to be normal but harms humans at critical moments.

In addition, developers are not always law-abiding citizens, and a small number of developers may maliciously implant certain code, which will be triggered under certain conditions, causing damaging events to occur. Many people have encountered computer viruses, mobile phone viruses, etc., which have proven the existence of malicious technicians.

4.5 Which Fields Can AI Be Used In

For human beings, science and technology often have two sides, and the key is how humans use them. The same is true for AI technology. AI is suitable for use in some cases. In some cases, it will be good for the welfare of human society if it is used in moderation. There are also many fields in which AI technology is not suitable for use in today's social systems.

Some dangerous occasions that are not suitable for human beings to stay in are very suitable for the use of artificial intelligence. For example, AI is suitable for use in space exploration and development activities such as Mars and asteroid exploration. Since the environment itself is extremely unsuitable for human survival, and there is no air or water necessary for human survival on asteroids and Mars, it will be very difficult for human beings to survive if we do not build a base suitable for human survival in the early stages. In this case, if intelligent robots are to land on them first to build a base suitable for human habitation, human beings will not have to directly face the significant problem of life and death when they arrive. For example, in some areas of the nuclear power plant where the radiation is strong and it is extremely unsuitable for humans to work, the use of robots is almost the best choice; thus, the maintenance of devices in some areas of nuclear power plants is suitable for using robots. Additionally, for the mining of underground minerals in certain geological structures that are not safe for humans, it is also a better choice to mine with robots or automated machinery.

AI is also suitable for the occasion where it is necessary to process a large amount of trivial and low-value data in a timely manner. If using human labor to finish such work, it would take too much manpower to process trivial data, making it challenging to complete tasks on time. For example, it is more suitable to apply artificial intelligence technology to identify traffic violations from video data and capture the scenes of violations. Due to the sheer size of today's road networks, a large number of cameras have been installed to monitor violations. Moreover, the amount of video data generated by each camera in 24-hour monitoring per day is staggeringly huge. The speed at which people process visual images is not fast, and if you watch the surveillance video frame by frame, a person can check the data from several cameras at most. So even if a lot of manpower is invested, it is difficult to identify illegal incidents in time. The occurrence of illegal acts is generally not too frequent. Most of the videos are unrelated to illegal phenomena. In a sense, these video data that have nothing to do with illegal phenomena are worthless. Therefore, it can be said that the average value of surveillance video data is not high, and investing a lot of manpower and other resources is a waste to society. In this case, the application of artificial intelligence technology can achieve visual image processing on mass video surveillance data at a fast and low cost, including identifying illegal phenomena and recording illegal scenes.

Artificial intelligence technology is also suitable for some particularly physically demanding and tiring occasions, such as the care of people with disabilities. Many people have unhappy experiences in caring for disabled elders, and they dream that if there were intelligent robots that could take care of the disabled, it would truly be a good liberation for their families. Nowadays, due to the lack of opportunities to face the existential crisis in terms of physical fitness, a considerable number of people have little physical exercise, do not grow strong muscles on their bodies, and have pitiful strength, so they are unable to lift and hold their bedridden relatives at all. It is even very difficult for them to turn over and scrub their bedridden relatives. If there are highly intelligent, tireless, and attentive robots that can take care of disabled people, they can obviously cater to the needs of many individuals. Especially in today's situation, where everyone has to go to work, having a capable, intelligent robot nanny at home is simply a great blessing for all.

Artificial intelligence is also suitable for some products with high precision requirements, and if it is operated by humans, it is limited by human capabilities and cannot meet the technical requirements. For example, for some steps in the production process of integrated circuits, it is most reasonable to apply automated machinery for production and processing.

When production dominated by human workers cannot keep up with the pace of demand, this paper argues that, after a certain review process, artificial intelligence can be appropriately introduced to improve labor productivity to some extent.

Under the condition of not undermining social ethics and morality, artificial intelligence technologies, including intelligent robots, can be appropriately allowed to be used by consumer end users. Intelligent robots only for consumer end users will not rob ordinary people of job opportunities, will not make ordinary people lose the opportunity to contribute to a sense of achievement, and will not make ordinary people lose the opportunity to obtain wealth for living. From the perspective of GDP and market consumption, the promotion of the use of intelligent robots for consumer end users is equivalent to increasing the types of consumer goods for human beings, which may expand the capacity of the consumer market and promote employment. This paper argues that if artificial intelligence continues to mature to a certain extent, intelligent robots for consumer end users will eventually become not only toys that satisfy human curiosity but will also greatly facilitate people's lives.

Of course, some applications of artificial intelligence involve both consumer end users and wealth creation, such as intelligent unmanned driving technology. For such artificial intelligence technology, people should seriously consider the issues of whether to permit its use or not, and if permitting its use, to what extent it can be used and how to open up the application, etc. This paper argues that applications of AI, such as intelligent unmanned driving technology, which have a significant impact on society, must have clear relevant licensing provisions at the legal level and can only be applied when there is a clear basis for how to enforce the law.

4.6 Rough Discussion on the Consequences of Using AI in Wealth Creation

This section mainly discusses the potential consequences of the comprehensive application of artificial intelligence technology in the field of wealth creation, primarily taking robots used in production and driverless intelligent vehicles as examples.

At present, using robots, not only industrial robots that simulate the function of human limbs but also automatic machines such as CNC automatic machine tools and automatic placement machines in the electronics industry, capitalists do not have to worry about legal problems, nor do they have to worry about a series of issues related to human nature caused by hiring human laborers.

At present, many countries have a five-day, 40-hour workweek; of course, some countries have a 35-hour workweek, and so on. As we all know, there are 168 hours in a week, so even if it is assumed that the productivity of a robot is the same as that of a human individual, a robot working at full load is equivalent to 4.2 human laborers. If the average work hour of laborers is the same as workers in Greece, which is about 1,255 hours, an industrial robot can even be equivalent to about 7 human laborers. Let's take a step back and assume that a robot needs to be maintained. For example, dozens of robots need a maintenance person, and if the robots are also shut down for a few hours a week due to maintenance needs, then the production capacity of one robot is still equivalent to the production capacity of several human laborers. In fact, for mechanical operations, because robots are tireless, they can move faster than humans, and the productivity per unit time can often be much higher than that of human labor; in other words, robots can be as productive as more human laborers.

The robot is mainly composed of a robot software system (including sensor information analysis and object recognition, judgment, decision-making, control, and other functional modules), a computer system, sensors (infrared, ultrasonic, camera, etc.), structural components made of steel and other materials, and electric, hydraulic, or pneumatic transmission components, as shown in Figure 4.6.1. In addition to the robot software system that concentrates on the cost of R&D, the cost of other components is very limited. For small robots that can be applied to the production field, a cost of tens of thousands of dollars or even lower, in addition to the robot software system, is sufficient. On the other hand, if robots are used on a large scale in the production field, and the robots are mass-produced, the cost of the robot software system distributed to each robot will become very low. As a result, the cost of robots used in industrial production will be low. As a result, the cost of robots used in industrial production will even be as low as the average monthly salary of a worker in developed countries today.

Robot = Software System + Computer System + Sensors

+ Structural Components Made of Steel and Other Materials

+ Electric, Hydraulic or Pneumatic Components

Fig. 4.6.1 Basic Robot Components

In order to obtain maximum profits, capitalists will naturally replace humans with robots in production. In fact, in recent years, the number of industrial robots equipped in China has been growing every year, and it has reached three to four hundred thousand units per year. This means that just the application of industrial robots may squeeze out more than one million people from the production field every year, which indicates that China will lose millions of jobs for human laborers on average each year.

Moreover, for a capitalist, if there is no intervention and restriction from public power, when competitors gain a competitive advantage with cheap robots, he is faced with several choices: either he has to follow by using robots, lower the remuneration of human laborers, or admit defeat. In this way, the race to catch up with the robots will quickly become a trend.

Let's take driverless cars as an example. At present, some companies represented by Baidu are trying to promote robotaxi in various parts of China and are stealing the jobs of ordinary people in the name of "high-tech" and "reducing labor consumption." Baidu launched the "Carrot Run" driverless travel service, and in August 2022, it began to implement fully unmanned commercial travel services in Chongqing and Wuhan. Taking Wuhan as an example, the robotaxis of "Carrot Run" exceeded 100 vehicles in February 2023 and had exceeded 500 vehicles by May 2024. Driverless taxis are rapidly crowding out the job opportunities of human taxi drivers in Wuhan. Moreover, relying on its advantage of capital, "Carrot Run" is engaging in low-price vicious competition by reducing the service price of its unmanned taxis to half or even fewer than that of ordinary taxis. It may be executing a so-called "strategic temporary loss-making competition policy." Referring to the speed at which ride-hailing software companies such as Didi Dache seized the taxi industry market in previous years, if there are no policy and regulatory constraints, it is very likely that human taxi drivers will be completely squeezed out of the taxi market in the next few years. If the government does not take restrictive measures, the jobs of about three million taxi drivers in China will be in jeopardy. It is also said that there are six to seven million online ride-hailing licenses in China. Whether it's three million or six to seven million, it represents a huge bottom group whose livelihoods are affected.

If there are no policy and regulatory restrictions, the use of mature unmanned vehicle technology will also be quickly applied to the freight industry. At present, there is also a lot of capital invested in the research of driverless trucks, and it has been experimented with and put into trial operation in many places. It is said that there are more than 30 million freight trucks in China, which means that the driverless delivery of freight trucks will lead to more than 30 million truck drivers facing a job crisis. Moreover, at present, unmanned express delivery vehicles are also being tried in many places, which directly threaten the livelihoods of tens of millions of human couriers in China.

Given the general level of skill literacy among taxi drivers, truck drivers, and couriers, if they all lose their jobs, what kind of employment opportunities could they find? In China alone, the use and promotion of driverless technologies in wealth creation will deal a fatal blow to three million taxi drivers, more than 30 million truck drivers, and so many couriers, who often have families to support. Even calculated as a family of three, it will endanger the lives of about one hundred million people.

Moreover, the key issue is that a large number of industries today are engaged in the so-called "high-tech," using intelligent machines to replace people to improve labor productivity and implementing automation and unmanned systems, etc. The fact that many new industrial robots are put into use every year is proof of this. Take the pillar industry of today's society, the automobile manufacturing industry, as an example. The major automobile companies are all engaging in the so-called "intelligent unmanned production line." The beneficiaries of this industry are becoming more and more concentrated in a few capitalists and a small number of other personnel, and the ordinary people who can benefit from the pillar industry will be fewer and fewer in the future. In the context of using robots, including CNC automated machines, in all walks of life, if an ordinary worker is squeezed out of one industry by robots, can he still dream of finding a livelihood in other industries? In the current context of the rapid development of artificial intelligence technology, if there are no laws and regulations on the application of robots in the field of wealth creation, the job opportunities for ordinary human workers will only become fewer and fewer.

China's situation is just a microcosm; the whole world is cheering for the so-called "unmanned intelligent driving" and applauding the so-called high-tech "artificial intelligence." You know, in fact, it is not China that is standing at the forefront of artificial intelligence technology, but the United States and other countries.

In the context of today's global economy, which basically operates according to the market economy system, if human workers are squeezed out of jobs by artificial intelligence technology on a large scale and become unemployed, it will bring many serious issues.

Firstly, it will bring a large number of family livelihood difficulties. After all, people are either unemployed or forced to lower their pay requirements to compete with cheap robots. With fewer sources of income and the difficulty in reducing daily family expenses, it will naturally become difficult for families to make ends meet.

The second is social unrest. If a normal laborer can't even find a job to support himself and his family, what else is there for him to worry about? For such people, they either starve to death or have to go out of their way to get the wealth they need to survive. There is a saying: there are two kinds of people in this world who are the most terrible; one is so rich that he is fearless, and the other is so poor that he has nothing. In the situation of comprehensive AI in wealth creation, people left in the world may all be classified into these two types. In this way, social order will naturally collapse, and social unrest will naturally take shape. In fact, the outbreak of the Arab Spring, which brought so much turmoil and war, was triggered by an incident related to people's access to the wealth they needed to live.

Third, the economy may be depressed. The consumption of a large number of unemployed people will either be downgraded or disappear, which will also affect the income of others and the prosperity of the economy as a whole. With the gradual rise of artificial intelligence in the field of wealth creation, society is likely to enter such a vicious circle: Some ordinary people are squeezed out of the job market by robots, resulting in unemployment and an inability to find jobs; their survival depends on relief, and their wealth and income are compressed, triggering a downgrade in consumption; the market pressure brought about by the downgrade of consumption has forced investors to further reduce costs and use more cheap robots to squeeze out more human laborers; the wealth and income of ordinary people have been further compressed, and consumption has been further downgraded... until the complete collapse of the economic order. The following is an analysis and discussion of the economic impact of AI, taking intelligent driverless taxis replacing human-driven taxis as an example.

The difference between human-driven taxis and intelligent driverless taxis mainly lies in the difference of drivers; one is driven by people, and the other is driven by intelligent driverless systems. From a technical point of view, today's intelligent driverless taxis can be considered to be the same as ordinary traditional taxis except for the intelligent driverless system. Since both human-driven taxis and intelligent driverless taxis have a variety of different configurations and brands, the acquisition cost is different for different configurations and brands of taxis. For the sake of discussion convenience, it is assumed that, except for the driver, the other parts of the two types of taxis are the same.

Table 4.6.1 lists the main cost components of human-driven taxis and intelligent driverless taxis (sorry, this table is only for comparison and illustration, and the item classification is not necessarily reasonable). From an accounting point of view, for human-driven taxi drivers, their net income is equal to the service income minus the cost of the car body, wherein the cost of the car body includes the depreciation of the car body, the energy consumption of the car, the maintenance cost, the insurance cost, the taxes and fees borne, etc. The fees borne include the fees charged by the government and the relevant fees charged by the taxi company if the taxi is rented from a taxi company. In principle, the taxes and fees incurred due to the operation should be the same for both types of taxis, so they are included in the cost of the car body here. Since the body part of the intelligent driverless taxi is the same as that of the human-driven taxi except for the driving system, the cost of the body part itself should be the same as that of the human-driven taxi. Therefore, it is assumed that the cost of the body part of the two types of taxis is the same. For intelligent driverless taxi companies, the net income gained from a single taxi is equal to the service income minus the cost of the car body and then the cost of the AI driver.

Table 4.6.1 the cost composition of the two types of taxis

	Human-driven taxis	Intelligent driverless taxis
The cost of car bodies	Vehicle wear and tear, depreciation	Vehicle wear and tear, depreciation
	Vehicle motion energy consumption cost	Vehicle motion energy consumption cost
	Vehicle maintenance and upkeep costs	Vehicle maintenance and upkeep costs
	Cost allocation of car insurance	Cost allocation of car insurance
	Taxes and fees	Taxes and fees
The cost of drivers		Depreciation cost allocation for autonomous driving systems
		Energy consumption cost of autonomous driving systems
		Costs of human employees for specific tasks (such as remote monitoring)

Assuming that the original society has formed a stable economic order; that is, the demand for funds, production, and consumption in the market has reached a balance. Assuming that the average monthly net income of taxi drivers is 7,000 yuan, and now suddenly human-driven taxis are replaced by driverless smart taxis, the demand and price of taxi services have not changed, and the monthly income of three million taxi drivers of 21 billion has all been transferred to the driverless smart taxi company. The driverless smart taxi company has hired 30,000 employees with a monthly salary of 30,000 yuan. Assume that the average monthly cost of an intelligent driverless system replacing a human driver is 2,000 yuan, including the acquisition cost sharing of the driverless intelligent system, energy consumption, and other operation and maintenance expenses. Now put aside the pain of unemployed past taxi drivers and purely analyze the incremental GDP in these two cases.

1) From the perspective of the total GDP, the total GDP value is equal to the total operating income of taxis, which is equal to the net GDP value added brought by pure taxi services plus the GDP value added brought by costs, where taxes and fees can be regarded as the GDP value added brought by government and related enterprises to provide services for taxis. Since the total service income is the same, the total GDP value added by the two types of taxis is the same. From the perspective of GDP value added brought by simple taxi services, according to the above assumption, the total incomes of both types of taxis are the same, and the costs of car bodies are the same, and then referring to Table 4.6.1, it can be seen that the total net GDP value added by taxi services provided by human drivers is greater than that provided by intelligent driverless systems. The difference in the net value added by pure rental services between these two types of taxis is equivalent to the cost related to intelligent unmanned systems. From the perspective of GDP value added in monthly statistics, the current GDP value added brought by pure taxi service is equal to the total operating income of taxis in the current period minus the current costs, which is more complicated to calculate. For the convenience of subsequent discussion, it is assumed that the GDP values added in each period for both types of taxis to provide taxi services are the same, and the value is represented by the net GDP value added by human drivers when they provide services; that is, it is substituted with the monthly net income of human drivers. The total monthly GDP increment is calculated as 21 billion.

2) Then analyze it from the perspective of subsequent GDP value added. Assuming that the receipt and payment of funds are electronic, the receipt and payment of funds are only manifested as the transfer between different accounts in the bank. This means that for both types of taxi services, there should be no essential difference in the subsequent increase in GDP brought by the financial system operations, including loans, investments, etc. For the sake of convenience, it is assumed that the funds in bank accounts do not produce subsequent value added; that is, the bank does not create GDP value. Now let's talk about the subsequent GDP value brought about by consumption and expenses.

A) Since human taxi drivers are not a high-income class, their monthly income is basically used to support the daily expenses of their families. Assuming that each driver spends an average of 6,000 yuan per month on consumption, and the remaining 1,000 yuan is reserved in their bank accounts, multiplying the average consumption by the number of drivers shows that the consumption of human drivers in the month directly drove the output value to 18 billion yuan.

B) In the case of using intelligent driverless taxis, assume that 30,000 employees have more monthly surplus due to a higher income, the average monthly money for expenses is 15,000 yuan, and the remaining 15,000 yuan is reserved in their bank accounts. The calculation shows that the consumption of these employees directly drives the output value of 450 million yuan. The monthly output value driven by the monthly consumption of three million sets of unmanned intelligent systems is 6 billion. The remaining 14.1 billion (21 billion – 30,000 × 30,000 – 6 billion) yuan is in the hands of driverless taxi companies. Due to the stable balanced economic order, there is no additional capital demand in the market, so there is no demand for the company's 14.1 billion yuan from the outside world. Suppose that the operator of the driverless taxi enterprise takes 20% of the money to invest for a certain purpose in the month, and the risky investment directly brings 2.82 billion yuan of GDP value added to society. In addition, the unemployed past human drivers take an average of 2,000 yuan per person per month from savings or social welfare benefits to maintain their survival, and the consumption that is to maintain survival directly drives 6 billion output value. It can be further calculated that in the situation of using intelligent driverless taxis, the subsequent direct GDP value added of the month is 15.27 billion (450 million + 6 billion + 2.82 billion + 6 billion) yuan.

According to the above discussion, if humans drive taxis, the total increase in monthly GDP is 39 billion (21 billion + 18 billion), and if intelligent driverless taxis are used, the total increase in monthly GDP is 36.27 billion (21 billion + 15.27 billion). It can be seen that artificial intelligence may bring about a decline in GDP. In addition, if the social economy is originally in a state of equilibrium, i.e., the input, output, and consumption have been balanced, the 2.82 billion risk investment of driverless taxi companies will have a crowding-out effect on the input side. Even if there are 2.82 billion inputs in the market, it may not have corresponding consumption output. In a sense, the 2.82 billion inputs are the same as the nature of end-user consumption, which are all one-time. In some sense, the $2.82 billion risk investment is a waste of resources.

In addition, since taxi drivers are not high-income, their consumption is used in large quantities for basic low-end consumption such as food and clothing, and their consumption providers are more likely to be small traders who earn money and have a short consumption cycle. The consumption of driverless taxi companies and their bosses is more likely to be provided by large enterprises, and the probability of money staying in bank accounts is higher. Of course, it is just a kind of assumption by the author; the author has no actual data. In reality, the problem will be more complicated. Different social development states and the time length with which money stays in people's hands will vary. For example, if a person barely makes ends meet, as long as he has no income for a day, he will fall into a state of eating the last meal and not the next meal; then he will spend his salary immediately every day. If a person's daily income is much greater than his daily expenses, then most of his income will be saved. If the above statement is true in a society, it means that the social output value driven by the consumption of human taxi drivers indirectly is likely to be higher than that driven by the consumption of high-income people.

The reasonableness of the above hypothetical discussion remains to be tested in the future. The assumption should be reasonable based on the price of cars equipped with intelligent driverless systems on the current market. It is said that each robotaxi in Wuhan consumes about 35 yuan per day for charging, 10 yuan for car washing, and 30 yuan for operation and maintenance. The charging fee of 35 yuan not only includes the electricity cost of the unmanned intelligent system but also includes the electricity cost of the car movement, and the electricity cost of the car movement should take up the majority. The human-driven taxi also consumes energy required for the movement of a car. As for the car washing fee and operation and maintenance fee, the human-driven taxi also needs them. The intelligent driverless system will be very cheap with the maturity of technology and mass production in the future. It is predicted that the cost of the sixth generation of Apollo can be reduced to about 200,000 yuan (https://www.autohome.com.cn/ask/13144469.html). While the intelligent driverless system is only a part of a car, the average monthly cost of 2,000 yuan for the intelligent driverless system in the above hypothetical discussion may be overestimated; that is, from the perspective of subsequent value added, the GDP value added after using robotaxis may be lower than that of the above hypothetical discussion. Thus, the total monthly GDP growth after the introduction of intelligent driverless taxis may be lower than it was before.

All in all, the indiscriminate use of artificial intelligence to replace human workers in the field of wealth creation will bring serious issues: human workers are squeezed out of the job market, thereby destroying the wealth chain of the market economy society, and then affecting people's life happiness, causing social unrest, eroding people's needs for a sense of security, and even leading to people's basic material needs for survival not being met.

After all, under the market economy system, every normal adult worker needs to make his or her own contribution in the process of social production, circulation, or social operation in order to obtain the material wealth needed to support himself or herself and their family.

Before the development of artificial intelligence and automation technology, human workers relied on their own intelligent advantages to obtain their jobs and make contributions in the process of wealth creation, circulation, or social operation, so as to obtain the living wealth needed by themselves and their families. Even manual laborers who are engaged in simple labor, such as moving bricks and twisting screws, rely on their own intellectual advantages, including strong environmental perception and behavioral decision-making abilities. After all, people can make reasonable responses according to specific situations. Artificial intelligence completely eliminates the intelligent advantages of human beings.

Comprehensive artificial intelligence means that ordinary workers have lost the opportunity to contribute their own talents, and it further means that ordinary people have lost the source of wealth in the market economy system, which means that the social wealth chain needed to ensure the operation of the market economy system has been broken, and it means that ordinary people have lost the right to survive under the market economy system. If ordinary people are difficult to survive, isn't it completely contrary to the original intention of developing artificial intelligence? Is it still worthy for society to engage in comprehensive artificial intelligence? It can be seen that comprehensive artificial intelligence is incompatible with the market economy system that prevails all over the world today. Ordinary people should also have the right to live; they should not lose the right to live because of artificial intelligence. They should get the wealth they need to survive, which requires society in the era of comprehensive artificial intelligence to change the way of wealth distribution, such as changing to an equal distribution mode. If the distribution of wealth is changed to equal distribution and other distribution methods, if wealth is falling from the sky, if almost all people have no contribution to wealth creation and society, for the sake of social fairness, the significance of the private property rights system is not very large, and the private property rights system basically has no value. Therefore, comprehensive artificial intelligence is also incompatible with the general recognition of private property rights in today's human society.

Further, comprehensive artificial intelligence requires fundamental changes in the social and economic system, including changes in the property rights system, the way social wealth is distributed, and so on. Such a fundamental change will inevitably bring about serious social contradictions and conflicts. What is embarrassing is that even if comprehensive artificial intelligence is realized, due to the scarcity of resources and other factors, human beings cannot enter the ideal society of "distribution according to needs." Therefore, changes in the property rights system will inevitably infringe on the vested interests of many people, and contradictions and conflicts will inevitably occur. This type of conflict will usually plunge society into turmoil, and even bloody wars and massacres may break out. It is too difficult to make a smooth transition to a fully AI-enabled society.

4.7 How to Plan the Use of Artificial Intelligence

The use of artificial intelligence technology will let some people enjoy the wealth that falls from the sky, so there will inevitably be people who will promote it. In the future, human beings will need a large number of intelligent robots to jump out of the Earth and go deep into space for development and exploration. In fact, automation and artificial intelligence are also needed in some areas of human society on the Earth today, such as dangerous occasions, occasions where the accuracy and other indicators do not meet the technical requirements with manual work, where the amount of data that needs to be processed is too large to be handled by humans in real time, and where the production capacity of human workers is seriously unable to keep up with demand. If human society is determined to move towards the era of comprehensive artificial intelligence in the future, how should our human society transition to the era of comprehensive artificial intelligence?

It should be emphasized that although the existence of country entities is a major feature of human society, human society is already in an era of globalization, and the economies and cultures of various countries are influencing each other. The implementation of AI in all areas is an epoch-making matter, and it is best for all countries to take a unified approach on whether to implement comprehensive AI or not, and on how to implement it if people decide to implement comprehensive AI, so as to prevent certain careerists from taking advantage of the loopholes in certain countries to create serious social disasters.

4.7.1 A Laissez-Faire Approach to Transition

One way to finish the transition is to go with the flow, not to set limits on the use of AI, and to be completely liberal in terms of the potential impact and consequences of comprehensive AI, adhering to the principle of accepting fate from heaven. At the heart of this line of thinking is the belief that the development and promotion of artificial intelligence technology might naturally promote the evolution and change of society. It is the prevailing attitude of the international community.

Following the habitual thinking that the development of science and technology has brought great progress to society in the past two hundred years, and with the history that whichever country was ahead in science and technology, that country would be developed in the past industrial revolutions, people in many countries are deeply afraid that the backwardness in the field of artificial intelligence technology will cause the country's decline and backwardness. Governments and other public power organizations of many countries have desperately encouraged the development of AI technology in terms of taxation and economic investment and have not made any restrictions on the use of AI technology within the existing legal framework, allowing it to be freely applied to various occasions. It can also be regarded as a laissez-faire way of transitioning to the era of comprehensive artificial intelligence.

The main issues of the laissez-faire way of transition are as follows.

First, the current background of comprehensive artificial intelligence is different from the backgrounds of the past industrial revolutions. The backgrounds of the past industrial revolutions were that the basic needs of human beings had not been met on a large scale, and society had called for new technologies and new products to meet people's basic needs. Moreover, in the past industrial revolutions, as far as the world was concerned, there were still a large number of people struggling to eat and wear, and there was a serious lack of satisfaction of many needs. Therefore, in the past industrial revolutions, although technological innovation had led to an increase in labor productivity, and some industries in the past needed to transfer labor out, a large number of new products and new industries had emerged, creating a large number of new jobs, and these new products and new industries needed a lot of labor. Even the rapid development of communication network-related industries in recent decades has brought great vitality to the social economy, but also because the "transportation" needs of information and data for human beings in the past had not been well satisfied. However, the current background of comprehensive artificial intelligence is that many needs of human beings, especially most of those needs related to daily life, have been met well enough.

Second, although the application of artificial intelligence technology on the consumer end can also meet some needs of human beings and promote the development and production of new products, artificial intelligence in wealth creation and distribution directly crowds human workers out of the job market. Moreover, under the liberal mindset, it is quite possible that the development and production of new products will also be done by artificial intelligence itself. What's more, even in the research and development of artificial intelligence technology, such as software writing, there is a lot of work that has been finished with the assistance of artificial intelligence. Now there is even a viewpoint in the software industry that there will be no programmers in future society. It is completely different from the past industrial revolutions in which new products and industries would absorb human labor. Artificial intelligence will obviously snatch people's jobs away only.

Third, it will take a long time for artificial intelligence technology to mature to the level of carrying out comprehensive AI, and the length of time may take another twenty to fifty years. In this period, people will lose employment opportunities one after another, and jobs will gradually be snatched away by robots and fully automated intelligent machinery in the wealth creation field. Most ordinary people do not have much savings, and they will often encounter an existential crisis if they are unemployed for half a year or even a few months. As a result, the unfortunate elements of human society will increase rapidly, and the factors of social unrest will become more and more intense. The following decades will be an insurmountable ordeal for ordinary people.

Fig. 4.7.1 The Backgrounds of AI and the Past Industrial Revolutions Are Different

Under the policies of laissez-faire freedom, human laborers will continue to be squeezed out of their jobs in the coming days, and the chain of social wealth will gradually lose its luster. The reform of the social wealth circulation and distribution system cannot be finished overnight, so what should be done about the large number of human laborers and their families who have been squeezed out of jobs? If AI is allowed to be used and promoted freely, social contradictions and turbulent factors will inevitably become more and more serious. When the turmoil does happen, it is likely that it will not be able to stop soon, and it will be turned upside down.

4.7.2 Regulatory and Timely Adjusting Strategies

Another idea is to set up a special agency to study and supervise the development and application of artificial intelligence, and social public management organizations such as governments, legislatures, and judiciaries should formulate, adjust, and enforce laws in a timely manner, and adjust society's labor-management relations, working hours, wealth distribution plans, etc., according to the development status.

Under this line of thinking, specialized research institutions and regulatory agencies should always keep abreast of the employment situation of human workers, the labor skills and labor quality of workers, and the potential impact of new products and technologies. Since it is estimated that a lot of social capital will invest resources in artificial intelligence, it should be expected that new products will be born from time to time. Regulators need to review the situations where new products and technologies can be applied and consider how many human workers will be squeezed out by new products and technologies. If the unemployment rate is higher than a certain standard, it is necessary to adjust the legal working hours in a timely manner, such as changing the current five-day-a-week, forty-hour workweek to four, three, or two days a week, and changing the daily working hours to seven, six, or four hours a day, to ensure a relatively high employment rate and prevent the wealth chain from collapsing.

4.7.3 Apply AI and Adjust the Social Mechanisms in a Very Short Period of Time Until the Maturity of AI

This transition routine is to wait for artificial intelligence technologies to be good enough and then quickly reform the social systems and promote the use of artificial intelligence. Under this line of thinking, it is mainly public organizations that are responsible for investing resources in the development of artificial intelligence technology and personnel training, and the developed artificial intelligence technology is generally experimentally verified on a small scale and is not promoted on a large scale. It is not until the highest level of public power management organizations in society determines that our society can carry out comprehensive artificial intelligence and begin to quickly replace human laborers with artificial intelligence, and at the same time comprehensively reorganize the social organizational structure and reform the social operation mechanisms, so that the wealth distribution mechanism can meet the needs of human beings in the era of comprehensive artificial intelligence.

Under this mindset, strict laws need to be enacted, and a strict regulatory body needs to be established. Except for some legally permitted applications, artificial intelligence technology involving the field of wealth production and creation can basically only be a technical reserve of R&D institutions. The experimental verification of the production and application of artificial intelligence technology must be carried out within the permitted range of regulatory agencies, and the scope cannot be expanded at will.

One important characteristic of this transition routine is that, because it is difficult to predict the future output of the investment in artificial intelligence technology, the enthusiasm for private capital investment in society will be relatively low; that is, the resource investment will be relatively limited, and the development of artificial intelligence technology will naturally be relatively slow. However, the slowness of development may help people have a longer time for understanding and psychological preparation in today's complex and diverse social conditions, help people build a clearer and more accurate understanding of the potential social state with comprehensive artificial intelligence, and help them finally decide whether to choose comprehensive artificial intelligence or not. The author believes that, following this way of transition to the era of comprehensive artificial intelligence, the probability of keeping social operation relatively stable will be relatively high.

5 Concluding Remarks

―――――――――⇒ ⇒⟱⟱⟱⟱⟱⟱⟱⟱⟱⟱⟱⟱⟱⟱⟱⟱― ―――――――――

Our society is a human society, and we should all be brave enough to abandon any technology if it does not bring benefits to mankind, rather than using it because it seems "complex and sophisticated." The normal purpose of our human development of science and technology is to gain benefits and meet the needs of humanity.

The target of human beings carrying out almost all activities, such as learning, research, production, and socializing, is to meet human needs. For human needs, firstly, this paper analyzes from a mechanical perspective and argues that human needs include food, heat preservation, rest, health, life continuity, housing, transportation, neuropsychological needs, knowledge and skills, etc.

In the ancient primitive times and the ancient agricultural and pastoral era, the scientific and technological level of human beings was low, and many basic needs of human beings were not met or often could not be met stably. In those times, there was an urgent need for mankind to develop science and technology and expand the capabilities of human beings to meet the various needs of humanity.

Along with the growth of the human population and the accumulation of knowledge, the development of science and technology has been accelerated continuously, especially since about 400 years ago. Human beings have achieved great advancements in the unveiling of the laws of the universe. With the application of scientific laws, labor productivity has also been greatly improved since then. A large number of new products have been invented and mass-produced to meet the various needs of humankind.

With the development of science and technology and productive forces, many needs of human beings have been basically satisfied. In fact, with the exception of a small number of countries and regions controlled by some bad people and those affected by certain historical factors, today's human society has generally solved the issues of food and clothing and entered the stage of a prosperous or moderately prosperous life. In particular, for the citizens of developed countries and moderately developed countries, which represent the frontier of human productivity today, food supply, heat preservation conditions, living conditions, health conditions, rest time, leisure, and entertainment, etc., have basically met the needs of the people. Even some needs have been over satisfied; for example, resisting the temptation of food to ensure good health, resisting the temptation of leisure and entertainment to ensure rest time to prevent decadence, and active exercise to prevent the deterioration of human ability, etc., have become very popular pursuits in modern human society.

The tremendous benefits brought about by scientific and technological progress are obvious to all, especially the tremendous improvement of the social outlook caused by the development of science and technology in the last two hundred years, which has created a relatively common tendency in human society to worship "profound" technology, so that many people tend to ignore the potential negative impact of science and technology, intentionally or unintentionally, and forget the key point that "technology is for people." Many people forget that there are many kinds of science and technology and that some technologies are mainly used to destroy the beauty and happiness of human beings. In the face of the negative impact of technology, many people often subconsciously only complain about why they can't grasp the dividends of technological development rather than questioning the negative impacts of technology itself.

Before the development of artificial intelligence, the machines built by humans mainly extended and expanded the capabilities of human hands, feet, eyes, ears, mouths, etc. When it comes to strength, speed, structural strength, fatigue resistance, etc., humans are nothing compared to machines. Compared with past machines, the main advantage of human workers is that they have brains and intelligence, can make reasonable decisions according to the changes in their working environments, and respond appropriately. What AI does is to simulate and surpass the intelligence of the human brain.

The current automation technology and artificial intelligence technology have made the advantages of human intelligence disappear on many occasions. As it stands, if the trend continues, it will soon eliminate the intellectual superiority of human workers in all fields. For ordinary people in human society, they have now reached a place very close to the edge of a cliff. If we do not take measures now, our society will be in danger.

As we all know, under the market economy system, every normal adult worker needs to make his or her own contribution in the process of production, circulation, or social operation in order to obtain the material wealth needed for life. Before the development of artificial intelligence and automation technology, human workers relied on their own intellectual advantages to obtain their jobs in the process of wealth creation and circulation, thereby obtaining wealth for themselves and their families.

The rapid development of automation and artificial intelligence technology is already breaking the monopoly of human workers on intelligence. Without the constraints of laws and regulations, it will inevitably disrupt the chain of wealth circulation in society. Even in the best-case scenario, it will also depress the status of human workers in the distribution of wealth. After all, unlike human workers who need to earn money to support their families, AI systems only need to pay for procurement, electricity, and maintenance costs for daily operation. A computer that can run a certain AI system is often very cheap, and the daily operating costs are not high. Plus, considering certain managerial factors, the capitalists themselves will be more inclined to use robots at the same cost, let alone if the financial cost of AI systems is lower than hiring human workers. Under the condition that the social wealth distribution system does not change, the comprehensive promotion and use of artificial intelligence systems will make ordinary people lose job opportunities which are vital for supporting their families. After all, in human society, the proportion of capitalists or business owners is extremely low, and the number of capitalists is basically far less than 1% of the total population, except for self-employed people who are not much different from ordinary wage laborers. Even if AI does not replace the R&D power of human workers, not all human individuals are smart enough to engage in R&D work, and because of the limited variety of products and resources, human society itself does not need or support too much R&D power. In fact, it is true that scientific and technological personnel engaged in R&D are less than 1% of the total population in most countries, and those whose proportion approaches 1% already are countries with superlative performance. According to the above proportional data, more than 90 percent of people are simply unable to find a source of wealth. How bad and horrible it must be when such a huge proportion of the population in a society has lost their source of subsistence wealth. Therefore, the comprehensive application of artificial intelligence technology is bound to disrupt the normal operational order of market economy countries, and society is very likely to enter a turbulent situation.

If artificial intelligence is to be allowed to completely replace human workers in wealth production and distribution, human society must be fully prepared and needs to make many adjustments, including operating systems, laws and regulations, cultural psychology, and so on. Is today's human society ready for the era of comprehensive artificial intelligence? Based on today's situation, it is clear that human society is still not ready.

Until humanity is ready to enter the era of comprehensive artificial intelligence, it is highly recommended that countries establish AI technology review committees and international cooperation committees. After all, since AI is better suited than humans in some areas, we still have to study it, develop it, and apply it in certain areas. Therefore, it would be better for our human society to set up special review committees to review the licensing of research and application of AI technology. Before an artificial intelligence technology or intelligent robot is put into use or put on the market, it must undergo a strict review, including the increase or decrease of employment opportunities, ethical conditions, application fields, carbon emissions, environmental impacts, etc. Heavy fines must be imposed for the indiscriminate use of artificial intelligence technology without permission.

For ordinary people, if conditions permit, we should consciously resist products produced using fully automatic unmanned production lines without the approval of relevant committees. The so-called intelligent unmanned production line is harming everyone's food and clothing sources.

Comprehensive artificial intelligence cannot change the state of scarce resources, and scarce resources will continue to be scarce. For example, the amount of gold on the Earth will not increase with the development of artificial intelligence technology, nor will the amount of energy sent by the Sun to the Earth per second increase or decrease.

Comprehensive artificial intelligence will bring about a huge change in the structure of social organization, and it is very likely that a small number of powerful people who control the robotic armament system and production system will control the world, while ordinary people will be marginalized to the point of dispensability. In the past, the elite still relied on ordinary laborers to provide material goods and the support of armed forces, and they relied on ordinary people to provide a sense of accomplishment, satisfaction, and so on. In a society with advanced artificial intelligence and the comprehensive application of artificial intelligence technology in all fields, including all aspects of material and spiritual emotions, the powerful will no longer need the support of ordinary people at all. There is a high probability that the lives of ordinary people will be unsecure, and it is very likely that they will be powerless to resist in the face of the AI armed forces. Therefore, even if our human society is ready to implement comprehensive artificial intelligence, we must also try to avoid the above situation in the design of social systems.

Human society is diverse in ideology and culture, the interests of national organizations, social systems, and so on, and there are many contradictions and conflicts, making it difficult to achieve harmony. Moreover, many individuals suffer from overt and recessive mental illnesses. There are signs that human society is not ready for full artificial intelligence at the cultural and psychological levels.

Nowadays, artificial intelligence technology is developing rapidly and showing more capabilities than humans. For the harmony of human society, we have reached the point where we must legislate to protect ordinary people. We need to constrain and limit the application fields of artificial intelligence, and it is urgent to protect ordinary humans.

Comprehensive artificial intelligence is incompatible with the market economic system prevailing in the world today, and it is also incompatible with the recognition of private property rights in today's most human societies. In order to comprehensively use artificial intelligence, it is necessary to adjust the social operation mechanism, which will inevitably involve huge social changes. This kind of revolutionary or huge social change is the most terrifying. If an individual doesn't deal with it right, they will be crushed to pieces. Do not start such a revolutionary social change easily until we have appropriate preparation. In particular, in the era of the global village, the most appropriate response to the full adoption of artificial intelligence is for all countries to work in unison. In today's international situation, there are so many overt or covert quarrels, so many social unrest events happening, and there are so many wars going on. It's a headache even to think about having all countries taking the same steps.

Before society is ready for the era of comprehensive artificial intelligence, we human beings should slow down the pace of using artificial intelligence. For the happiness of the majority of the people, restricting the use of AI is very necessary and urgent.